A2

Edexcel
Economics

Peter Smith

Philip Allan Updates, an imprint of Hodder Education, an Hachette UK company, Market Place, Deddington, Oxfordshire OX15 0SE

Orders

Bookpoint Ltd, 130 Milton Park, Abingdon, Oxfordshire OX14 4SB
tel: 01235 827720   fax: 01235 400454
e-mail: uk.orders@bookpoint.co.uk

Lines are open 9.00 a.m.–5.00 p.m., Monday to Saturday, with a 24-hour message answering service. You can also order through the Philip Allan Updates website: www.philipallan.co.uk

© Philip Allan Updates 2009

ISBN 978-0-340-94926-9

First printed 2009
Impression number   5   4   3
Year 2014   2013   2012   2011   2010

This textbook has been written specifically to support students studying Edexcel A2 Economics. The content has been neither approved nor endorsed by Edexcel and remains the sole responsibility of the author.

All website addresses included in this book are correct at the time of going to press but may subsequently change.

All photographs are reproduced by permission of Topfoto, except where otherwise specified.

Printed in Italy

Environmental information
Hachette UK's policy is to use papers that are natural, renewable and recyclable products and made from wood grown in sustainable forests. The logging and manufacturing processes are expected to conform to the environmental regulations of the country of origin.

P01396

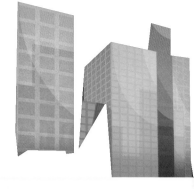

Contents

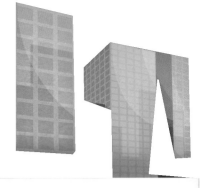

This textbook provides an introduction to economics. It has been tailored explicitly to cover the content of the Edexcel specification for A2 economics, module by module, and follows on from the companion volume *Edexcel AS Economics*.

The text provides the foundation for studying Edexcel A2 economics, but you will no doubt wish to keep up to date by referring to additional topical sources of information about economic events. This can be done by reading the serious newspapers, visiting key sites on the internet, and by reading such magazines as *Economic Review*.

The text is in two parts, corresponding to the two units that make up the A2 specification as follows:

Edexcel unit	Text
A2 Unit 3	**Part 1:** Business economics and economic efficiency
Business economics and economic efficiency	Chapters 1–5
A2 Unit 4	**Part 2:** The global economy
The global economy	Chapters 6–12

The text features the following:

➤ a statement of the intended learning outcomes for each chapter

➤ clear and concise but comprehensive explanation and analysis of economic terms and concepts

➤ examples to show these concepts applied to real-world situations

➤ definitions of key terms

➤ exercises to provide active engagement with economic analysis

A separate *Teacher Guide* is available that provides complete answers to all exercises, plus additional support material and exercises.

Assessment objectives

In common with other economics specifications, Edexcel economics entails four assessment objectives. Candidates will thus be expected to:

- demonstrate knowledge and understanding of the specified content
- apply knowledge and critical understanding to problems and issues arising from both familiar and unfamiliar situations
- analyse economic problems and issues
- evaluate economic arguments and evidence, making informed judgements

In the overall assessment of the A-level, the four assessment objectives count equally. However, there is a greater weighting given to the first two objectives in AS, and a greater weighting to the final two objectives in A2.

Both the A2 units include an element of *synoptic* assessment. Synoptic assessment sets out to test '...candidates' understanding of the connections between different elements of the subject'. This will test the ability to:

- understand the ways in which many economic issues, problems and institutions are interrelated
- understand how economic concepts, theories and techniques may be relevant to a range of different contexts
- apply such concepts, theories and techniques in the analysis of economic issues and problems and in evaluating arguments and evidence

'The emphasis will be on the students' ability to think as economists and to use the economist's toolkit of concepts, theories and techniques that they have built up during their course of study.'

(See the Edexcel AS/A GCE in Economics specification at **www.edexcel.com***.)*

In approaching the A2 part of the A-level programme, it is therefore important not to discard what has been learnt from the AS section. Where appropriate, this text will provide references to relevant chapters of *Edexcel AS Economics* to allow connections to be made. These references will appear in the form '*AS Economics, Chapter x*'. By studying these books, you should develop an awareness of the economist's approach to issues and problems, and the economist's way of thinking about the world.

Economics and the real world

The study of economics also requires a familiarity with recent economic events in the UK and elsewhere, and candidates will be expected to show familiarity with 'recent historical data' − broadly defined as the last 7–10 years. The following websites will help you to keep up to date with recent trends and events.

- Recent and historical data about the UK economy can be found at the website of the Office for National Statistics (ONS) at: **www.statistics.gov.uk**
- Also helpful is the site of HM Treasury at: **www.hm-treasury.gov.uk**
- The Bank of England site is well worth a visit, especially the *Inflation Report* and the Minutes of the Monetary Policy Committee: **www.bankofengland.co.uk**

➤ The Institute for Fiscal Studies offers an independent view of a range of economic topics: **www.ifs.org.uk**

For information about other countries, visit the following:

➤ **www.oecd.org/home**

➤ **europa.eu.int/**

➤ **www.worldbank.org**

➤ **www.undp.org**

Another way of keeping up to date with economic topics and events is to read *Economic Review*, a magazine specifically written for A-level economics students, also published by Philip Allan Updates.

How to study economics

There are two crucial aspects of studying economics. The first stage is to study the theory, which helps us to explain economic behaviour. However, in studying AS and A2 economics it is equally important to be able to *apply* the theories and concepts that you meet, and to see just how these relate to the real world.

If you are to become competent at this, it is vital that you get plenty of practice. In part, this means carrying out the exercises that you will find in this text. However, it also means thinking about how economics helps us to explain news items and data that appear in the newspapers and on the television. Make sure that you practise as much as you can.

In economics, it is also important to be able to produce examples of economic phenomena. In reading this text, you will find some examples that help to illustrate ideas and concepts. Do not rely solely on the examples provided here, but look around the world to find your own examples, and keep a note of these ready for use in essays and exams. This will help to convince the examiners that you have under-stood economics. It will also help you to understand the theories.

Enjoy economics

Most important of all, I hope you will enjoy your study of economics. I have always been fascinated by the subject, and hope that you will capture something of the excitement and challenge of learning about how markets and the economy operate. I also wish you every success with your AS/A-level studies.

Acknowledgements

I would like to express my deep gratitude to Russell Dudley-Smith, whose thorough reading of the book's precursor and thoughtful and helpful comments were invaluable in improving the scope and focus of the book. I would also like to thank everyone at Philip Allan Updates, especially Rachel Furse and Penny Fisher, for their efficiency in production of this book, for their support and encouragement.

Many of the data series shown in figures in this book are drawn from the data obtained from the National Statistics website: **www.statistics.gov.uk** Crown copyright material is reproduced with the permission of the Controller of HMSO (PSI licence number C2007001851).

Other data were from various sources, including OECD, World Bank, United Nations Development Programme and other sources as specified.

While every effort has been made to trace the owners of copyright material, I would like to apologise to any copyright holders whose rights may have unwittingly been infringed.

Peter Smith

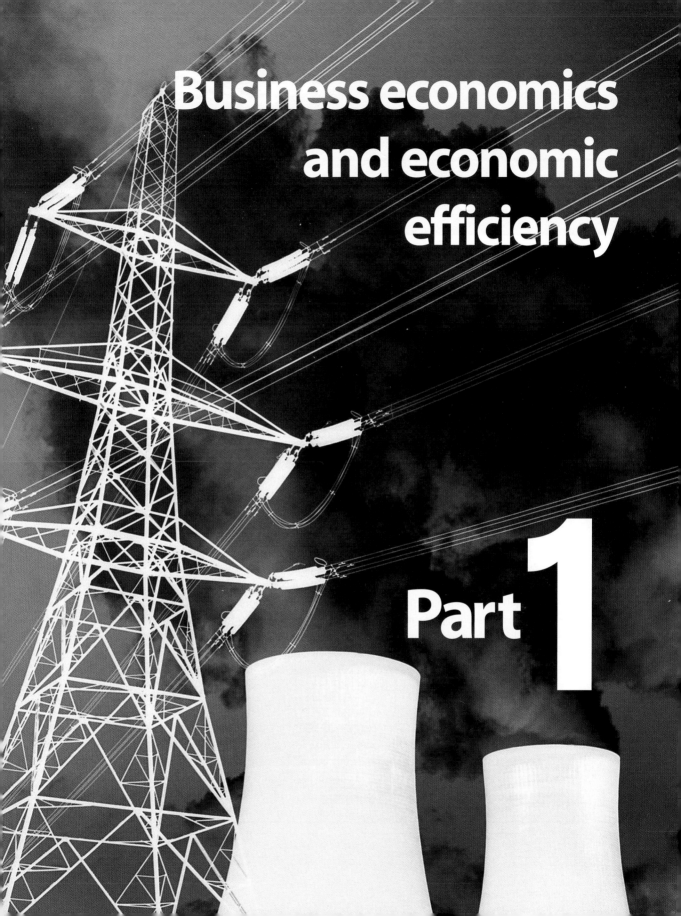

Business economics and economic efficiency

Part 1

Firms and their motivations

In studying AS economics, you will have come to realise the importance of firms in the operation of markets. Business economics looks more closely at the decisions made by firms, and the implications of those decisions for the effectiveness of markets in allocating resources within an economy. This chapter examines some of the key concepts that are needed for this important part of economic analysis. In studying this chapter, you may find it helpful to review some of the material that has appeared in AS Economics.

Learning outcomes

After studying this chapter, you should:
- ➤ be aware of the reason for the birth of firms, and the desire for their growth
- ➤ be familiar with alternative ways in which firms grow
- ➤ be able to distinguish between horizontal, vertical and conglomerate mergers
- ➤ be aware of the need for firms to grow if they wish to compete in global markets
- ➤ be familiar with short- and long-run cost curves and their characteristics
- ➤ understand the significance of economies of scale in the context of the growth of firms
- ➤ understand the profit maximisation motive and its implications for firms' behaviour
- ➤ be aware of the principal–agent issue, and its influence on the motivations of firms
- ➤ be familiar with alternative motivations for firms and how these affect decision-making
- ➤ be able to interpret productive and allocative efficiency in terms of a firm's cost curves

Supply and the firm

In *AS Economics*, the notion of the supply curve in a competitive market was introduced. This is a key component of the demand and supply model, which was seen to be powerful in enabling the interpretation of changes in market conditions. In order to construct the supply curve, it was argued that a firm will respond to price in taking decisions about how much output to produce. The starting point of *A2 Economics* is to look more closely at the decisions made by firms.

What is a firm?

One way of answering this question is to say that **firms** exist in order to organise production: they bring together various factors of production, and organise the production process in order to produce output.

Key *term*

firm: an organisation that brings together factors of production in order to produce output

There are various forms that the organisation of a firm can take. The simplest is perhaps that of *sole proprietor*, in which the owner of the firm also runs the firm. Examples would be an independent newsagent/corner shop, plumber or hairdresser, where the owner is liable for the debts of the enterprise, but also gets to keep any profits.

In some professions firms are operated on a *partnership* basis. Examples here are doctors, dentists and solicitors. Profits are shared between the partners, as are debts, according to the contract drawn up between them.

Private *joint stock companies* are owned by shareholders, each of whom has contributed funds to the business by buying shares. However, each shareholder's responsibility for the debts of the company is limited to the amount he/she paid for the shares. Profits are distributed to shareholders as dividends. The shares in a private company of this kind are not traded on the stock exchange, and the firms tend to be controlled by the shareholders themselves. Many local businesses are operated on this basis, for example double glazing installation firms or computer consultancies. If you look in your local yellow pages, you will see that some firms indicate that they are this sort of company by the 'Ltd' after their name, which indicates that they have *limited liability*, meaning that the liability of shareholders for the firm's debt is limited to the amount that they paid for their shares.

Firms that are owned by shareholders but are listed on the stock exchange are *public joint stock companies*. Again, the liability of the shareholders is limited to the amount they have paid for their shares. However, such companies are required to publish their annual accounts and also to publish an annual report to their shareholders. Day-to-day decision-making is normally delegated to a board of directors, appointed at the annual general meeting (AGM) of the shareholders. Examples of this sort of company abound — Tesco, HSBC, BP and so on. Again, your local yellow pages will reveal the names of some companies with 'plc' after the name, standing for *public limited company*.

Later in the chapter you will see that the way in which a firm is organised may influence the way in which decisions are taken on key economic issues — indeed, it may affect the whole motivation of a firm in decision-taking. However, for now all such forms of organisation will be referred to simply as 'firms'.

The nature of the activity being undertaken by the firm and its scale of operation will help to determine its most efficient form of organisation. For firms to operate successfully, they must minimise the transaction costs of undertaking business.

The Sheffield College
Hillsborough LRC
Telephone: 0114 260 2254

Identify firms that are operating in your town or city. Which of them would you classify as being relatively small-scale enterprises, and which operate on a more national basis?

The growth of firms

A feature of the economic environment in recent years has been the increasing size of firms. Some, e.g. Microsoft, Wal-Mart and Shell, have become giants. Why is this happening?

Firms may wish to increase their size in order to gain market power within the industry in which they are operating. A firm that can gain market share, and perhaps become dominant in the market, may be able to exercise some control over the price of its product, and thereby influence the market. However, firms may wish to grow for other reasons, which will be explained later in the chapter.

Organic growth

Some firms grow simply by being successful. For example, a successful marketing campaign may increase a firm's market share, and provide it with a flow of profits that can be reinvested to expand the firm even more. Some firms may choose to borrow in order to finance their growth, perhaps by issuing shares (equity).

Such *organic growth* may encounter limits. A firm may find that its product market is saturated, so that it can grow further only at the expense of other firms in the market. If its competitors are able to maintain their own market shares, the firm may need to diversify its production activities by finding new markets for its existing product, or perhaps offering new products.

There are many examples of such activity. Tesco, the leading UK supermarket, has launched itself into new markets by opening branches overseas, and has also introduced a range of new products, including financial services, to its existing customers. Microsoft has famously used this strategy, by selling first its internet browser and later its media player as part of its Windows operating system, in an attempt to persuade existing customers to buy its new products.

Diversification may be a dangerous strategy: moving into a market in which the firm is inexperienced and existing rival firms already know the business may pose quite a challenge. In such circumstances much may depend on the quality of the management team.

Mergers and acquisitions

Instead of growing organically – i.e. based on the firm's own resources – many firms choose to grow by merging with, or acquiring, other firms. The distinction here is that an *acquisition* (or takeover) may be hostile, whereas a *merger* may be the coming together of equals, with each firm committed to forming a single entity.

Growth in this way has a number of advantages; for example, it may overcome the management problem, and allow some rationalisation to take place. On the other hand, firms tend to develop their own culture, or way of doing things, and some mergers have foundered because of an incompatibility of corporate cultures.

Mergers (or acquisitions) can be of three different types. A **horizontal merger** is a merger between firms operating in the same industry and at the same stage of the production process, for example the merger of two car assembly firms. The car industry has been characterised by such mergers, including the takeover of Rover by BMW in 1994 and the merger of Daimler-Benz with Chrysler in 1998.

A horizontal merger can affect the degree of market concentration, because after the merger takes place there are fewer independent firms operating in the market. This may increase the market power held by the new firm.

A car assembly plant merging with a tyre producer, on the other hand, is an example of a **vertical merger**. A real-life example of this is the brewing company Bass, which has acquired a chain of pubs in the UK.

Vertical mergers may be either upstream or downstream. If a car company merges with a component supplier, that is known as backward integration, as it involves merging with a firm that is involved in an earlier part of the production process. Forward integration entails merging in the other direction, as for example if the car assembly plant decided to merge with a large distributor.

Key terms

horizontal merger: a merger between two firms at the same stage of production in the same industry

vertical merger: a merger between two firms in the same industry, but at different stages of the production process

The coming together of pharmaceutical giants GlaxoWellcome and SmithKline Beecham is an example of a horizontal merger.

Vertical integration may allow rationalisation of the process of production. Car producers often work on a just-in-time basis, ordering components for the production line only as they are required. This creates a potential vulnerability, because if the supply of components fails then production has to stop. If a firm's component supplier is part of the firm rather than an independent operator, this may improve the reliability of, and confidence in, the just-in-time process, and in consequence may make life more difficult for rival firms. However, vertical mergers have different implications for concentration and market power.

The third type of merger involves the merging of two firms that are operating in quite different markets or industries. For example, companies like Unilever or Nestlé operate in a wide range of different markets, partly as a result of acquisitions.

One argument in favour of **conglomerates** is that they reduce the risks faced by firms. Many markets follow fluctuations that are in line with the business cycle but are not always fully synchronised. By operating in a number of markets that are on different cycles, the firm can even out its activity overall. However, it is not necessarily an efficient way of doing business, as the different activities undertaken may require different skills and specialisms. In recent years conglomerate mergers seem to have become less popular.

Not all mergers turn out to be successful, and there may be circumstances in which merged firms choose to 'demerge' and split. A common factor that can lead to this happening is where firms from different countries merge, only to find that their corporate cultures are incompatible. This can even happen with firms from the same country, where management styles in the individual companies do not fit well together. In other situations, it may be that expected synergies between the production activities of the firms are not as strong as had been thought. Demergers can turn out to be costly and acrimonious.

Exercise 1.2

Categorise each of the following as a horizontal, vertical or conglomerate merger:

a the merger of a firm operating an instant coffee factory with a coffee plantation

b the merger of a brewer and a bakery

c the merger of a brewer and a crisp manufacturer

d the merger of a soft drinks manufacturer with a chain of fast-food outlets

e the merger of an internet service provider with a film studio

f a merger between two firms producing tyres for cars

Globalisation

Globalisation, which has been on the increase since the 1980s, has had a significant effect on the growth of firms. In particular, transactions have become quicker and easier with the development of transport and communication technology. The whole process of marketing goods and services has been revolutionised with the spread of the internet and e-commerce.

In some markets this has led to the growth of giant firms operating in global markets. The **multinational corporations** will make a number of appearances in the following chapters of the book, and their increasing role in the global economy will be evaluated. One motive for mergers and acquisitions has been defensive, i.e. to try to compete with other large firms in the global market.

Summary

➤ A firm is an organisation that exists to bring together factors of production in order to produce goods or services.

➤ Firms range, in the complexity of their organisation, from sole proprietors to public limited companies.

➤ Firms may undergo organic growth, building upon their own resources and past profits.

➤ If limited by the size of their markets, firms may diversify into new markets or products.

➤ Firms may also grow through horizontal, vertical or conglomerate mergers and acquisitions.

➤ Globalisation has enabled the growth of giant firms operating on a global scale.

Costs facing firms

To understand why firms wish to grow, it is important to examine the costs of production that they face, as the pursuit of economies of scale (introduced in *AS Economics, Chapter 4*) provides one of the major motivations for growth — although there are other reasons, as will be explained later in the chapter. This section focuses on the relationship between costs and the level of output produced by a firm. Diagrams will illustrate this relationship using a series of cost curves that apply in various circumstances.

For simplicity, it is assumed that the firm under consideration produces a single product — analysis of conglomerates is a little more complicated. It is also assumed that the firm uses just two factors of production — labour (L) and capital (K). This seems a stronger assumption, but again is made for simplicity. 'Labour' and 'capital' can be thought of as the representative factors of production, although in real life a firm organises a whole range of factors of production — including different types of labour and capital.

These two factors are representative in a particular way. In the short run the firm faces limited flexibility. Varying the quantity of labour input the firm uses may be relatively straightforward — it can increase the use of overtime, or hire more workers, fairly quickly. However, varying the amount of capital the firm has at its disposal may take longer. For example, it takes time to commission a new piece of machinery, or to build a new factory — or a Channel Tunnel! Hence labour is regarded as a flexible factor and capital as a fixed factor. This may not always be correct; for example, it may sometimes be easier to bring in new computers than to train new staff to use them. However, in this chapter 'labour' will be regarded as flexible and 'capital' as inflexible, and the definitions of the **short run** and **long run** are based on this assumption.

The production function

As the firm changes its volume of production, it needs to vary the inputs of its factors of production. Thus, the total amount of output produced in a given period depends upon the inputs of labour and capital used in the production process. Of course, there are many different ways of combining labour and capital inputs, some combinations being more efficient than others. The **production function** summarises the technically most efficient combinations for any given output level.

The nature of technology in an industry will determine the way in which output varies with the quantity of inputs. However, one thing is certain. If the firm increases the amount of inputs of the variable factor (labour) while holding constant the input of the other

 terms

short run: the period over which a firm is free to vary the input of one of its factors of production (labour), but faces a fixed input of the other (capital)

long run: the period over which the firm is able to vary the inputs of all its factors of production

production function: function embodying information about technically efficient ways of combining labour and capital to produce output

law of diminishing returns: law stating that if a firm increases its inputs of one factor of production while holding inputs of the other factor fixed, it will eventually derive diminishing marginal returns from the variable factor

factor (capital), it will gradually derive less additional output per unit of labour for each further increase. This is known as the **law of diminishing returns**, and is one of the few 'laws' in economics. It is a *short-run* concept, as it relies on the assumption that capital is fixed.

It can readily be seen why this should be the case. Suppose a firm has 10 computer programmers working in an office, using 10 computers. The 11th worker may add some extra output, as the workers may be able to 'hot-desk' and take their coffee breaks at different times. The 12th worker may also add some extra output, perhaps by keeping the printers stocked with paper. However, if the firm keeps

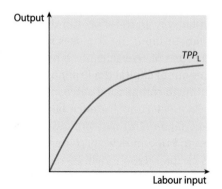

Figure 1.1 *A short-run production function*

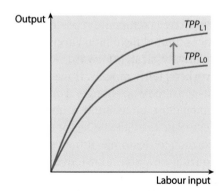

Figure 1.2 *The effect of an increase in capital*

adding programmers without increasing the number of computers, each extra worker will be adding less additional output to the office. Indeed, the 20th worker may add nothing at all, being unable to get access to a computer.

Figure 1.1 illustrates the short-run relationship between labour input and total physical product (TPP_L), with capital held constant. The curvature of the TPP_L relationship reflects the law of diminishing returns: as labour input increases, the amount of additional output produced gets smaller. An increase in the amount of capital available will raise the amount of output produced for any given labour input, so the TPP_L will shift upwards, as shown in Figure 1.2.

The production function thus carries information about the physical relationship between the inputs of the factors of production and the physical quantity of output. With this information and knowledge of the prices the firm must pay for its inputs of the factors of production, it is possible to map out the way in which costs will change with the level of output.

Costs in the short run

Because the firm cannot vary some of its inputs in the short run, some costs may be regarded as fixed, and some as variable. In this short run, some **fixed costs** are **sunk costs**, i.e. costs that the firm cannot avoid paying even if it chooses to produce no output. Total costs are the sum of fixed and **variable costs**:

total costs = total fixed costs + total variable costs

Total costs will increase as the firm increases the volume of production, because more of the variable input is needed to increase output. The way in which the costs will vary depends on the nature of the production function, and on whether the prices of labour or capital alter as output increases.

A common assumption made by economists is that in the short run, at very low levels of output, total costs will rise more slowly than output, but that as diminishing returns set in total costs will accelerate, as shown in Figure 1.3.

Total, marginal and average costs

An important relationship exists between total, marginal and **average costs**. Remember from *AS Economics, Chapter 4* that **marginal cost** is the additional cost of producing an additional unit of output.

Key terms

fixed costs: costs that do not vary with the level of output

sunk costs: short-run costs that cannot be recovered if the firm closes down

variable costs: costs that vary with the level of output

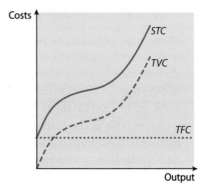

Figure 1.3 *Costs in the short run*

Key terms

average cost: total cost divided by the quantity produced

marginal cost: the cost of producing an additional unit of output

Table 1.1 provides an arithmetic example to illustrate the relationship between these different aspects of costs. The firm represented here faces fixed costs of £225 per week. The table shows the costs of production for up to 6000 units of the firm's product per week. Column (3) shows total variable costs of production: you can see that these rise quite steeply as the volume of production increases. Adding fixed and variable costs gives the short-run total costs (*STC*) at each output level. This is shown in column (4), which is the sum of columns (2) and (3).

(1) Output ('000 units per week)	(2) Fixed costs	(3) Total variable costs	(4) Short-run total costs (2) + (3)	(5) Short-run average total cost (4)/(1)	(6) Short-run marginal cost Δ(4)/Δ(1)	(7) Short-run average variable cost (3)/(1)	(8) Short-run average fixed cost (2)/(1)
1	225	85	310	310		85	225
					65		
2	225	150	375	187.5		75	112.5
					60		
3	225	210	435	145		70	75
					90		
4	225	300	525	131.25		75	56.25
					175		
5	225	475	700	140		95	45
					395		
6	225	870	1095	182.5		145	37.5

Table 1.1 *The short-run relationship between output and costs (in £s)*

The short-run average cost (*SATC* – column (5)) is calculated as short-run total cost divided by output. To calculate short-run marginal cost, you need to work out the additional cost of producing an extra unit of output at each output level. This is calculated as the change in costs divided by the change in output (Δ column (4) divided by Δ column (1), where Δ means the 'change in').

Finally, average variable costs (*SAVC*, i.e. column (3)/column (1)) and average fixed costs (*SAFC*, i.e. column (2)/column (1)) can be calculated.

These relationships are plotted in Figure 1.4, which shows how they relate to each other. First, notice that short-run average total costs (*SATC*) takes on a U-shape. This is the form often assumed in economic analysis. *SATC* is the sum of average fixed and variable costs (*SAFC* and *SAVC*, respectively). Average fixed costs slope downwards

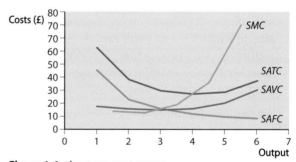

Figure 1.4 *short-run cost curves*

throughout – this is because fixed costs do not vary with the level of output, so as output increases *SAFC* must always get smaller, as the fixed costs are spread over more and more units of output. However, *SAVC* also shows a U-shape, and it is this that gives the U-shape to *SATC*.

A very important aspect of Figure 1.4 is that the short-run marginal cost cuts both *SAVC* and *SATC* at their minimum points. This is always the case. If you think about this for a moment, you will realise that it makes good sense. If you are adding on something that is greater than the average, the average must always increase. For a firm, when the marginal cost of producing an additional unit of a good is higher than the average cost of doing so, the average cost must rise. If the marginal is the same as the average, then the average will not change. This is quite simply an arithmetic property of the average and the marginal, and always holds true. So when you draw the average and marginal cost curves for a firm, the marginal cost curve will always cut average cost at the minimum point of average cost. Another way of viewing marginal cost is as the *slope* or gradient of the total cost curve.

Remember that the short-run cost curves show the relationship between the volume of production and costs under the assumption that the quantity of capital is fixed, so that in order to change output the firm has to vary the amount of labour. The *position* of the cost curves thus depends on the quantity of capital. In other words, there is a short-run average total cost curve for each given level of capital.

Costs in the long run

In the long run, a firm is able to vary both capital and labour. It is thus likely to choose the level of capital that is appropriate for the level of output that it expects to produce. Figure 1.5 shows a number of short-run average total cost curves corresponding to different expected output levels.

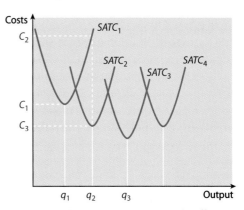

Figure 1.5 *Short-run cost curves with different levels of capital input*

Extension material

For the firm in Figure 1.5, the choice of capital is important. Suppose the firm wants to produce the quantity of output q_1. It would choose to install the amount of capital corresponding to the short-run total cost curve $SATC_1$, and could then produce q_1 at an average cost of C_1 in the short run. However, if the firm finds that demand is more buoyant than expected, and so wants to increase output to q_2, in the short run it has no option but to increase labour input and expand output along $SATC_1$, taking cost per unit to C_2.

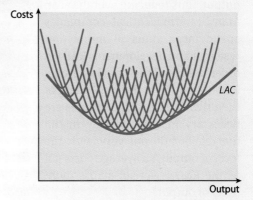

Figure 1.6 *The long-run average cost curve*

In the longer term, the firm will be able to adjust its capital stock and move on to $SATC_2$, reducing average cost to C_3. Thus, as soon as the firm moves away from the output level for which capital stock is designed, it incurs higher average cost in the short run than is possible in the long run.

In this way a long-run average cost curve can be derived to illustrate how the firm chooses to vary its capital stock for any given level of output. Figure 1.6 shows what such a curve would look like for the firm of the previous figure under the assumption that there is an infinite number of short-run costs curves, each corresponding to a particular desired output level, of which only some are shown! The long-run average cost curve just touches each of the short-run average cost curves, and is known as the 'envelope' of the *SATC* curves.

With the set of *SATC* curves in Figure 1.5, the long-run average cost curve also takes on a U-shape. *AS Economics, Chapter 4* introduced the notion of **economies of scale**. It pointed out that there are several reasons why average cost might be expected to fall as a firm expanded its scale of operations. It is now clear that this refers to a situation in which the firm expands its inputs of both fixed and variable factors in order to increase its scale of operation. Economies of scale thus correspond to a situation in which long-run average cost falls as output is increased. There may be several reasons why economies of scale may arise. Some may arise from factors that are internal to the firm, whereas others may be external – arising when the whole industry expands.

Internal economies of scale arise as a firm expands its production. For example, there may be *indivisibilities* in production, whereby some inputs can only be used in certain quantities. A train would be a very inefficient way of carrying a single passenger between two destinations, and only becomes cost-effective when there are more travellers. There may also be fixed costs in the production process that must be incurred before any production takes place at all. As the volume of production expands, these fixed costs are spread out over more units of output, thus reducing average cost. Many pharmaceutical companies spend large sums of money on research and development (R&D) in order to expand their product range (and to match the R&D spending of their rivals). These expenditures are necessary in order to stay in the market, but do not vary with the level of output, so average costs fall as the R&D is spread across more units of output.

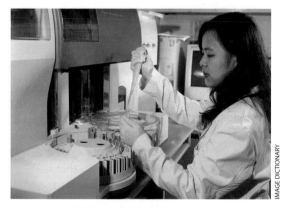

Spending on R&D is a fixed cost that has to be spread across units of output.

Specialisation may be another source of economies of scale – as noted by Adam Smith in his discussion of the division of labour (see *AS Economics, Chapter 1*). Large-scale production enables the process to be broken into a series of parts, and this then allows workers to become adept at their part of that process, again reducing costs. There may also be managerial economies of scale, by which a larger firm can have specialist departments dealing with procurement or human resources. A large firm may also be able to obtain better deals on its purchases of inputs, or on its borrowing. All these things may reduce average cost for the larger firm.

External economies of scale arise as an industry expands. For example, when a new industry first sets up in an economy it may be difficult to recruit workers with the skills needed for the new activity, and firms may need to provide their own training. However, as the industry expands, there will be more workers that have acquired the necessary skills. It may even be that local colleges find it worthwhile to set up courses that provide these skills. Firms thus find they need to spend less on providing training, and this element of costs falls. One example of this was the proliferation of courses in computer programming and computer science when computers began to be used by firms.

In Figure 1.7, if the firm expands its output up to q^*, long-run average cost falls. Up to q^* of output is the range over which there are economies of scale. To the right of q^*, however, long-run average cost rises as output continues to be increased, and the firm experiences **diseconomies of scale**. The output q* itself is at the intermediate state of **constant returns to scale**.

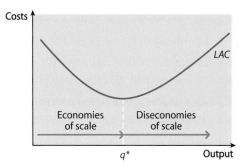

Figure 1.7 The long-run average cost curves

A common source of diseconomies of scale is in management. As a firm continues to grow, additional layers of management may be needed to cope with the increasing complexity of operations – especially if the firm is spread between many locations. As the firm becomes more cumbersome in its organisation, the average cost of running and monitoring activity within the firm tends to rise. The rapid developments in technology in recent years may have enabled some of these problems to be overcome, as it becomes easier to use technology to assist in the administration of the firm. This may help to explain the appearance of some giant firms.

Key terms

economies of scale: what happens if an increase in a firm's scale of production leads to production at lower long-run average cost

diseconomies of scale: said to occur when long-run average cost rises as output increases

constant returns to scale: found when long-run average cost remains constant with an increase in output, i.e. when output and costs rise at the same rate

It is also possible that there could be external diseconomies of scale – for example, if the industry grows so rapidly that the supply of workers runs dry. This helps to explain why average costs may start to rise at some level of output. This point may come at different points for different sorts of activities.

It is important not to confuse the notion of returns to scale with the idea introduced earlier of diminishing marginal returns to a factor. The two concepts arise in

different circumstances. The law of diminishing returns to a factor applies in the *short run*, when a firm increases its inputs of one factor of production while facing fixed amounts of other factors. It is thus solely a short-run phenomenon. Diseconomies of scale (sometimes known as *decreasing returns to scale*), can occur in the *long run*, and the term refers to how output changes as a firm varies the quantities of *all* factors.

The point at which long-run average cost stops falling is known as the **minimum efficient scale**. This is the smallest level of output that a firm can produce at the minimum level of long-run average cost.

 Key term

minimum efficient scale: the level of output at which long-run average cost stops falling as output increases

If the firm is operating at the lowest possible level of long-run average costs it is in a position of *productive efficiency*, which was defined and discussed in *AS Economics, Chapter 4*. Remember that the long-run average cost curve (*LAC*) is drawn as a U-shape because of the assumptions that were made about the technology of production. The underlying assumption here is that the firm faces economies of scale at relatively low levels of output, so that *LAC* slopes downwards. However, at some point decreasing returns to scale set in, and *LAC* then begins to slope upwards.

This turns out to be a convenient representation, but in practice the *LAC* curve can take on a variety of shapes. Figure 1.8 shows some of these. LAC_1 is the typical U-shape — which you will meet again. LAC_2 is an example of a situation in which there are economies of scale up to a point, after which long-run average cost levels out and there is a long flat range over which the firm faces constant returns to

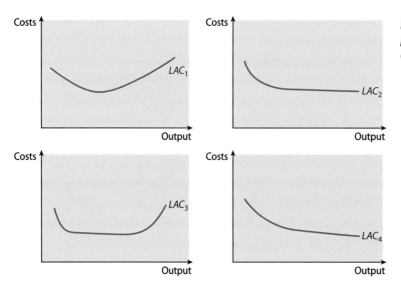

Figure 1.8
possible shapes of the LAC curve

scale. LAC_3 is a bit similar, except that the constant returns to scale (flat) segment eventually runs out and diseconomies of scale set in. In LAC_4 the economies of scale continue over the whole range of output shown. This could occur in a market where the fixed costs are substantial, dominating the influence of variable costs.

Exercise 1.3

Which of the following reflects a movement *along* a long-run average cost curve, and which would cause a shift *of* a long-run average cost curve?

a A firm becomes established in a market, learning the best ways of utilising its factors of production.

b A firm observes that average cost falls as it expands its scale of production.

c The larger a firm becomes, the more difficult it becomes to manage, causing average cost to rise.

d A firm operating in the financial sector installs new, faster computers, enabling its average cost to fall for any given level of service that it provides.

Summary

➤ A firm may face inflexibility in the short run, with some factors being fixed in quantity and only some being variable.

➤ The short run is defined in this context as the period over which a firm is free to vary some factors but not others.

➤ The long run is defined as the period over which the firm is able to vary the input of all of its factors of production.

➤ The production function shows how output can be efficiently produced through the input of factors of production.

➤ The law of diminishing returns states that, if a firm increases the input of a variable factor while holding input of the fixed factor constant, eventually the firm will get diminishing marginal returns from the variable factor.

➤ Short-run costs can be separated into fixed, sunk and variable costs.

➤ There is a clear and immutable relationship between total, average and marginal costs.

➤ For a U-shaped average cost curve, marginal cost always cuts the minimum point of average cost.

➤ The minimum efficient scale is the point at which the long-run average cost curve stops sloping downwards.

➤ In practice, long-run average cost curves may take on a variety of shapes, according to the technology of the industry concerned.

Exercise 1.4

A firm faces long-run total cost conditions as in Table 1.2:

Output ('000 units per week)	Total cost (£'000)
0	0
1	32
2	48
3	82
4	140
5	228
6	352

Table 1.2 *Output and long-run costs*

a Calculate long-run average cost and long-run marginal cost for each level of output.

b Plot long-run average cost and long-run marginal cost curves on a graph. (*Hint*: don't forget to plot *LMC* at points that are halfway between the corresponding output levels.)

c Identify the output level at which long-run average cost is at a minimum.

d Identify the output level at which *LAC* = *LMC*.

e Within what range of output does this firm enjoy economies of scale?

f Within what range of output does the firm experience diseconomies of scale?

g If you could measure the nature of returns to scale, what would characterise the point where *LAC* is at a minimum?

Case study of a failed merger

Earlier discussion identified the quest for economies of scale as one of the motivating forces for a firm to look for growth through merger activity. However, not all mergers are able to deliver the expected benefits. This case study examines one episode in which a merger did not turn out the way that the firms involved anticipated.

In 2001 negotiations began between two firms in the telecoms-equipment business — the French firm Alcatel and Lucent Technologies of America. At the time, the negotiations came to nothing, as the two firms could not come to an agreement over who would control the merged firm. However, 5 years later in April 2006 an agreement was reached that the two firms would merge.

On the face of it, there seemed to be good commercial reasons for coming together in this way. Alcatel, the bigger of the two firms, would gain entry into the lucrative American market, and the merger would make the combined firm one of the largest in the world in the market. The combined revenue of the two firms from sales of network equipment would be slightly larger than Cisco Systems, the existing market leader at the time.

It was expected that the merger would not only give the firm a higher profile in the two key markets of America and Europe, but would also enable the exploitation of economies of scale. By combining the companies, it was expected that about 10%

of the existing workforce could be cut, saving $1.7 billion. This would be achieved by eliminating overlapping administrative, procurement and marketing costs, as well as reducing the workforce. This demonstrates one of the benefits of a larger firm that arise because of economies of scale.

However, not all commentators at the time were convinced that this was the best way forward in the industry. Other firms had been growing more slowly, acquiring smaller firms that had complementary products that expanded the firm's product range. A problem with the merger of two large firms was anticipated to lie in the difficulty of killing off duplicate products, as previous customers using the product of one of the firms would be reluctant to switch to an alternative product, even if it provided a similar specification. This would therefore restrict the degree to which the larger firm would be able to rationalise its activity.

In the event, the merged company did indeed run into problems. The firm found cost savings difficult to realise, in spite of 16,500 job losses from a workforce of 88,000 — and found that prices in the market were falling, squeezing profitability. The firm faced competition from new entrants, in particular two Chinese firms, and found difficulty in keeping up with the pace of technological change. It was also reported that the firm was suffering from a clash of cultures between the French and American parts of the business.

The result of all this was that in July 2008 it was announced that the French chairman (who was formerly the boss of Alcatel) and the American chief executive (formerly the boss of Lucent) were leaving the company and being replaced by a new executive team charged with the task of taking the company forward. The new chairman was neither French nor American.

The Alcatel-Lucent merger failed to deliver the expected economies of scale.

Motivations of firms

The opening section of this chapter stated that firms exist to organise production, by bringing together the factors of production in order to produce output. This begs the question of what motivates them to produce particular *levels* of output, and at what price. In the remainder of this chapter consideration will be given to alternative objectives that firms may set out to achieve.

Profit maximisation

Traditional economic analysis has tended to start from the premise that firms set out with the objective of maximising profits. In analysing this, economists define profits as the difference between the total revenue received by a firm and the total costs that it incurs in production:

profits = total revenue − total cost

Total revenue here is seen in terms of the quantity of the product that is sold multiplied by the price. Total cost includes the fixed and variable costs that have already been discussed. However, one important item of costs should be highlighted before going any further.

Consider the case of a sole proprietor — a small local business. It seems reasonable to assume that such a firm will set out to maximise its profits. However, from the entrepreneur's perspective there is an *opportunity cost* (see *AS Economics, Chapter 1*) of being in business, which may be seen in terms of the earnings that the proprietor could make in an alternative occupation. This required rate of return is regarded as a fixed cost, and is included in the total cost of production.

The same procedure applies to cost curves for other sorts of firm. In other words, when economists refer to costs, they include the rate of return that a firm needs to make to stay in a particular market in the long run.

supernormal profits/abnormal profits/ economic profit: terms referring to profits that exceed normal profit

Accountants dislike this, as 'opportunity cost' cannot be identified as an explicit item in the accounts. This part of costs is known as *normal profit*. Profits made by a firm above that level are known as **supernormal profits**, **abnormal profits** or **economic profits**.

In the short run, a firm may choose to remain in a market even if it is not covering its opportunity costs, provided its revenues are covering its variable costs. Since the firm has already incurred fixed costs, if it can cover its variable costs in the short run it will be better off remaining in business and paying off part of the fixed costs than exiting the market and losing all of its fixed costs. Thus, the level of average variable costs represents the shut-down price, below which the firm will exit from the market in the short run.

How does a firm choose its output level if it wishes to maximise profits? Suppose a firm is a relatively small player in a big market, and thus has no influence over the price of its product. Its total revenue is then proportional to the amount of output it sells. If it faces the shape of short-run total cost curve that was introduced earlier in the chapter, its output decision can be analysed by reference to Figure 1.9.

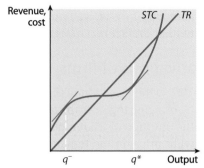

Figure 1.9 Profit maximisation

To maximise profits, the firm needs to choose the output level at which the total revenue curve (*TR*) is as far above the total cost curve as possible. This happens at q^*, which is the point at which the slope of *STC* is the same as the slope of *TR*.

Notice that the slope of *STC* is in fact the short-run marginal cost, as noted earlier. Similarly, the slope of *TR* is **marginal revenue**; this is the additional revenue that the firm gains from selling an additional unit of output. Thus it can be seen that profits will be maximised where marginal cost is equal to marginal revenue – with one proviso: total revenue must exceed total cost. After all, the slopes of *STC* and *TR* are also equal at q^-, but at that point total costs are way higher than total revenue, and the firm makes a substantial loss.

An alternative way of looking at this decision is to draw the marginal cost and marginal revenue curves as in Figure 1.10. Because it was assumed that the firm could not influence price, the marginal revenue received from selling each additional unit of output is constant, and equal to the price. The marginal cost curve is U-shaped as usual.

Again, you can see that q^* will be the output that maximises profits. If the firm is producing less output than this, it will find that the marginal revenue from selling an additional unit of output is higher than the marginal cost of producing it, so the firm can add to its profits by increasing output. In contrast, if the firm is producing beyond q^*, it will find that the marginal revenue from selling an extra unit fails to cover the cost of producing the unit, so it will not pay the firm to produce beyond q^*. Therefore, q^* can be seen as the level of output that maximises the firm's profits.

The *MC* = *MR* rule is a general rule for firms that want to maximise profits, and it holds in all market situations. For example, suppose the firm faces a downward-sloping demand curve for its product, such that it can sell more by reducing the price. In *AS Economics, Chapter 2* it was seen that a linear demand curve is associated with a total revenue curve like that shown in Figure 1.11. Assume that the firm faces the usual shape of short-run total cost curve *STC*.

Profits are again maximised where the slopes of *STC* and *TR* are equal, with *TR* exceeding *STC*. This occurs at q_π.

Key term

marginal revenue: the additional revenue gained by a firm from selling an additional unit of output

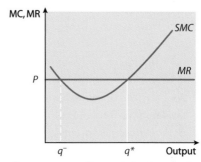

Figure 1.10 *Profit maximisation again*

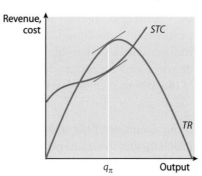

Figure 1.11 *Profit maximisation with a downward-sloping demand curve*

Exercise 1.5

Figure 1.12 shows a firm in short-run equilibrium. The firm is operating in a market in which it has no influence over price, so it gains the same marginal revenue from the sale of each unit of output. Marginal revenue and average revenue are thus the same. P_1, P_2 and P_3 represent three possible prices that could prevail in the market.

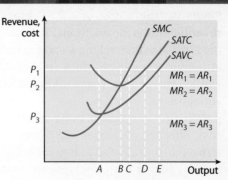

Figure 1.12 Profit maximisation in the short run

a For each price level, identify the output level that the firm would choose in order to maximise profits.

b For each of these output levels, compare the level of average revenue with that of average cost, and consider what this means for the firm's profits.

The principal–agent problem

The discussion so far seems reasonable when considering a relatively small owner-managed firm. In this context, profit maximisation makes good sense as the firm's motivation.

However, for many larger firms — especially public limited companies — the owners may not be involved in running the business. This gives rise to the **principal–agent** (or **agency**) **problem**. In a public limited company, the shareholders delegate the day-to-day decisions concerning the operation

 term

principal–agent (agency) problem: a problem arising from conflict between the objectives of the principals and those of the agents who take decisions on their behalf

of the firm to managers who act on their behalf. In this case the shareholders are the *principals*, and the managers are the *agents* who run things for them.

If the agents are fully in sympathy with the objectives of the owners there is no problem, and the managers will take exactly the decisions that the owners would like. Problems arise when there is conflict between the aims of the owners and those of the managers.

One simple explanation of why this problem arises is that the managers like a quiet life, and therefore do not push for the absolute profit-maximising position, but do just enough to keep the shareholders off their backs. Herbert Simon referred to this as 'satisficing' behaviour, where managers aim to produce satisfactory profits rather than maximum profits.

Another possibility is that managers become negligent because they are not fully accountable. One manifestation of this may be *organisational slack* in the

organisation: costs will not be minimised, as the firm is not operating as efficiently as it could. This is an example of what is called **X-inefficiency**. For example, in Figure 1.13 LAC represents the long-run average cost curve showing the most efficient cost positions for the firm at any output level. With X-inefficiency, a firm could end up producing output q_1 at average cost AC_1. Thus, in the presence of X-inefficiency the firm will be operating *above* its long-run average cost curve.

Some writers have argued that the managers may be pursuing other objectives. For example, some managers may enjoy being involved in the running of a *large* business, and may prefer to see the firm gaining market share — perhaps beyond the profit-maximising level. Others may like to see their status rewarded and so will want to divert part of the profits into managerial perks — large offices, company cars and so on. Or they may feel that having a large staff working for them increases their prestige inside the company. These sorts of activity tend to reduce the profitability of firms.

Key term

X-inefficiency: situation arising when a firm is not operating at minimum cost, perhaps because of organisational slack

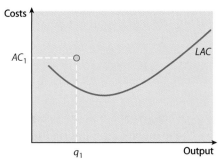

Figure 1.13 *X-inefficiency*

Revenue maximisation

William Baumol argued that managers may set out with the objective of maximising revenue. The effects of such action can be seen in Figure 1.14. As before, q_π represents the profit-maximising level of output. However, you can see that total revenue is maximised at the peak of the TR curve (where $MR = 0$) at q_r. Thus, a revenue-maximising firm will produce more output than a profit-maximising one, and will need to charge a lower price in order to sell the extra output.

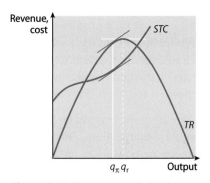

Figure 1.14 *Revenue maximisation*

Baumol pointed out that the shareholders might not be too pleased about this. The way the firm behaves then depends upon the degree of accountability that the agents (managers) have to the principals (shareholders). For example, the shareholders may have sufficient power over their agents to be able to insist on some minimum level of profits. The result may then be a compromise solution between the principals and the agents, with output being set somewhere between q_π and q_r.

Sales maximisation

In some cases managers may focus more on the volume of sales than on the resulting revenues. This could lead to output being set even higher, as shown in

Figure 1.15. The firm would now push for higher sales up to the point where it just breaks even at q_s. This is the point at which total revenue only just covers total cost. Remember that total cost includes normal profit – the opportunity cost of the resources tied up in the firm. The firm would have to close down if it did not cover this opportunity cost.

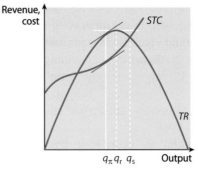

Figure 1.15 *Sales maximisation*

Again, the extent to which the managers will be able to pursue this objective without endangering their positions with the shareholders depends on how accountable the managers are to the shareholders. Remember that the managers are likely to have much better information about the market conditions and the internal functioning of the firm than the shareholders, who view the firm only remotely. This may be to the managers' advantage.

Efficiency

An important question is what this analysis implies for the efficiency of markets. How likely are firms to produce in ways that bolster the overall efficiency with which markets work to allocate resources? *AS Economics, Chapter 4* introduced two important aspects of efficiency: productive efficiency and allocative efficiency. The conditions necessary for these aspects to be met can be seen in terms of the cost curves.

Productive efficiency itself has two such conditions. First, it requires that firms choose an appropriate set of factor inputs. Second, it requires that those inputs be used in the best possible way in order to minimise costs. These requirements will be met in a market if firms are operating at minimum long-run average cost.

Allocative efficiency in an individual market requires that firms charge a price that is equal to marginal cost. To determine whether this condition will be met, it is necessary to explore how prices are set, which is what the next chapter sets out to do.

Summary

> Traditional economic analysis assumes that firms set out to maximise profits, where profits are defined as the excess of total revenue over total cost.

> This analysis treats the opportunity cost of a firm's resources as a part of fixed costs. The opportunity cost is known as normal profit.

> Profits above this level are known as supernormal profits.

> A firm maximises profits by choosing output such that marginal revenue is equal to marginal cost.

➤ For many larger firms, where day-to-day control is delegated to managers, a principal–agent problem may arise if there is conflict between the objectives of owners (principals) and those of the managers (agents).

➤ This may lead to satisficing behaviour and to X-inefficiency.

➤ William Baumol suggested that managers may set out to maximise revenue rather than profits; others have suggested that sales or the growth of the firm may be the managers' objectives.

➤ For an individual firm, productive efficiency can be regarded as having been achieved when the firm is operating at minimum long-run average cost.

Market structure: perfect competition and monopoly

The AS Economics course introduced the notion of market failure — describing situations in which free markets may not produce the best outcome for society in terms of efficiency. One of the reasons given for this concerned what is termed 'imperfect competition'. It was argued that, if firms can achieve a position of market dominance, they may distort the pattern of resource allocation. It is now time to look at market structure more closely in order to evaluate the way that markets work, and the significance of this for resource allocation. The fact that firms try to maximise profits is not in itself bad for society. However, the structure of a market has a strong influence on how well the market performs. 'Structure' here is seen in relation to a number of dimensions, but in particular to the number of firms operating in a market and the way in which they interact. This chapter considers two extreme forms of market structure: perfect competition and monopoly.

Learning outcomes

After studying this chapter, you should:
- ➤ understand what is meant by market structure, and why it is important for firms
- ➤ appreciate the significance of barriers to entry to a market in influencing the market structure
- ➤ be familiar with the assumptions of the model of perfect competition
- ➤ understand how a firm chooses profit-maximising output under perfect competition
- ➤ appreciate how a perfectly competitive market reaches long-run equilibrium
- ➤ understand how the characteristics of long-run equilibrium affect the performance of the market in terms of productive and allocative efficiency
- ➤ be familiar with the assumptions of the model of monopoly

➤ understand how the monopoly firm chooses output and sets price
➤ understand why a monopoly can arise in a market
➤ understand how the characteristics of the monopoly equilibrium affect the performance of the market in terms of productive and allocative efficiency
➤ be aware of the relative merits of perfect competition and monopoly in terms of market performance

Market structure

Firms cannot take decisions without some awareness of the market in which they are operating. In some markets, firms find themselves to be such a small player that they cannot influence the price at which they sell. In others, a firm may find itself to be the only firm, which clearly gives it much more discretion in devising a price and output strategy. There may also be many intermediate situations where the firm has some control over price, but needs to be aware of rival firms in the market.

Economists have devised a range of models that allow such different **market structures** to be analysed. Before looking carefully at the most important types of market structure, the key characteristics of alternative market structures will be introduced. The main models are summarised in Table 2.1. In many ways, we can regard these as a spectrum of markets with different characteristics.

market structure: the market environment within which firms operate

	Perfect competition	**Monopolistic competition**	**Oligopoly**	**Monopoly**
Number of firms	Many	Many	Few	One
Freedom of entry	Not restricted	Not restricted	Some barriers to entry	High barriers to entry
Firm's influence over price	None	Some	Some	Price maker, subject to the demand curve
Nature of product	Homogeneous	Differentiated	Varied	No close substitutes
Examples	Cauliflowers	Fast-food outlets	Cars	PC operating systems
	Carrots	Travel agents	Mobile phones	Local water supply

Table 2.1 *A spectrum of market structures*

Perfect competition

At one extreme is *perfect competition.* This is a market in which each individual firm is a *price taker.* This means that there is no individual firm that is large enough to be able to influence the price, which is set by the market as a whole. This situation would arise where there are many firms operating in a market, producing a product that is much the same whichever firm produces it. You might think of a market for a particular sort of vegetable, for example. One cauliflower is very much like another, and it would not be possible for a particular cauliflower-grower to set a premium price for its product.

Such markets are also typified by freedom of entry and exit. In other words, it is relatively easy for new firms to enter the market, or for existing firms to leave it to produce something else. The market price in such a market will be driven down to that at which the typical firm in the market just makes enough profit to stay in business. If firms make more than this, other firms will be attracted in, and thus abnormal profits will be competed away. If some firms in the market do not make sufficient profit to want to remain in the market, they will exit, allowing price to drift up until again the typical firm just makes enough to stay in business.

Monopoly

At the other extreme of the spectrum of market structures is *monopoly*. This is a market where there is only one firm in operation. Such a firm has some influence over price, and can choose a combination of price and output in order to maximise its profits. The monopolist is not entirely free to set any price that it wants, as it must remain aware of the demand curve for its product. Nonetheless, it has the freedom to choose a point along its demand curve.

The nature of a monopolist's product is that it has no close substitutes — either actual or potential — so faces no competition. An example might be Microsoft, which for a long time held a global monopoly for operating systems for PC computers. At the time of the famous trial in 1998, Microsoft was said to supply operating systems for about 95% of the world's PCs.

Another condition of a monopoly market is that there are barriers to the entry for new firms. This means that the firm is able to set its price such as to make profits that are above the minimum needed to keep the firm in business, without attracting new rivals into the market.

Bill Gates held a global monopoly on PC operating systems through his company Microsoft.

Monopolistic competition

Between the two extreme forms of market structure are many intermediate situations in which firms may have some influence over their selling price, but still have to take account of the fact that there are other firms in the market. One such market is known as *monopolistic competition*. This is a market in which there are many firms operating, each producing similar but not identical products, so that there is some scope for influencing price, perhaps because of brand loyalty. However, firms in such a market are likely to be relatively small. Such firms may find it profitable to make sure that their own product is differentiated from other goods, and may advertise in order to convince potential customers that this is the case. For example, small-scale local restaurants may offer different styles of cooking.

Small-scale local restaurants differentiate what they have to offer by serving particular kinds of food.

Oligopoly

Another intermediate form of market structure is *oligopoly*, which literally means 'few sellers'. This is a market in which there are just a few firms that supply the market. Each firm will take decisions in close awareness of how other firms in the market may react to their actions. In some cases, the firms may try to collude – to work together in order to behave as if they were a monopolist – thus making higher profits. In other cases, they may be intense rivals, which will tend to result in abnormal profits being competed away. The question of whether firms in an oligopoly collude or compete has a substantial impact on how the overall market performs in terms of resource allocation, and whether consumers will be disadvantaged as a result of the actions of the firms in the market.

Barriers to entry

It has been argued that if firms in a market are able to make abnormal profits this will act as an inducement for new firms to try to gain entry into that market in order to share in those profits. A *barrier to entry* is a characteristic of a market that prevents new firms from joining the market. The existence of such barriers is thus of great importance in influencing the market structure that will evolve.

For example, if a firm holds a patent on a particular good, this means that no other firm is permitted by law to produce the product, and the patent-holding firm thus has a monopoly. The firm may then be able to set price such as to make abnormal profits without fear of rival firms competing away those profits. On the other hand, if there are no barriers to entry in a market, and if the existing firms set price to make abnormal profits, new firms will join the market, and the increase in market supply will push price down until no abnormal profits are being made.

Summary

➤ The decisions made by firms must be taken in the context of the market environment in which they operate.

➤ Under conditions of perfect competition, each firm must accept the market price as given, but can choose how much output to produce in order to maximise profits.

➤ In a monopoly market, where there is only one producer, the firm can choose output and price (subject to the demand curve).

➤ Monopolistic competition combines some features of perfect competition, and some characteristics of monopoly. Firms have some influence over price, and will produce a differentiated product in order to maintain this influence.

➤ Oligopoly exists where a market is occupied by just a few firms. In some cases, these few firms may work together to maximise their joint profits; in other cases, they may seek to outmanoeuvre each other.

Exercise 2.1

For each of the market situations listed below, select the form of market structure that is most likely to apply. In each case, comment on the way in which the firm's actions may be influenced by the market structure.

Forms of market structure: A perfect competition
                            B monopoly
                            C monopolistic competition
                            D oligopoly

a A fairly large number of fast-food outlets in a city centre, offering various different styles of cooking (Indian, Chinese, fish and chips, burgers, etc.) at broadly similar prices.

b An island's only airport.

c A large number of farmers selling parsnips at the same price.

d A small number of large firms that between them supply most of the market for commercial vans.

The model of perfect competition

At one end of the spectrum of market structures is **perfect competition**. This model has a special place in economic analysis, because if all its assumptions were fulfilled, and if all markets operated according to its precepts, the best allocation of resources would be ensured for society as a whole. Although it may be argued that this ideal is not often achieved, perfect

Key term

perfect competition: a form of market structure that produces allocative and productive efficiency in long-run equilibrium

competition nonetheless provides a yardstick by which all other forms of market structure can be evaluated.

Assumptions

The assumptions of the model of perfect competition are as follows:

1 Firms aim to maximise profits.
2 There are many participants (both buyers and sellers).
3 The product is homogeneous.
4 There are no barriers to entry to or exit from the market.
5 There is perfect knowledge of market conditions.
6 There are no externalities.

Profit maximisation

The first assumption is that firms act to maximise their profits. You might think that this means that firms, acting in their own self-interest, are unlikely to do consumers any favours. However, it transpires that this does not interfere with the operation of the market. Indeed, it is the pursuit of self-interest by firms and consumers that ensures that the market works effectively.

Many participants

This is an important assumption of the model: that there are so many buyers and so many sellers that no individual trader is able to influence the market price. The market price is thus determined by the operation of the market.

On the sellers' side of the market, this assumption is tantamount to saying that there are limited economies of scale in the industry. If the minimum efficient scale is small relative to market demand, then no firm is likely to become so large that it will gain influence in the market.

A homogeneous product

This assumption means that buyers of the good see all products in the market as being identical, and will not favour one firm's product over another. If there were brand loyalty, such that one firm was more popular than others, then that firm would be able to charge a premium on its price. By ruling out this possibility the previous assumption is reinforced, and no individual seller is able to influence the selling price of the product.

No barriers to entry or exit

By this assumption, firms are able to join the market if they perceive it to be a profitable step, and they can exit from the market without hindrance. This assumption is important when it comes to considering the long-run equilibrium towards which the market will tend.

Perfect knowledge

It is assumed that all participants in the market have perfect information about trading conditions in the market. In particular, buyers always know the prices that firms are charging, and thus can buy the good at the cheapest possible price. Firms

that try to charge a price above the market price will get no takers. At the same time, traders are aware of the product quality.

No externalities

AS Economics, Chapter 8 described externalities as a form of market failure that prevents the attainment of allocative efficiency. Here externalities are ruled out in order to explore the characteristics of the perfect competition model.

Perfect competition in the short run

The firm under perfect competition

With the above assumptions, it is possible to analyse how a firm will operate in the market. An important implication of these assumptions is that no individual trader can influence the price of the product. In particular, this means that the firm is a **price taker**, and has to accept whatever price is set in the market as a whole.

Key term

price taker: a firm that must accept whatever price is set in the market as a whole

This means that the firm faces a perfectly elastic demand curve for its product, as is shown in Figure 2.1. In this figure, P_1 is the price set in the market, and the firm cannot sell at any other price. If it tries to set a price above P_1 it will sell nothing, as buyers are fully aware of the market price and will not buy at a higher price, espe-

cially as they know that there is no quality difference between the product as produced by different firms in the market. What this also implies is that the firm can sell as much output as it likes at that going price – which means there is no incentive for any firm to set a price below P_1. Thus, all firms charge the same price, P_1.

The firm's short-run supply decision

If the firm can sell as much as it likes at the market price, how does it decide how much to produce?

Chapter 1 explained that to maximise profits a firm needs to set output at such a level that marginal revenue is equal to marginal cost. Figure 2.2 illustrates this rule by adding the short-run cost curves to the demand curve. (Remember that *SMC* cuts the *SATC* at the minimum point of *SAVC* and *SATC*.) As the demand curve is horizontal,

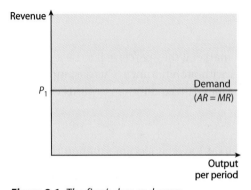

Figure 2.1 *The firm's demand curve*

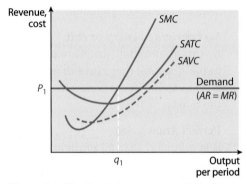

Figure 2.2 *The firm's short-run supply decision*

the firm faces constant average and marginal revenue and will choose output at q_1, where $MR = MC$.

If the market price were to change, the firm would react by changing output, but always choosing to supply output at the level at which $MR = MC$. This suggests that the short-run marginal cost curve represents the firm's short-run supply curve; in other words, it shows the quantity of output that the firm would supply at any given price.

However, there is one important proviso to this statement. If the price falls below short-run average variable cost, the firm's best decision will be to exit from the market, as it will be better off just incurring its fixed costs. So the firm's **short-run supply curve** is the SMC curve above the point where it cuts $SAVC$ (at its minimum point).

Key term

short-run supply curve: for a firm operating under perfect competition, the curve given by its short-run marginal cost curve above the price at which $MC = SAVC$; for the industry, the horizontal sum of the supply curves of the individual firms

Industry equilibrium in the short run

One crucial question not yet examined is how the market price comes to be determined. To answer this, it is necessary to consider the industry as a whole. In this case there is a conventional downward-sloping demand curve, of the sort met in *AS Economics*. This is formed according to preferences of consumers in the market and is shown in Figure 2.3.

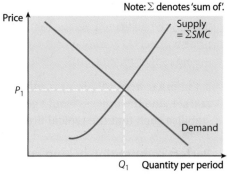

Figure 2.3 *A perfectly competitive industry in short-run equilibrium*

On the supply side, it has been shown that the individual firm's supply curve is its marginal cost curve above $SAVC$. If you add up the supply curves of each firm operating in the market, the result is the industry supply curve, also shown in Figure 2.3. The price will then adjust to P_1 at the intersection of demand and supply. The firms in the industry between them will supply Q_1 output, and the market will be in equilibrium.

The firm in short-run equilibrium revisited

As this seems to be a well-balanced situation, with price adjusting to equate market demand and supply, the only question is why it is described as just a *short-run equilibrium*. The clue to this is to be found back with the individual firm.

Figure 2.4 returns to the position facing an individual firm in the market. As before, the firm maximises profits by accepting the price P_1 as set in the market and producing up to the point where $MR = MC$, which is at q_1. However, now the firm's average revenue (which is equal to price) is greater than its average cost (which is given by AC_1 at this level of output). The firm is thus making supernormal profits

at this price. (Remember that 'normal profits' are included in average cost.) Indeed, the amount of total profits being made is shown as the shaded area on the graph. Notice that average revenue minus average costs equals profit per unit, so multiplying this by the quantity sold determines total profit.

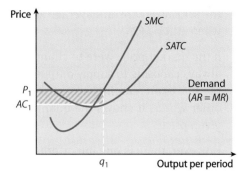

Figure 2.4 *The firm in short-run supply equilibrium*

This is where the assumption about freedom of entry becomes important. If firms in this market are making profits above opportunity cost, the market is generating more profits than other markets in the economy. This will prove attractive to other firms, which will seek to enter the market — and the assumption is that there are no barriers to prevent them from doing so.

This process of entry will continue for as long as firms are making supernormal profits. However, as more firms join the market, the *position* of the industry supply curve, which is the sum of the supply curves of an ever-larger number of individual firms, will be affected. As the industrial supply curve shifts to the right, the market price will fall. At some point the price will have fallen to such an extent that firms are no longer making supernormal profits, and the market will then stabilise.

If the price were to fall even further, some firms would choose to exit from the market, and the process would go into reverse. Therefore price can be expected to stabilise such that the typical firm in the industry is just making normal profits.

Perfect competition in long-run equilibrium

Figure 2.5 shows the situation for a typical firm and for the industry as a whole once long-run equilibrium has been reached and firms no longer have any incentive to enter or to exit the market. The market is in equilibrium, with demand equal to supply at the going price. The typical firm sets marginal revenue equal to marginal cost to maximise profits, and just makes normal profits.

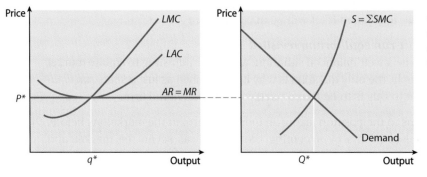

Figure 2.5 *Long-run equilibrium under perfect competition*

The long-run supply curve

Comparative static analysis can be used to explore this equilibrium a little more deeply. Suppose there is an increase in the demand for this product. Perhaps, for some reason, everyone becomes convinced that the product is really health-promoting, so demand increases at any given price. This disturbs the market equilibrium, and the question then is whether (and how) equilibrium can be restored.

Figure 2.6 reproduces the long-run equilibrium that was shown in Figure 2.5. Thus, in the initial position market price is at P^*, the typical firm is in long-run equilibrium producing q^*, and the industry is producing Q^*. Demand was initially at D_0, but with the increased popularity of the product it has shifted to D_1. In the short run this pushes the market price up to P_1 for the industry, because as market price increases existing firms have the incentive to supply more output; that is, they move along their short-run supply curves. So in the short run a typical firm starts to produce q_1 output. The combined supply of the firms then increases to Q_1.

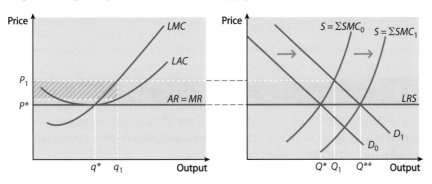

Figure 2.6
Adjusting to an increase in demand under perfect competition

However, at the higher price the firms start making supernormal profits (shown by the shaded area in Figure 2.6), so in time more firms will be attracted into the market, pushing the short-run industry supply curve to the right. This process will continue until there is no further incentive for new firms to enter the market – which occurs when the price has returned to P^*, but with increased industry output at Q^{**}. In other words, the adjustment in the short run is borne by existing firms, but the long-run equilibrium is reached through the entry of new firms.

This suggests that the **industry long-run supply curve (LRS)** is horizontal at the price P^*, which is the minimum point of the long-run average cost curve for the typical firm in the industry.

Strictly speaking, the LRS is perfectly flat only if all firms face equal cost conditions, and if factor prices remain constant as the industry expands. For example, if there is a labour shortage, then industrial expansion may drive up labour costs, causing firms to face higher costs at any output level. In these sorts of circumstances the LRS is slightly upward sloping.

Key term

industry long-run supply curve (LRS): under perfect competition, the curve that, for the typical firm in the industry, is horizontal at the minimum point of the long-run average cost curve

Exercise 2.2

Figure 2.7 shows the short-run cost curves for a firm that is operating in a perfectly competitive market.

a At what price would the firm just make 'normal' profits?

b What area would represent total fixed cost at this price?

c What is the shut-down price for the firm?

d Within what range of prices would the firm choose to operate at a loss in the short run?

e Identify the firm's short-run supply curve.

f Within what range of prices would the firm be able to make short-run supernormal profits?

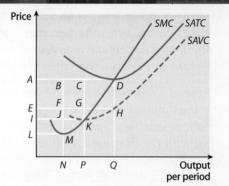

Figure 2.7 A firm operating under short-run perfect competition

Exercise 2.3

Starting from a diagram like Figure 2.5, track the response of a perfectly competitive market to a decrease in market demand for a good — in other words, explain how the market adjusts to a leftward shift of the demand curve.

Efficiency under perfect competition

Having reviewed the characteristics of the long-run equilibrium of a perfectly competitive market, you may wonder what is so good about such a market in terms of productive and allocative efficiency.

Productive efficiency

For an individual market, productive efficiency is reached when a firm operates at the minimum point of its long-run average cost curve. Under perfect competition, this is indeed a feature of the long-run equilibrium position. So productive efficiency is achieved in the long run — but not in the short run, when a firm need not be operating at minimum average cost.

Allocative efficiency

For an individual market, allocative efficiency is achieved when price is set equal to marginal cost. Again, the process by which supernormal profits are competed away through the entry of new firms into the market ensures that price is equal to marginal cost within a perfectly competitive market in long-run equilibrium. So allocative efficiency is also achieved. Indeed, firms set price equal to marginal cost even in the short run, so allocative efficiency is a feature of perfect competition in both the short run and the long run.

Evaluation of perfect competition

A criticism sometimes levelled at the model of perfect competition is that it is merely a theoretical ideal, based on a sequence of assumptions that rarely holds in the real world. Perhaps you have some sympathy with that view.

It could be argued that the model does hold for some agricultural markets. One study in the USA estimated that the elasticity of demand for an individual farmer producing sweetcorn was −31,353, which is pretty close to perfect elasticity.

However, to argue that the model is useless because it is unrealistic is to miss a very important point. By allowing a glimpse of what the ideal market would look like, at least in terms of resource allocation, the model provides a measure against which alternative market structures can be compared. Furthermore, economic analysis can be used to investigate the effects of relaxing the assumptions of the model, which can be another valuable exercise. For example, it is possible to examine how the market is affected if firms can differentiate their products, or if traders in the market are acting with incomplete information. This scenario was in fact explored in *AS Economics, Chapter 8*, describing the effects of asymmetric information on a market.

So, although there may be relatively few markets that display all the characteristics of perfect competition, that does not destroy the usefulness of the model in economic theory. It will continue to be a reference point when examining alternative models of market structure.

Extension material: a word of warning

Some writers, e.g. Nobel prize winner Friedrich von Hayek, have disputed the idea that perfect competition is the best form of market structure. Hayek argued that supernormal profits can be seen as the basis for investment by firms in new technologies, research and development (R&D) and innovation. If supernormal profits are always competed away, as happens under perfect competition, such activity will not take place. Similarly, Joseph Schumpeter argued that only in monopoly or oligopoly markets can firms afford to undertake R&D. Under this sort of argument, it is not quite so clear that perfect competition is the most desirable market structure.

Summary

> The model of perfect competition describes an extreme form of market structure. It rests on a sequence of assumptions.

> Its key characteristics include the assumption that no individual trader can influence the market price of the good or service being traded, and that there is freedom of entry and exit.

> In such circumstances each firm faces a perfectly elastic demand curve for its product, and can sell as much as it likes at the going market price.

> A profit-maximising firm chooses to produce the level of output at which marginal revenue (MR) equals marginal cost (MC).

▶ The firm's short-run marginal cost curve, above its short-run average variable cost curve, represents its short-run supply curve.

▶ The industry's short-run supply curve is the horizontal summation of the supply curves of all firms in the market.

▶ Firms may make supernormal profits in the short run, but because there is freedom of entry these profits will be competed away in the long run by new firms joining the market.

▶ The long-run industry supply curve is horizontal, with price adjusting to the minimum level of the typical firm's long-run average cost curve.

▶ Under perfect competition in long-run equilibrium, both productive efficiency and allocative efficiency are achieved.

The model of monopoly

At the opposite end of the spectrum of market structures is **monopoly**, which is a market with a single seller of a good.

Key *term*

monopoly: a form of market structure in which there is only one seller of a good or service

There is a bit more to it than that, and economic analysis of monopoly rests on some important assumptions. In the real world, the Competition Commission, the official body in the UK with the responsibility of monitoring monopoly markets, is empowered to investigate a merger if it results in the combined firm having more than 25% of a market. The operations of the Competition Commission will be discussed in Chapter 5.

Assumptions
The assumptions of the monopoly model are as follows:

1 There is a single seller of a good.

2 There are no substitutes for the good, either actual or potential.

3 There are barriers to entry into the market.

It is also assumed that the firm aims to maximise profits. You can see that these assumptions all have their counterparts in the assumptions of perfect competition, and that in one sense this model can be described as being at the opposite end of the market structure spectrum.

If there is a single seller of a good, and if there are no substitutes for the good, the monopoly firm is thereby insulated from competition. Furthermore, any barriers to entry into the market will ensure that the firm can sustain its market position into the future. The assumption that there are no potential substitutes for the good reinforces the situation. (Chapter 4 will explore what happens if this assumption does not hold.)

A monopoly in equilibrium
The first point to note is that a monopoly firm faces the market demand curve directly. Thus, unlike perfect competition, the demand curve slopes downwards. For

the monopolist, the demand curve may be regarded as showing average revenue. Unlike a firm under perfect competition, therefore, the monopolist has some influence over price, and can make decisions regarding price as well as output. This is not to say that the monopolist has complete freedom to set the price, as the firm is still constrained by market demand. However, the firm is a *price maker* and can choose a location *along* the demand curve.

As a preliminary piece of analysis, recall a piece of analysis in *AS Economics, Chapter 2*, which looked at the relationship between the own-price elasticity of demand along a straight-line demand curve and total revenue. The key graphs are reproduced here as Figure 2.8. The analysis pointed out that the price elasticity of demand is elastic above the mid-point of the demand curve and inelastic in the lower half, with total revenue increasing with a price fall when demand is elastic and falling when demand is inelastic.

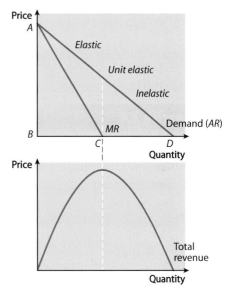

The marginal revenue curve (*MR*) has been added to the figure, and it has a fixed relationship with the average revenue curve (*AR*). This is for similar mathematical reasons as those that explained the relationship between marginal and average costs in the previous chapter. *MR* shares the intercept point on the vertical axis (point *A* in Figure 2.8) and has exactly twice the slope of *AR*. Whenever you have to draw this figure, remember that *MR* and *AR* have this relationship — meeting at *A*, and with the distance *BC* being the same as the distance *CD*. *MR* is zero (meets the horizontal axis) at the maximum point of the total revenue curve.

Figure 2.8 *Elasticity and total revenue*

As with the firm under perfect competition, a monopolist aiming to maximise profits will choose to produce at the level of output at which marginal revenue equals marginal cost. This is at Q_m in Figure 2.9. Having selected output, the monopolist then identifies the price that will clear the market for that level of output — in Figure 2.9 this is P_m.

This choice allows the monopolist to make supernormal profits, which can be identified as the shaded area in the figure. As before, this area is average revenue minus average cost, which gives profit per unit, multiplied by the quantity.

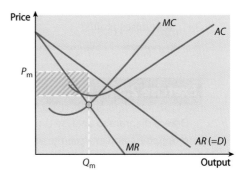

Figure 2.9 *Profit maximisation and monopoly*

It is at this point that barriers to entry become important. Other firms may see that the monopoly firm is making healthy supernormal profits, but the existence of barriers to entry will prevent those profits from being competed away, as would happen in a perfectly competitive market.

It is important to notice that the monopolist cannot be guaranteed always to make such substantial profits as are shown in Figure 2.9. The size of the profits depends upon the relative position of the market demand curve and the position of the cost curves. If the cost curves in the diagram were higher, the monopoly profits would be much smaller, as the distance between average revenue and average costs would be less. It is even possible that the cost curves could be so high as to force the firm to incur losses, in which case it would probably shut down.

Exercise 2.4

Table 2.2 shows the demand curve faced by a monopolist.

a   Calculate total revenue and marginal revenue for each level of demand.

b   Plot the demand curve (AR) and marginal revenue on a graph.

c   Plot total revenue on a separate graph.

d   Identify the level of demand at which total revenue is at a maximum.

e   At what level of demand is marginal revenue equal to zero?

f   At what level of demand is there unit own-price elasticity of demand?

g   If the monopolist maximises profits, will the chosen level of output be higher or lower than the revenue-maximising level?

h   What does this imply for the price elasticity of demand when the monopolist maximises profits?

Demand (000 per week)	Price (£)
0	80
1	70
2	60
3	50
4	40
5	30
6	20
7	10

Table 2.2 *Demand curve for a monopolist*

Exercise 2.5

Draw a diagram to analyse the profit-maximising level of output and price for a monopolist, and analyse the effect of an increase in demand.

How do monopolies arise?

Monopolies may arise in a market for a number of reasons. In a few instances, a monopoly is created by the authorities. For example, for 150 years the UK Post Office held a licence giving it a monopoly on delivering letters. This service is now open

For 150 years, the Post Office held a licence giving it a monoply on delivering letters.

to some competition, although any company wanting to deliver packages weighing less than 350 grams and charging less than £1 can do so only by applying for a licence. The Post Office monopoly formerly covered a much wider range of services, but its coverage has been eroded over the years, and competition in delivering larger packages has been permitted for some time. Nonetheless, it remains an example of one way in which a monopoly can be created.

The patent system offers a rather different form of protection for a firm. The patent system was designed to provide an incentive for firms to innovate through the development of new techniques and products. By prohibiting other firms from copying the product for a period of time, a firm is given a temporary monopoly.

In some cases the technology of the industry may create a monopoly situation. In a market characterised by substantial economies of scale, there may not be room for more than one firm in the market. This could happen where there are substantial fixed costs of production but low marginal costs; for example, in establishing an underground railway in a city, a firm faces very high fixed costs in building the network of rails and stations and buying the rolling stock. However, once in operation, the marginal cost of carrying an additional passenger is very low.

Figure 2.10 illustrates this point. The firm in this market enjoys economies of scale right up to the limit of market demand. The largest firm operating in

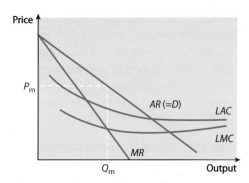

Figure 2.10 A natural monopoly

the market can always produce at a lower cost than any potential entrant, so will always be able to price such firms out of the market. Here the economies of scale act as an effective barrier to the entry of new firms and the market is a **natural monopoly**. A profit-maximising monopoly would thus set $MR = MC$, produce at quantity Q_m and charge a price P_m.

Key *term*

natural monopoly: monopoly that arises in an industry in which there are such substantial economies of scale that only one firm is viable

Such a market poses particular problems regarding allocative efficiency. Notice in the figure that marginal cost is below average cost over the entire range of output. If the firm were to charge a price equal to marginal cost it would inevitably make a loss, so such a pricing rule would not be viable. This problem is analysed in Chapter 5.

The sort of market where a natural monopoly may emerge is one in which there may be substantial fixed costs of operation but relatively low marginal cost. An example might be an underground railway system in a city or a Channel Tunnel. The setup costs of building a rail network under a city or a tunnel under the Channel are enormous compared with the marginal cost of carrying an additional passenger. Some cities (e.g. Kuala Lumpur) do have more than one underground railway

system, but they do not compete on the same routes. It would not make economic sense to have parallel rail systems competing for the same passengers on a particular route, any more than it would be sensible to have two Channel Tunnels close to each other. Notice that although the Channel Tunnel may seem an obvious natural monopoly, it does not mean that the firm operating it faces no competition. The Tunnel has to compete with ferry companies and airlines.

A city underground railway is a good example of a natural monopoly.

Another example of a natural monopoly might seem to be the manufacture of passenger aircraft. Building a plane capable of carrying large numbers of passengers on long-haul routes has large economies of scale. There are indivisibilities in the production process, and any firm producing such aircraft has to make substantial investment in research and development upfront. Thus there are large economies of scale in the production process. Furthermore, the market is relatively small, in the sense that the number of aircraft sold in a year is modest. However, looking at the market, it is clear that it is not a monopoly as there are two firms operating in the market — Boeing and Airbus. These are the only effective global competitors.

Does this negate the natural monopoly theory? The answer is no. In fact, this market has aroused much transatlantic debate and contention. Boeing, the US producer, has accused European governments of unfairly subsidising Airbus's R&D programme. In return, Airbus has responded by pointing to the benefits that

Edexcel A2 Economics

Boeing has received from the US military research programme. Without being drawn into this debate at this stage, the net effect of the interventions has been to create a duopoly situation (a market with just two firms) in which Boeing and Airbus compete for market share. Later discussion will examine why such competition is regarded as being more favourable for consumers than allowing an unregulated natural monopoly to develop.

There are markets in which firms have risen to become monopolies by their actions in the market. Such a market structure is sometimes known as a *competitive monopoly*. Firms may get into a monopoly position through effective marketing, through a process of merger and acquisition, or by establishing a new product as a widely accepted standard.

In the first Microsoft trial in 1998, it was claimed that Microsoft had gained 95% of the world market for operating systems for PC computers. The firm claimed that this was because it was simply very good at what it does. However, part of the reason why it was on trial was that not everyone agreed with it, and alleged unfair market tactics. This will be examined in Chapter 5.

Exercise 2.6

In 2000, AOL merged with Time Warner, bringing together an internet service provider with an extensive network and a firm in the entertainment business.

One product that such a merged company might produce would be a digitised music performance that could be distributed through the internet. Think about the sorts of costs entailed in producing and delivering such a product, and categorise them as fixed or variable costs. What does this imply for the economies of scale faced by the merged company?

Monopoly and efficiency

The characteristics of the monopoly market can be evaluated in relation to productive and allocative efficiency (see Figure 2.9).

Productive efficiency

A firm is said to be productively efficient if it produces at the minimum point of long-run average cost. It is clear from the figure that this is extremely unlikely for a monopoly. The firm will produce at the minimum point of long-run average cost only if it so happens that the marginal *revenue* curve passes through this exact point — and this would happen only by coincidence.

Allocative efficiency

For an individual firm, allocative efficiency is achieved when price is set equal to marginal cost. It is clear from Figure 2.9 that this will not be the case for a profit-maximising monopoly firm. The firm chooses output where *MR* equals *MC*; however, given that *MR* is below *AR* (i.e. price), price will always be set above marginal cost.

Perfect competition and monopoly compared

It is possible to identify the extent to which a monopoly by its behaviour distorts resource allocation, by comparing the monopoly market with the perfectly competitive market. To do this, the situation can be simplified by setting aside the possibility of economies of scale. This is perhaps an artificial assumption to make, but it can be relaxed later.

Suppose that there is an industry with no economies of scale, which can be operated either as a perfectly competitive market with many small firms, or as a monopoly firm running a large number of small plants.

Figure 2.11 shows the market demand curve ($D = AR$), and the long-run supply curve under perfect competition (LRS). If the market is operating under perfect competition, the long-run equilibrium will produce a price of P_{pc}, and the firms in the industry will

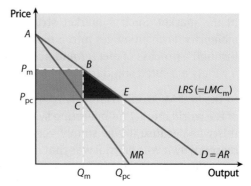

Figure 2.11 *Comparing perfect competition and monopoly*

together supply Q_{pc} output. Consumer surplus is given by the area $AP_{pc}E$, which represents the surplus that consumers gain from consuming this product. In other words, it is a measure of the welfare that society receives from consuming the good, as was explained in *AS Economics, Chapter 4*.

Now suppose that the industry is taken over by a profit-maximising monopolist. The firm can close down some of the plants to vary its output over the long run, and the *LRS* can be regarded as the monopolist's long-run marginal cost curve. As the monopoly firm faces the market demand curve directly, it will also face the *MR* curve shown, so will maximise profits at quantity Q_m and charge a price P_m.

Thus, the effect of this change in market structure is that the profit-maximising monopolist produces less output than a perfectly competitive industry and charges a higher price.

It is also apparent that consumer surplus is now very different, as in the new situation it is limited to the area AP_mB. Looking more carefully at Figure 2.11, you can see that the loss of consumer surplus has occurred for two reasons. First, the monopoly firm is now making profits shown by the shaded area P_mBCP_{pc}. This is a redistribution of welfare from consumers to the firm, but, as the monopolist is also a member of society, this does not affect overall welfare. However, there is also a deadweight loss, which represents a loss to society resulting from the monopolisation of the industry. This is measured by the area of the triangle *BCE*. Chapter 5 returns to this issue to examine whether the authorities need to worry about this situation and to explore the sort of policy that could be adopted to tackle the issue.

Summary

➤ A monopoly market is one in which there is a single seller of a good.

➤ The model of monopoly used in economic analysis also assumes that there are no substitutes for the goods or services produced by the monopolist, and that there are barriers to the entry of new firms.

➤ The monopoly firm faces the market demand curve, and is able to choose a point along that demand curve in order to maximise profits.

➤ Such a firm may be able to make supernormal profits, and sustain them in the long run because of barriers to entry and the lack of substitutes.

➤ A monopoly may arise because of patent protection or from the nature of economies of scale in the industry (a 'natural monopoly').

➤ A profit-maximising monopolist does not achieve allocative efficiency, and is unlikely to achieve productive efficiency in the sense of producing at the minimum point of the long-run average cost curve.

➤ A comparison of perfect competition with monopoly reveals that a profit-maximising monopoly firm operating under the same cost conditions as a perfectly competitive industry will produce less output, charge a higher price and impose a deadweight loss on society.

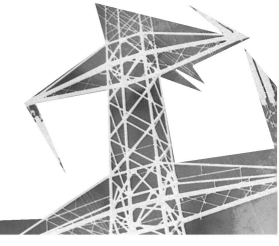

Market structure: monopolistic competition and oligopoly

The previous chapter introduced the models of perfect competition and monopoly, and described them as being at the extreme ends of a spectrum of forms of market structure. In between those two extremes are other forms of market structure, which have some but not all of the characteristics of either perfect competition or monopoly. It is in this sense that there is a spectrum of structures. Attention in this chapter is focused on some of these intermediate forms of market structure.

Learning outcomes

After studying this chapter, you should:

- ➤ understand the significance of concentration in a market and how to measure it
- ➤ be familiar with the range of market situations that exists between the extremes of perfect competition and monopoly
- ➤ understand the meaning of product differentiation and its role in the model of monopolistic competition
- ➤ understand the conditions under which price discrimination is possible and how this affects consumers and producers
- ➤ understand the notion of oligopoly and be familiar with approaches to modelling firm behaviour in an oligopoly market
- ➤ understand the benefits that firms may gain from forming a cartel — and the tensions that may result

Market concentration

Chapter 2 pointed out that the models of perfect competition and monopoly produce very different outcomes for productive and allocative efficiency. Perfect competition produces a 'good' allocation of resources, but monopoly results in a deadweight loss. In the real-world economy it is not quite so simple. In particular, not every market is readily classified as following either of these extreme models. Indeed, you might think that the majority of markets do not correspond to either of the models, but instead display a mixture of characteristics.

An important question is whether such markets behave more like a competitive market or more like a monopoly. There are many different ways in which markets with just a few firms operating can be modelled, because there are many ways in which the firms may interact. Some of these models will be explored later in the chapter.

It is helpful to have some way of gauging how close a particular market is to being a monopoly. One way of doing this is to examine the degree of concentration in the market. Later it will be seen that this is not all that is required to determine how efficiently a market will operate; but it is a start.

Concentration is normally measured by reference to the **concentration ratio**, which measures the market share of the largest firms in an industry. For example, the three-firm concentration ratio measures the market share of the largest three firms in the market; the five-firm concentration ratio calculates the share of the top five firms, and so on. Concentration can also be viewed in terms of employment, reflected in the proportion of workers in any industry that are employed in the largest firms.

Key *term*

_n_-firm concentration ratio: a measure of the market share of the largest *n* firms in an industry

Consider the following example. Table 3.1 gives average circulation figures for the firms that publish national newspapers in the UK. In the final column these are converted into market shares. Where one firm produces more than one newspaper, their circulations have been combined (e.g. News International publishes both the *Sun* and *The Times*).

Firm	Average circulation	Market share (%)
News International Newspapers Ltd	3,470,711	36.3
Associated Newspapers Ltd	2,077,545	21.7
Trinity Mirror plc	1,318,168	13.8
Express Newspapers Ltd	1,292,330	13.5
Telegraph Group Ltd	799,021	8.4
Guardian Newspapers Ltd	292,909	3.1
Independent Newspapers (UK) Ltd	178,576	1.9
Financial Times Ltd	130,695	1.4

Table 3.1
Concentration in the UK newspaper industry, July 2008

Source: **www.abc.org.uk**

The three-firm concentration ratio is calculated as the sum of the market shares of the biggest three firms: that is, 36.3 + 21.7 + 13.8 = 71.8%.

Concentration ratios may be calculated on the basis of either shares in output or shares in employment. In the above example the calculation was on the basis of output (daily circulation). The two measures may give different results, because the largest firms in an industry may be more capital-intensive in their production methods, which means that their share of employment in an industry will be smaller than their share of output. For purposes of examining market structure, however, it is more helpful to base the analysis of market share on output.

This might seem an intuitively simple measure, but it is *too* simple to enable an evaluation of a market. For a start, it is important to define the market appropriately; for instance, in the above example are *The Financial Times* and the *Sun* really part of the same market?

There may be other difficulties too. Table 3.2 gives some hypothetical market shares for two markets. The five-firm concentration ratio is calculated as the sum of the market shares of the largest five firms. For market A this is 68 + 3 + 2 + 1 + 1 = 75; for market B it is 15 + 15 + 15 + 15 + 15 = 75. In each case the market is perceived to be highly concentrated, at 75%. However, the nature of likely interactions

Largest firms in rank order	Market A	Market B
Firm 1	68	15
Firm 2	3	15
Firm 3	2	15
Firm 4	1	15
Firm 5	1	15

Table 3.2 *Market shares (% of output)*

between the firms in these two markets is very different, because the large relative size of firm 1 in market A is likely to give it substantially more market power than any of the largest five firms in market B. Nonetheless, the concentration ratio is useful for giving a first impression of how the market is likely to function.

Figure 3.1 shows the five-firm concentration ratio for a number of industrial sectors in the UK. Concentration varies from 14.1% in tools and 15.6% in paper, printing and publishing to 96% in iron and steel and 99.2% in tobacco. In part, the difference between sectors might be expected to reflect the extent of economies of scale, and this makes sense for many of the industries shown.

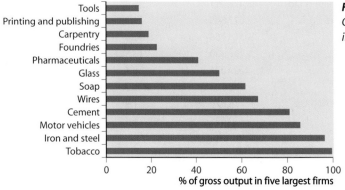

Figure 3.1
Concentration in UK industry, 1992

Summary

➤ Real-world markets do not often conform to the models of perfect competition or monopoly — which are extreme forms of market structure.

➤ It is important to be able to evaluate the degree of concentration in a market.

➤ While not a perfect measure, the concentration ratio is one way of doing this, by calculating the market share of the largest firms.

Monopolistic competition

The theory of **monopolistic competition** was devised by Edward Chamberlin, writing in the USA in the 1930s, and his name is often attached to the model, although Joan Robinson published her book on imperfect competition in the UK at the same time. The motivation for the analysis was to explain how markets operated when they were operating neither as monopolies nor under perfect competition.

 term

monopolistic competition: a market that shares some characteristics of monopoly and some of perfect competition

The model describes a market in which there are many firms producing similar, but not identical, products, e.g. travel agents, hairdressers or fast-food outlets. In the case of fast-food outlets, the high streets of many cities are characterised by large numbers of different types of takeaway — burgers, fish and chips, Indian, Chinese, fried chicken and so on.

Fast-food restaurants operate in monopolistic conditions.

Model characteristics

Three important characteristics of the model of monopolistic competition distinguish this sort of market from others.

Product differentiation

First, firms produce differentiated products, and face downward-sloping demand curves. In other words, each firm competes with the others by making its product slightly different. This allows the firms to build up brand loyalty among their regular customers, which gives them some influence over price. It is likely that firms will engage in advertising in order to maintain such brand loyalty, and heavy advertising is a common characteristic of a market operating under monopolistic competition.

 term

product differentiation: a strategy adopted by firms that marks their product as being different from their competitors'

Because other firms are producing similar goods, there are substitutes for each firm's product, which means that demand will be relatively price-elastic. However, it is not perfectly price-elastic, as was the case with perfect competition. These features — that the product is not homogeneous and demand is not perfectly price-elastic — represent significant differences from the model of perfect competition.

Freedom of entry

Second, there are no barriers to entry into the market. Firms are able to join the market if they observe that existing firms are making supernormal profits. New entrants to the market will be looking for some way to differentiate their product slightly from the others — perhaps the next fast-food restaurant will be Nepalese, or Peruvian.

This characteristic distinguishes the market from the monopoly model, as does the existence of fairly close substitutes.

Low concentration

Third, the concentration ratio in the industry tends to be relatively low, as there are many firms operating in the market. For this reason, a price change by one of the firms will have negligible effects on the demand for its rivals' products.

This characteristic means that the market is also different from an oligopoly market, where there are a few firms that interact strategically with each other.

Overview

Taking these three characteristics together, it can be seen that a market of monopolistic competition has some of the characteristics of perfect competition and some features of monopoly; hence its name.

Short-run equilibrium

Figure 3.2 represents short-run equilibrium under monopolistic competition. D_S is the demand curve, and MR_S is the corresponding marginal revenue curve. AC and MC are the average and marginal cost curves for a representative firm in the industry. If the firm is aiming to maximise profits, it will choose the level of output such that $MR_S = MC$. This occurs at output Q_S, and the firm will then choose the price that clears the market at P_S.

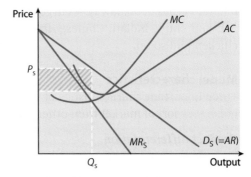

Figure 3.2 *Short-run equilibrium under monopolistic competition*

This closely resembles the standard monopoly diagram that was introduced in Chapter 2. As with monopoly, a firm under monopolistic competition faces a downward-sloping demand curve, as already noted. The difference is that now it is assumed that there is free entry into the market under monopolistic competition, so that Figure 3.2 represents equilibrium only in the short run. This is because the firm shown in the figure is making supernormal profits, shown by the shaded area (which is $AR - AC$ multiplied by output).

The importance of free entry

This is where the assumption of free entry into the market becomes important. In Figure 3.2 the profits being made by the representative firm will attract new firms into the market. The new firms will produce differentiated products, and this will have two important effects on demand for the representative firm's product. First, the new firms will attract some customers away from this firm, so that its demand curve will tend to shift to the left. Second, as there are now more substitutes for the original product, the demand curve will become more elastic – remember that the availability of substitutes is an important influence on the own-price elasticity of demand.

Long-run equilibrium

This process will continue as long as firms in the market continue to make profits that attract new firms into the activity. It may be accelerated if firms are persuaded to spend money on advertising in an attempt to defend their market shares. The advertising may help to keep the demand curve downward sloping, but it will also affect the position of the average cost curve, by pushing up average cost at all levels of output.

Figure 3.3 shows the final position for the market. The typical firm is now operating in such a way that it maximises profits (by setting output such that $MR = MC$); at the same time, the average cost curve (AC) at this level of output is at a tangent to the demand curve. This means that $AC = AR$, and the firm is just making normal profit (i.e. is just covering opportunity cost). There is thus no further incentive for more firms to join the market. In Figure 3.3 this occurs when output is at Q_l and price is set at P_l.

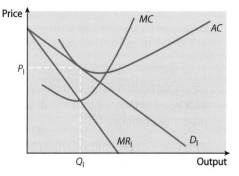

Figure 3.3 *Long-run equilibrium under monopolistic competition*

Efficiency

One way of evaluating the market outcome under this model is to examine the consequences for productive and allocative efficiency. It is clear from Figure 3.3 that neither of these conditions will be met. The representative firm does not reach the minimum point on the long-run average cost curve, and so does not attain productive efficiency; furthermore, the price charged is above marginal cost, so allocative efficiency is not achieved.

Evaluation

If the typical firm in the market is not fully exploiting the possible economies of scale that exist, it could be argued that product differentiation is damaging society's total welfare, in the sense that it is the product differentiation that allows firms to keep their demand curves downward sloping. In other words, too many different products are being produced. However, this argument could be countered by pointing out that consumers may enjoy having more freedom of choice. The very

fact that they are prepared to pay a premium price for their chosen brand indicates that they have some preference for it.

Another crucial difference between monopolistic competition and perfect competition is that under monopolistic competition firms would like to sell more of their product at the going price, whereas under perfect competition they can sell as much as they like at the going price. This is because price under monopolistic competition is set above marginal cost. The use of advertising to attract more customers and to maintain consumer perception of product differences may be considered a problem with this market. It could be argued that excessive use of advertising to maintain product differentiation is wasteful, as it leads to higher average cost curves than needed. On the other hand, the need to compete in this way may result in less X-inefficiency than could arise under a complacent monopolist.

Examples of monopolistic competition

The theory of monopolistic competition describes a market with some features of monopoly and some features of perfect competition. Entry barriers are low, so the market has many firms. However, firms in the market use product differentiation to influence consumers, and thus face downward-sloping demand curves. What sorts of market in the real world might typify this structure?

Take a drive along a motorway or trunk road in the UK, and observe the heavy goods vehicles (HGVs) and smaller vans that you pass. You will see HGVs and vans in a wide variety of liveries, from a wide range of countries and carrying a wide diversity of loads.

This is a market characterised by many competing firms, many of which operate in niche markets. Firms try to differentiate their offering by carrying particular categories of products — building materials, perhaps, or electronic goods. Some may trade between certain destinations. They advertise by broadcasting these specialisms on their vehicles, in the *Yellow Pages* or on the internet.

Another part of the road transport market that may typify monopolistic competition is local taxi markets. Count the local taxi companies in your local *Yellow Pages*. Again, firms may seek to differentiate their products through having a fleet livery, by advertising pre-booking only or by offering a limousine service. There may also be firms that specialise in longer-distance trips, say to airports.

Another example is food outlets. The number of restaurants and fast-food outlets has mushroomed in recent decades, and on many high streets in UK towns there is a proliferation of eating places and takeaways. One of the characteristics of a market operating under monopolistic competition is the product differentiation that takes place. Each individual seller sets out to be different from its competitors. This is certainly a characteristic of the fast-food sector, where outlets offer different styles of cuisine — burgers, Indian, Chinese, Thai, Mexican and so on. Before condemning such a market as being damaging to consumers because of the effect on productive and allocative efficiency, it is worth being aware that this market offers consumers a wide range of choice for fast food. If they value this choice, then this should be seen as a benefit that arises because of the market structure.

Exercise 3.1

Figure 3.4 shows a firm under monopolistic competition.

a Identify the profit-maximising level of output.

b At what price would the firm sell its product?

c What supernormal profits (if any) would be made by the firm?

d Is this a short-run or a long-run equilibrium? Explain your answer.

e Describe any subsequent adjustment that might take place in the market (if any).

f At what level of output would productive efficiency be achieved? (Assume that 'AC' represents long-run average cost for this part of the question.)

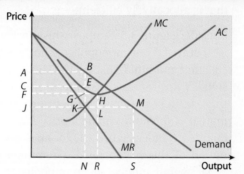

Figure 3.4 *A firm under monopolistic competition*

Summary

➤ The theory of monopolistic competition has its origins in the 1930s, when economists such as Edward Chamberlin and Joan Robinson were writing about markets that did not conform to the models of perfect competition and monopoly.

➤ The model describes a market where there are many firms producing similar, but not identical, products.

➤ By differentiating their product from those of other firms, it is possible for firms to maintain some influence over price.

➤ To do this, firms engage in advertising to build brand loyalty.

➤ There are no barriers to entry into the market, and concentration ratios are low.

➤ Firms in the short run may make supernormal profits.

➤ In response, new entrants join the market, shifting the demand curves of existing firms and affecting their shape.

➤ The process continues until supernormal profits have been competed away, and the typical firm has its average cost curve at a tangent to its demand curve.

➤ Neither productive nor allocative efficiency is achieved in long-run equilibrium.

➤ Consumers may benefit from the increased range of choice on offer in the market.

Price discrimination

One thing that monopoly and monopolistic competition have in common is that, by setting price above marginal cost, a deadweight loss is imposed on society, with output lower than would be implied by the $P = MC$ outcome. This section examines a special case of monopoly, in which a monopolist will produce the level of output that is allocatively efficient.

Consider Figure 3.5. Suppose this market is operated by a monopolist who faces constant marginal cost *LMC*. (This is to simplify the analysis.) Chapter 2 showed that under perfect competition the market outcome would be a price P^* and quantity Q^*. (See Figure 2.11 for an explanation of this if you need a reminder.) What would induce the monopolist to produce at Q^*?

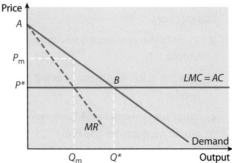

Figure 3.5 *Perfect price discrimination*

One of the assumptions made throughout the analysis so far is that all consumers in a market get to pay the same price for the product. This leads to the notion of consumer surplus. In Figure 3.5, if the market were operating under perfect competition and all consumers were paying the same price, consumer surplus would be given by the area AP^*B. If the market were operated by a monopolist, also charging the same price to all buyers, then profits would be maximised where $MC = MR$, i.e. at quantity Q_m and price P_m.

But suppose this assumption is now relaxed; suppose that the monopolist is able to charge a different price to each individual consumer. A monopolist is then able to charge each consumer a price that is equal to his/her willingness to pay for the good. In other words, the demand curve effectively becomes the marginal revenue curve, as it represents the amount that the monopolist will receive for each unit of the good. It will then maximise profits at point B in Figure 3.5, where MR (i.e. AR) is equal to *LMC*. The difference between this situation and that under perfect competition is that the area AP^*B is no longer consumer surplus, but producer surplus, i.e. the monopolist's profits. The monopolist has hijacked the whole of the original consumer surplus as its profits.

From society's point of view, total welfare is the same as it is under perfect competition (but more than under monopoly without discrimination). However, now there has been a redistribution, from consumers to the monopoly — and presumably to the shareholders of the firm. This situation is known as **perfect price discrimination**, or **first-degree price discrimination**.

> **Key term**
>
> **perfect/first-degree price discrimination:** situation arising in a market whereby a monopoly firm is able to charge each consumer a different price

Perfect price discrimination is fairly rare in the real world, although it might be said to exist in the world of art or fashion, where customers may commission a painting, sculpture or item of designer jewellery and the price is a matter of negotiation between the buyer and supplier.

However, there are situations in which partial price discrimination is possible. For example, students or old-age pensioners may get discounted bus fares, the young and/or old may get cheaper access to sporting events or theatres etc. In these instances individual consumers are paying different prices for what is in fact the same product.

There are three conditions under which a firm may be able to price discriminate:

1 The firm must have market power.

2 The firm must have information about consumers and their willingness to pay – and there must be identifiable differences between consumers (or groups of consumers).

3 The consumers must have limited ability to resell the product.

Market power

Clearly, price discrimination is not possible in a perfectly competitive market, where no seller has the power to charge other than the going market price. So price discrimination can take place only where firms have some ability to vary the price.

Information

From the firm's point of view, it needs to be able to identify different groups of consumers with different willingness to pay. What makes price discrimination profitable for firms is that different consumers display different sensitivities to price; i.e. they have different price elasticities of demand.

Ability to resell

If consumers could resell the product easily, then price discrimination would not be possible, as consumers would engage in **arbitrage**. In other words, the group of consumers who qualified for the low price could buy up the product and then turn a profit by reselling to consumers in the other segment/s of the market. This would mean that the firm would no longer be able to sell at the high price, and would no longer try to discriminate in pricing.

> **Key** *term*
>
> **arbitrage:** a process by which prices in two market segments are equalised by the purchase and resale of products by market participants

In the case of student discounts and OAP concessions, the firm can identify particular groups of consumers; and such 'products' as bus journeys or dental treatment cannot be resold. But why should a firm undertake this practice?

The simple answer is that, by undertaking price discrimination, the firm is able to increase its profits. This is shown in Figure 3.6, which separates two distinct groups

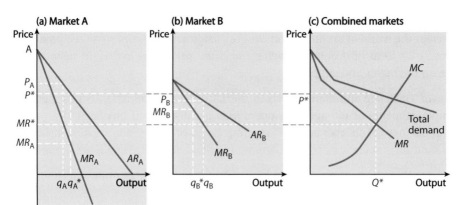

Figure 3.6 *A price-discriminating monopolist*

of consumers with differing demand curves. Thus, panel (a) shows market A and panel (b) shows market B, with the combined demand curve being shown in panel (c), which also shows the firm's marginal cost curve.

If a firm has to charge the same price to all consumers, it sets marginal revenue in the combined market equal to marginal cost, and produces Q^* output, to be sold at a price of P^*. This maximises profits when all consumers pay the same price. The firm sells q_A^* in market A, and q_B^* in market B.

However, if you look at panels (a) and (b), you will see that marginal revenue in market A is much lower (at MR_A) than that in market B (at MR_B). It is this difference in marginal revenue that opens up a profit-increasing opportunity for the firm. By taking sales away from market A and selling more in market B, the firm gains more extra revenue in B than it loses in A. This increases its profit. The optimal position for the firm is where marginal revenue is equalised in the two markets. In Figure 3.6 the firm sells q_A in market A at the higher price of P_A. In market B sales increase to q_B with price falling to P_B. Notice that in both situations the amounts sold in the two sub-markets sum to Q^*.

The consumers in market B seem to do quite well by this practice, as they can now consume more of the good. Indeed, it is possible that with no discrimination the price would be so high that they would not be able to consume the good at all.

An extreme form of price discrimination was used by NAPP Pharmaceutical Holdings, as a result of which the firm was fined £3.2 million by the Office of Fair Trading. NAPP sold sustained-release morphine tablets and capsules in the UK. These are drugs administered to patients with incurable cancer.

NAPP realised that the market was segmented. The drugs were sold partly to the NHS for use in hospitals, but were also prescribed by GPs. As these patients were terminally ill, they tended to spend a relatively short time in hospital before being sent home. NAPP realised that GPs tended to prescribe the same drugs as the patients had received in hospital. It therefore reduced its price to hospitals by 90%, thereby forcing all competitors out of the market and gaining a monopoly in that market segment. It was then able to increase the price of these drugs prescribed through GPs, and so maximise profits. The OFT investigated the firm, fined it and instructed it to stop its actions, thus saving the NHS £2 million per year.

Exercise 3.2

In which of the following products might price discrimination be possible? Explain your answers.

a Hairdressing

b Peak and off-peak rail travel

c Apples

d Air tickets

e Newspapers

f Plastic surgery

g Beer

Summary

➤ In some markets a monopolist may be able to engage in price discrimination by selling its product at different prices to different consumers or groups of consumers.

➤ This enables the firm to increase its profits by absorbing some or all of the consumer surplus.

➤ Under first-degree price discrimination, the firm is able to charge a different price to each customer and absorb all consumer surplus.

➤ The firm can practise price discrimination only where it has market power, where consumers have differing elasticities of demand for the product, and where consumers have limited ability to resell the product.

Oligopoly

A number of markets seem to be dominated by relatively few firms — think of motor vehicle manufacturing or commercial banking in the UK, or the newspaper industry. A market with just a few sellers is known as an **oligopoly** market. An important characteristic of such markets is that when making economic decisions each firm must take account of its rivals' behaviour and reactions. The firms are therefore interdependent.

Key term

oligopoly: a market with a few sellers, in which each firm must take account of the behaviour and likely behaviour of rival firms in the industry

An important characteristic of oligopoly is that each firm has to act strategically, both in reacting to rival firms' decisions and in trying to anticipate their future actions.

There are many different ways in which a firm may take such strategic decisions, and this means that there are many ways in which an oligopoly market can be modelled, depending on how the firms are behaving. This chapter reviews just a few such models.

Oligopolies may come about for many reasons, but perhaps the most convincing concerns economies of scale. An oligopoly is likely to develop in a market where there are modest economies of scale — economies that are not substantial enough to require a natural monopoly, but are large enough to make it difficult for too many firms to operate at minimum efficient scale.

Within an oligopoly market, firms may adopt rivalrous behaviour or they may choose to cooperate with each other. The two attitudes have implications for how markets operate.

High-street banking is an oligopoly market.

Cooperation will tend to take the market towards the monopoly end of the spectrum, whereas non-cooperation will take it towards the competitive end. In either scenario, it is likely that the market outcome will be somewhere between the two extremes.

The kinked demand curve model

One such model revolves around how a firm *perceives* its demand curve. This is called the kinked demand curve model, and was developed by Paul Sweezy in the USA in the 1930s.

The model relates to an oligopoly in which firms try to anticipate the reactions of rivals to their actions. One problem that arises is that a firm cannot readily observe its demand curve with any degree of certainty, so it must form expectations about how consumers will react to a price change.

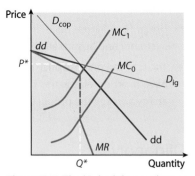

Figure 3.7 The kinked demand curve

Figure 3.7 shows how this works. Suppose the price is currently set at P^*; the firm is selling Q^*, and is trying to decide whether to alter price. The problem is that it knows for sure about only one point on the demand curve: that is, when price is P^*, the firm sells Q^*.

However, the firm is aware that the degree of sensitivity to its price change will depend on whether or not the other firms in the market will follow its lead. In other words, if its rivals ignore the firm's price change, there will be more sensitivity to this change than if they all follow suit.

Figure 3.7 shows the two extreme possibilities for the demand curve the firm perceives that it faces. If other firms ignore its action, D_{ig} will be the relevant demand curve, which is relatively elastic. On the other hand, if the other firms copy the firm's moves, D_{cop} will be the relevant demand curve.

The question then is under what conditions will the other firms copy the price change, and when will they not? The firm may imagine that if it raises price there is little likelihood that its rivals will copy. After all, this is a non-threatening move that gives market share to the other firms. So for a price *increase*, it is D_{ig} that is the relevant section.

On the other hand, a price reduction is likely to be seen by the rivals as a threatening move, and they are likely to copy in order to preserve their market positions. For a price *decrease*, then, it is D_{cop} that is relevant.

Putting these together, the firm perceives that it faces a kinked demand curve (*dd*). Furthermore, if the marginal revenue curve is added to the picture, it is seen to have a discontinuity at the kink. It thus transpires that Q^* is the profit-maximising level of output under a wide range of cost conditions from MC_0 to MC_1; so, even in the face of a change in marginal costs, the firm will not alter its behaviour.

Thus, the model predicts that, if the firm perceives its demand curve to be of this shape, it has a strong incentive to do nothing, even in the face of changes in costs. However, it all depends upon the firm's perceptions. If there is a general increase in costs that affects all producers, this may affect the firm's perception of rival reaction, and thus encourage it to raise price. If other firms are reading the market in the same way, they are likely to follow suit. Notice that this model does not explain how the price reaches P^* in the first place.

Game theory

A more recent development in the economic theory of the firm has been in the application of **game theory**. This began as a branch of mathematics, but it became apparent that it had wide applications in explaining the behaviour of firms in an oligopoly.

 Key *term*

game theory: a method of modelling the strategic interaction between firms in an oligopoly

Game theory itself has a long history, with some writers tracing it back to correspondence between Pascal and Fermat in the mid-seventeenth century. Early applications in economics were by Antoine Augustin Cournot in 1838, Francis Edgeworth in 1881 and J. Bertrand in 1883, but the key publication was the book by John von Neumann and Oskar Morgenstern (*Theory of Games and Economic Behaviour*) in 1944. Other famous names in game theory include John

Russell Crowe playing the part of mathematician and game theorist John Nash in A Beautiful Mind.

Nash (played by Russell Crowe in the film *A Beautiful Mind*), John Harsanyi and Reinhard Selton, who shared the 1994 Nobel prize for their work in this area.

Almost certainly, the most famous game is the **Prisoners' Dilemma**, introduced in a lecture by Albert Tucker (who taught John Nash at Princeton) in 1950. This simple example of game theory turns out to have a multitude of helpful applications in economics.

 Key term

Prisoners' Dilemma: an example of game theory with a range of applications in oligopoly theory

Two prisoners, Al Fresco and Des Jardins, are being interrogated about a major crime, and the police know that at least one of the prisoners is guilty. The two are kept in separate cells and cannot communicate with each other. The police have enough evidence to convict them of a minor offence, but not enough to convict them of the major one.

Each prisoner is offered a deal. If he turns state's evidence and provides evidence to convict the other prisoner, he will get off — *unless* the other prisoner also confesses. If both refuse to deal, they will just be charged with the minor offence. Table 3.3 summarises the sentences that each will receive in the various circumstances.

		Des			
		Confess		**Refuse**	
Al	**Confess**	10	10	0	15
	Refuse	15	0	5	5

Table 3.3 *The Prisoners' Dilemma: possible outcomes (years in jail)*

In each case, Al's sentence (in years) is shown in orange and Des's in blue. In terms of the entries in the table, if both Al and Des refuse to deal, they will be convicted of the minor offence, and each will go down for 5 years. However, if Al confesses and Des refuses to deal, Al will get off completely free, and Des will take the full rap of 15 years. If Des confesses and Al refuses, the reverse happens. However, if both confess they will each get 10 years.

Think about this situation from Al's point of view, remembering that the prisoners cannot communicate, so Al does not know what Des will choose to do and vice versa. You can see from Table 3.3 that, whatever Des chooses to do, Al will be better off confessing. John Nash referred to such a situation as a **dominant strategy**.

 Key term

dominant strategy: a situation in game theory where a player's best strategy is independent of those chosen by others

The dilemma is, of course, symmetric, so for Des too the dominant strategy is to confess. The inevitable result is that if both prisoners are selfish they will both confess — and both will then get 10 years in jail. If they had both refused to deal they would *both* have been better off; but this is too risky a strategy for either of them to adopt. A refusal to deal might have led to 15 years in jail.

What has this to do with economics? Suppose there are two firms (Diamond Tools and Better Spades) operating in a duopoly market (i.e. a market with only two firms). Each firm has a choice of producing 'high' output or 'low' output. The profit made by one firm depends on two things: its own output, and the output of the other firm.

Table 3.4 shows the range of possible outcomes for a particular time period. Consider Diamond Tools: if it chooses 'low' when Better Spades also chooses 'low', it will make £2 million profit (and so will Better Spades); but if Diamond Tools chooses 'low' when Better Spades chooses 'high', Diamond Tools will make zero profits and Better Spades will make £3 million.

		Better Spades			
		High		Low	
Diamond	High	1	1	3	0
Tools	Low	0	3	2	2

Table 3.4 *Diamond Tools and Better Spades: possible outcomes (profits in £m)*

The situation that maximises joint profits is for both firms to produce low; but suppose you were taking decisions for Diamond Tools — what would you choose?

If Better Spades produces 'low' you will maximise profits by producing 'high', whereas if Better Spades produces 'high' you will still maximise profits by producing high! So Diamond Tools has a dominant strategy to produce high — it is the profit-maximising action whatever Better Spades does, even though it means that joint profits will be lower.

Given that the table is symmetric, Better Spades faces the same decision process, and also has a dominant strategy to choose high, so they always end up in the northwest corner of the table, even though southeast would be better for each of them. Furthermore, after they have made their choices and seen what the other has chosen, each firm feels justified by its actions, and thinks that it took the right decision, given the rival's move. This is known as a **Nash equilibrium**, which has the characteristic that neither firm needs to amend its behaviour in any future period. This model can be used to investigate a wide range of decisions that firms need to take strategically.

Key term

Nash equilibrium: situation occurring within a game when each player's chosen strategy maximises pay-offs given the other player's choice, so that no player has an incentive to alter behaviour

Exercise 3.3

Suppose there are two cinemas in a market, X and Y; you are taking decisions for firm X. You cannot communicate with the other firm; both firms are considering only the next period. Each firm is choosing whether to set price 'high' or 'low'. Your expectation is that the pay-offs (in terms of profits) to the two firms are as shown in Table 3.5 (**firm X in brown, firm Y in blue**):

		Firm Y chooses:			
		High price		Low price	
Firm X	High price	0	10	1	15
chooses:	Low price	15	1	4	4

Table 3.5 *Cinemas X and Y: possible outcomes*

a If firm Y sets price high, what strategy maximises profits for firm X?

b If firm Y sets price low, what strategy maximises profits for firm X?

c So what strategy will firm X adopt?

d What is the market outcome?

e What outcome would maximise the firms' joint profit?

f How might this outcome be achieved?

g Would the outcome be different if the game were played over repeated periods?

Cooperative games and cartels

Look back at the Prisoners' Dilemma game in Table 3.4. It is clear that the requirement that the firms be unable to communicate with each other is a serious impediment from the firms' point of view. If both firms could agree to produce 'low' they would maximise their joint profits, but they will not risk this strategy if they cannot communicate.

If they could join together in a **cartel**, the two firms could come to an agreement to adopt the low–low strategy. However, if they were to agree to this each firm would have a strong incentive to cheat, because if each now knew that the other firm was going to produce low, they would also know that they could produce high and dominate the market — at least, given the pay-offs in the table.

Key term

cartel: an agreement between firms on price and output with the intention of maximising their joint profits

This is a common feature of cartels. Collusion can bring high joint profits, but there is always the temptation for each of the member firms to cheat and try to sneak some additional market share at the expense of the other firm/s in the cartel.

Extension material

You can see how a cartel might operate in Figure 3.8, which shows the situation facing a two-firm cartel (a duopoly). Panels (a) and (b) show the cost conditions for each of the firms, and panel (c) shows the whole market.

If the firms aim to maximise their joint profits, then they set $MR = MC$ at the level of the market (shown in panel (c)). This occurs at the joint level of output $Q_1 + Q_2$, with the price set at P^*. Notice that the joint marginal cost curve is the sum of the two firms' marginal cost curves.

The critical decision is how to divide the market up between the two firms. In the figure, the two firms have different cost conditions, with firm 1 operating at lower short-run average cost than firm 2. If the firms agree to set price at P^*, and each produces up to the point where marginal cost equals the level of (market) marginal revenue at MR^*, then the market should work well. Firm 1 produces Q_1 and firm 2 produces Q_2. Joint profits are maximised, and there is a clear rule enabling the division of the market between the firms.

However, notice that firm 2 is very much the junior partner in this alliance, as it gets a much smaller market share. The temptation to cheat is obvious. If firm 2 accepts price P^*, it sees that its profits will be maximised at Q_2^*, so there is a temptation to try to steal an extra bit of market share.

Of course, the temptation is also there for firm 1, but as soon as either one of the firms begins to increase output the market price will have to fall to maintain equilibrium, and the cartel will be broken: the market will move away from the joint profit-maximising position.

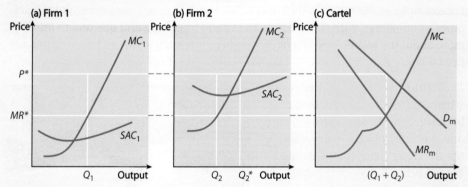

Figure 3.8 *Market allocation in a two-firm cartel*

There is another downside to the formation of a cartel. In most countries around the world (with one or two exceptions such as Hong Kong) they are illegal. For example, in the UK the operation of a cartel is illegal under the UK Competition Act, under which the Office of Fair Trading is empowered to fine firms up to 10% of their turnover for each year the cartel is found to have been in operation.

This means that overt collusion is rare. The most famous example is not between firms but between nations, in the form of the Organisation of Petroleum Exporting Countries (OPEC), which over a long period of time has operated a cartel to control the price of oil.

Conditions favouring collusion

Some conditions may favour the formation of cartels – or at least, some form of collusion between firms. The most important of these is the ability of each of the firms involved to monitor the actions of the other firms, and so ensure that they are keeping to the agreement.

In this context, it helps if there is a relatively small number of firms; otherwise it will be difficult to monitor the market. It also helps if they are producing similar goods; otherwise one firm could try to steal an advantage by varying the quality of the product. When the economy is booming it may be more difficult to monitor market shares, because all firms are likely to be expanding. If firms have excess capacity, this may increase the temptation to cheat by increasing output and stealing market share; on the other hand, it also makes it possible for the other

firms to retaliate quickly. The degree of secrecy about market shares and market conditions is also important.

Collusion in practice

Although cartels are illegal, the potential gains from collusion may tempt firms to find ways of working together. In some cases firms have joined together in rather loose strategic alliances, in which they may work together on part of their business, perhaps in undertaking joint research and development or technology swaps.

For example, in 2000 General Motors (GM) and Fiat took an equity stake in each other's companies, with GM wanting to expand in Europe and needing to find out more about the technology of making smaller cars. Such alliances have not always been a success, and in the GM–Fiat case GM and Fiat separated in 2005.

The airline market is another sector where strategic alliances have been important, with the Star Alliance and the One World Alliance carving up the long-haul routes between them. Such alliances offer benefits to passengers, who can get access to a wider range of destinations and business class lounges and frequent-flier rewards, and to the airlines, which can economise on airport facilities by pooling their resources. However, the net effect is to reduce

STAR ALLIANCE

Strategic alliances in the airline industry are promoted as benefiting customers, but are potentially anti-competitive.

competition, and the regulators have interfered with some suggested alliances, such as that between British Airways and American Airlines in 2001, which was investigated by regulators on both sides of the Atlantic. The conditions under which the alliance would have been permitted were such that British Airways withdrew the proposal.

Alternatively, firms may look for **tacit collusion**, in which the firms in a market observe each other's behaviour very closely and refrain from competing on price, even if they do not actually communicate with each other. Such collusion may emerge gradually over time in a market, as the firms become accustomed to market conditions and to each other's behaviour.

One way in which this may happen is through some form of *price leadership*. If one firm is a dominant producer in a market, then it may take the lead in setting the price, with the other firms following its example. It has been suggested that the OPEC cartel operated according to this model in some periods, with Saudi Arabia acting as the dominant firm.

Key term

tacit collusion: situation occurring when firms refrain from competing on price, but without communication or formal agreement between them

An alternative is *barometric price leadership*, in which one firm tries out a price increase and then waits to see whether other firms follow. If they do, a new higher price has been reached without the need for overt discussions between the firms. On the other hand, if the other firms do not feel the time is right for the change they will keep their prices steady, and the first firm will drop back into line or else lose market share. The initiating firm need not be the same one in each round. It has been argued that the domestic air travel market in the USA has operated in this way on some internal routes. The practice is facilitated by the ease with which prices can be checked via the computerised ticketing systems, so that each firm knows what the other firms are doing.

The frequency of anti-cartel cases brought by regulators in recent years suggests that firms continue to be tempted by the gains from collusion. The operation of a cartel is now a criminal act in the UK, as it has been in the USA for some time. This will be discussed in Chapter 5.

An example of an oligopoly — travel agents

The market for package holidays is big business. In 2006 UK residents made 45.3 million holiday visits abroad, of which package holidays made up a large proportion. This represents a major change in habits over recent decades — in 1971, the number of holiday visits abroad was just 6.7 million. To what extent does the market operate efficiently? In order to evaluate efficiency, economic analysis suggests that a starting point is to examine the market structure.

The Association of British Travel Agents (ABTA) is an organisation that acts as a trade association for tour operators and travel agents in the UK. In early 2006, ABTA covered more than 6,000 travel agency offices and more than 1,000 tour operators. According to the ABTA website, between them, these accounted for 85% of UK-sold holidays.

Superficially, the fact that there are more than 6,000 travel agency offices seems to suggest a competitive market, but this is misleading, as it is not only the number of offices that is important, but also the number of firms in the market, and the distribution of the business between them. ABTA's membership comprises about 1,722 individual member companies, but the four largest control a significant part of the market. These are Thomson, Thomas Cook, My Travel and First Choice.

With just four major operators in the market, it would be classified as an *oligopoly*. If the firms were to collude together in order to exploit their market power, this could have an adverse effect on allocative efficiency. A monopolist attempting to maximise profits would restrict output and raise price, thus pushing the market away from the point at which price is equal to marginal cost. However, the question is whether the firms do collude in this way, or whether there are other forces within the market that constrain or prevent them from exploiting their position.

One of the problems in evaluating whether an oligopoly market is typified by collusion or competition is that, in general, it is not possible to observe marginal cost, so that it is not possible to check whether price is being set above marginal

cost. An alternative might be to look at profits, and ask whether firms in a market seem to be making excessive profits. In the case of the travel companies, recent experience may not help in this respect. The substantial reduction in demand for foreign holidays following the terrorist attacks of 11 September 2001 in the USA created difficulties for many of the tour operators and travel agents, many of which posted sharp reductions in profits, or even losses. But this is not conclusive evidence that firms were not abusing their market power; it might just be a process of adjustment to lower demand for their products.

The growth of the internet may be the key factor that determines the intensity of competition in the travel industry. The growing ability of consumers to by-pass the local travel agent by making their own bookings online suggests that the travel market is highly contestable. It is now possible for a potential holidaymaker to find their flights, hotel accommodation, car rentals or hotel transfers from their PCs. This can be done either by booking direct with airlines and hotels, or by using one of the growing number of online firms, such as Expedia, the world's largest online travel agent.

The travel agents have thus had to respond to these new online entrants to their market. They have done so partly by themselves going online, and developing their own websites and online sales. They have also responded by looking for niche markets, offering specialist advice on long-haul holidays, adventure trips or skiing packages.

The intensity of this competition is likely to be beneficial for consumers in terms of the prices that can be obtained for package holidays. Inevitably, there may also be dangers. For example, it may be that online purchase of the separate components of a holiday is more risky than buying from a travel agent backed by the code of conduct now issued by ABTA. Or it may be that the online companies themselves will go through a process of merger, acquisition and increasing concentration that may lead at some point to market power.

Exercise 3.4

For each of the following markets, identify the model that would most closely describe it (i.e. perfect competition, monopoly, monopolistic competition or oligopoly):

a a large number of firms selling branded varieties of toothpaste

b a sole supplier of postal services

c a large number of farmers producing cauliflowers, sold at a common price

d a situation in which a few large banks supply most of the market for retail banking services

e a sole supplier of rail transport

Summary

➤ An oligopoly is a market with a few sellers, each of which takes strategic decisions based on likely rival actions and reactions.

➤ Because there are many ways in which firms may interact, there is no single way of modelling an oligopoly market.

➤ One example is the kinked demand curve model, which argues that firms' perceptions of the demand curve for their products is based on their views about whether or not rival firms will react to their own actions.

➤ This suggests that price is likely to remain stable over a wide range of market conditions.

➤ Game theory is a more recent and more flexible way of modelling interactions between firms.

➤ The Prisoners' Dilemma can demonstrate the potential benefits of collusion, but also shows that in some market situations each firm may have a dominant strategy to move the market away from the joint profit-maximising position.

➤ If firms could join together in a cartel, they could indeed maximise their joint profits — but there would still be a temptation for firms to cheat, and try to steal market share. Such action would break up the cartel, and move the market away from the joint profit-maximising position.

➤ However, cartels are illegal in most societies.

➤ Firms may thus look for covert ways of colluding in a market, for example through some form of price leadership.

Chapter 4

Pricing strategies and contestable markets

Having examined a range of models of market structure, it is time to investigate the sorts of pricing strategies that firms may adopt, and how they decide which to go for. This chapter also discusses ways in which firms may try to prevent new firms from joining a market, in terms of both pricing and non-price strategies. The theory of contestable markets is investigated as well.

Learning outcomes

After studying this chapter, you should:
➤ be aware of the possible pricing rules that can be adopted by firms
➤ understand the notion of cost-plus pricing, and how this may relate to profit maximisation
➤ be familiar with the idea of predatory pricing
➤ be aware of the concept of limit pricing
➤ understand the notion of contestable markets and its implication for firms' behaviour
➤ be familiar with other entry deterrence strategies

Pricing rules

In the analysis of market structure, it was assumed that firms set out to maximise profits. However, Chapter 1 pointed out that sometimes they may set out to achieve other objectives. The price of a firm's product is a key strategic variable that must be manipulated in order to attain whatever objective the firm wishes to achieve.

Figure 4.1 illustrates the variety of pricing rules that are possible. The figure shows a firm operating under a form of market structure that is not perfect competition — because the firm faces a downward-sloping demand curve for its product shown by AR ($= D$).

Profit maximisation

If the firm chooses to maximise profits, it will choose output such that marginal revenue is equal to marginal cost, and will then set the price to clear the market. In terms of the figure, it will set output at Q_1 and price at P_1.

Revenue maximisation

The economist William Baumol argued that, if there is a divorce of ownership from control in the organisation of a firm, whereby the shareholders have delegated day-to-day decision making to

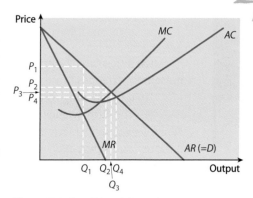

Figure 4.1 *Possible pricing rules*

managers (a principal–agent situation), the managers may find themselves with some freedom to pursue other objectives, such as revenue maximisation. A revenue maximiser in Figure 4.1 would choose to produce at the output level at which marginal revenue is zero. This occurs at Q_2 in the figure, with the price set at P_2.

Sales maximisation

If instead managers set out to maximise the volume of sales subject to covering opportunity cost, they will choose to set output at a level such that price equals average cost, which will clear the market. In Figure 4.1 this happens at Q_4 (with price at P_4).

Allocative efficiency

It has been argued that allocative efficiency in an individual market occurs at the point where price is equal to marginal cost. In Figure 4.1 this is at Q_3 (with price P_3). However, from the firm's perspective there is no obvious reason why this should become an objective of the firm, as it confers no particular advantage.

Exercise 4.1

For each of the following situations, identify the pricing rule most appropriate to achieve the firm's objectives, and comment on the implications that this has for efficiency.

a A firm producing computers tries to achieve as high a market share as possible, measured in value terms.

b A firm producing DVDs tries to make as high a surplus over costs as can be achieved.

c A national newspaper sets out to maximise circulation (subject to covering its costs), knowing that this will affect advertising revenues.

d A farmer producing cabbages finds that she cannot influence the price of her product.

Pricing in practice

It seems clear that in practice most firms do not know the shape of their revenue and cost curves with any great precision. It might thus be argued that they cannot

actually adopt any of these rules, and need to find alternative ways of devising a pricing strategy.

One such approach would be to make a series of small (marginal) changes, and observe the effects each time, thereby moving gradually towards whatever objective the firm wishes to attain. However, if you were to ask managers how they decide on price, many of them would probably say that they use **cost-plus pricing** (sometimes known as mark-up pricing). In other words, they calculate average cost at their chosen output level, and then add on a mark-up to bring them some profit per unit. Indeed, when in 1996 the Bank of England conducted a survey of British companies to see how they set their prices, 37% said that they set prices using a mark-up pricing rule.

Key term

cost-plus pricing: pricing policy whereby firms set their price by adding a mark-up to average cost

Does this nullify the profit-maximising hypothesis? Not necessarily. Saying that a firm sets price as a mark-up on average cost leaves a very important question unanswered: namely, what determines the size of the mark-up that the firm can add to average cost?

The Bank of England survey also discovered that firms in markets in which there were few competitors set higher mark-ups than those in markets in which there were more firms. Mark-ups were also higher in markets where there were differentiated products than in markets producing homogeneous ones.

This pattern of behaviour is entirely compatible with the profit-maximisation hypothesis, where mark-ups are expected to be lower in the presence of a high degree of competition. In other words, mark-up pricing may be a strategy used by firms to find the profit-maximising level of price and output.

Summary

➤ There are many pricing rules that a firm may choose to adopt, depending on the objectives it wishes to achieve.

➤ In practice, firms may not know their cost and revenue curves with any accuracy.

➤ By making marginal changes and observing the effects, they may be able to move towards the price that would achieve their chosen objective.

➤ Many firms use mark-up pricing, adding a profit margin to average cost.

➤ The size of the mark-up may depend upon the degree of competition in the market and the extent to which the product is differentiated.

➤ Mark-up pricing is not inconsistent with profit maximisation.

Price wars

Another finding of the Bank of England's survey was that firms were very strong in saying that they wished to avoid price wars. This could be expected from the kinked demand curve model, where firms in an oligopoly realise that a price reduction is likely to be matched by rivals, leaving all firms with lower profits but having relatively little effect on market shares.

And yet, price wars do break out from time to time. For example, in May 2002 a price war broke out in the UK tabloid newspaper market. It was initiated by the *Express*, but the main protagonists were the *Mirror* and the *Sun*, which joined in after a couple of weeks. The *Mirror* cut its price from 32p to 20p, and the *Sun* from 30p to 20p.

After a week at these lower prices, the editor of the *Sun* was serving champagne in the newsroom in celebration. Their reading of the situation was that the *Mirror* had not expected the *Sun* to follow the price cut. Three weeks after the *Mirror's* price cut, it put its price back up again — followed by the *Sun*. Analysts and observers commented that the only gainers had been the readers, who had enjoyed three weeks of lower prices.

Why should firms act in this way? The *Mirror* argued that it was trying to re-brand itself, and capture new readers who would continue to read the paper even after the price returned to its normal level. This may hint at the reason for a price war — to affect the long-run equilibrium of the market. The *Sun's* retaliation was a natural defensive response to an aggressive move.

In some cases a price war may be initiated as a strategy to drive a weaker competitor out of the market altogether. The motivation then is clear, especially if the initiator of the price war ends up with a monopoly or near-monopoly position in the market. It could be argued that this represents an attempt to maximise profits in the long run by establishing a monopoly position.

Predatory pricing

Perhaps the most common context in which price wars have broken out is where an existing firm or firms have reacted to defend the market against the entry of new firms.

One such example occurred in 1996, in the early years of easyJet, the low-cost air carrier, which was then trying to become established. When easyJet started flying the London–Amsterdam route, charging its now well-known low prices, the incumbent firm (KLM) reacted very aggressively, driving its price down to a level just below that of easyJet's. The response from easyJet was to launch legal action against KLM, claiming it was using unfair market tactics.

Was there a winner in the price war?

So-called **predatory pricing** is illegal under English, Dutch and EU law. It should be noted that, in order to declare an action illegal, it is necessary to define that action very carefully — otherwise it will not be possible to prove the case in the courts. In the case of predatory pricing, the legal definition is based on economic analysis.

Key *term*

predatory pricing: an anti-competitive strategy in which a firm sets price below average variable cost in an attempt to force a rival or rivals out of the market and achieve market dominance

Remember that Chapter 2 defined the shut-down price for the firm, pointing out that if a firm was failing to cover average variable costs its strategy should be to close down immediately, as it would be better off doing so. The courts have backed this theory, and state that a pricing strategy should be interpreted as being predatory if the price is set below average variable costs, as the only motive for remaining in business while making such losses must be to drive competitors out of business and achieve market dominance. This is known as the *Areeda–Turner principle* (after the case in which it was first argued in the USA).

On the face of it, it would seem that consumers have much to gain from such strategies through the resulting lower prices. However, a predator that is successful in driving out the opposition is likely to recoup its losses by putting prices back up to profit-maximising levels thereafter, so the benefit to consumers is short lived.

Having said that, the low-cost airlines survived the attempts of the established airlines to hold on to their market shares. Indeed, in the post-9/11 period, which was a tough one for the airlines for obvious reasons, the low-cost airlines flourished while the more conventional established airlines went through a very difficult period indeed.

In some cases, the very threat of predatory pricing may be sufficient to deter entry by new firms, if the threat is a credible one. In other words, the existing firms need to convince potential entrants that they, the existing firms, will find it in their best interests to fight a price war, otherwise the entrants will not believe the threat. The existing firms could do this by making it known that they had surplus capacity, so that they would be able to increase output very quickly in order to drive down the price.

Whether entry will be deterred by such means may depend in part on the characteristics of the potential entrant. After all, a new firm may reckon that, if the existing firm finds it worth sacrificing profits in the short run, the rewards of dominating the market must be worth fighting for. It may therefore decide to sacrifice short-term profit in order to enter the market — especially if it is diversifying from other markets and has resources at its disposal. The winner will then be the firm that can last the longest; but, clearly, this is potentially very damaging for all concerned.

Exercise 4.2

Discuss the extent to which consumers benefit from a price war.

Limit pricing

An associated but less extreme strategy is **limit pricing**. This assumes that the incumbent firm has some sort of cost advantage over potential entrants, for example economies of scale.

Figure 4.2 shows a firm facing a downward-sloping demand curve, and thus having some influence over the price of its product. If the firm is maximising profits, it is setting output at Q_0 and price at P_0. As average revenue is comfortably above average cost at this price, the firm is making healthy supernormal profits.

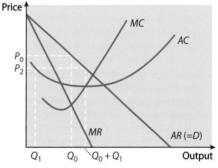

Figure 4.2 Limit pricing

Suppose that the natural barriers to entry in this industry are weak. The supernormal profits will be attractive to potential entrants. Given the cost conditions, the incumbent firm is enjoying the benefit of economies of scale, although producing below the minimum efficient scale.

If a new firm joins the market, producing on a relatively small scale, say at Q_1, the impact on the market can be analysed as follows. The immediate effect is on price, as now the amount $Q_0 + Q_1$ is being produced, pushing price down to P_2. The new firm (producing Q_1) is just covering average cost, so is making normal profits and feeling justified in having joined the market. The original firm is still making super-normal profits, but at a lower level than before. The entry of the new firm has competed away part of the original firm's supernormal profits.

One way in which the firm could have guarded against entry is by charging a lower price than P_0 to begin with. For example, if it had set output at $Q_0 + Q_1$ and price at P_2, then a new entrant joining the market would have pushed the price down to a level below P_2, and without the benefit of

Key term

limit price: the highest price that an existing firm can set without enabling new firms to enter the market and make a profit

economies of scale would make losses and exit the market. In any case, if the existing firm has been in the market for some time it will have gone through a process of learning by doing, and therefore will have a lower average cost curve than the potential entrant. This makes it more likely that limit pricing can be used.

Thus, by setting a price below the profit-maximising level, the original firm is able to maintain its market position in the longer run. This could be a reason for avoiding making too high a level of supernormal profits in the short run, in order to make profits in the longer term.

Notice that such a strategy need not be carried out by a monopolist, but could also occur in an oligopoly, where existing firms may jointly seek to protect their market against potential entry.

Contestable markets

It has been argued that in some markets, in order to prevent the entry of new firms, the existing firm would have to charge such a low price that it would be unable to reap any supernormal profits at all.

This theory was developed by industrial economist William Baumol, and is known as the theory of **contestable markets.** It was in recognition of this theory that the monopoly model in Chapter 2 included the assumption that there must be no substitutes for the good, *either actual or potential.*

www.econ.nyu.edu/user/baumol/w

William Baumol.

For a market to be contestable, it must have no barriers to entry or exit and no sunk costs. *Sunk costs* refers to costs that a firm incurs in setting up a business and which cannot be recovered if the firm exits the market. Furthermore, new firms in the market must have no competitive disadvantage compared with the incumbent firm/s; in other words, they must have access to the same technology, and there must be no significant learning-by-doing effects. Entry and exit must be rapid.

> **Key term**
>
> **contestable market:** a market in which the existing firm makes only normal profit, as it cannot set a higher price without attracting entry, owing to the absence of barriers to entry and sunk costs

Under these conditions, the incumbent firm cannot set a price that is higher than average cost, because as soon as it does it will open up the possibility of *hit-and-run entry* by new firms, which can enter the market and compete away the super-normal profits.

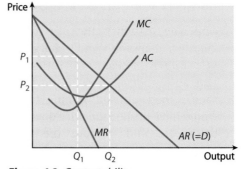

Figure 4.3 Contestability

Consider Figure 4.3, which shows a monopoly firm in a market. The argument is that, if the monopolist charges the profit-maximising price, then if the market is contestable the firm will be vulnerable to hit-and-run entry — a firm could come into the market, take some of the supernormal profits, then exit again. The only way the monopolist can avoid this happening is to set price equal to average cost, so that there are no supernormal profits to act as an incentive for entry.

On the face of it, the conditions for contestability sound pretty stringent. In particular, the firm in Figure 4.3 enjoys some economies of scale, so you would think that some sunk costs had been incurred.

However, suppose a firm has a monopoly on a domestic air route between two destinations. An airline with surplus capacity — i.e. a spare aircraft sitting in a hangar — could enter this route and exit again without incurring sunk costs in response to profits being made by the incumbent firm. This is an example of how contestability may limit the ability of the incumbent firm to use its market power.

Notice in this example that, although the firm only makes normal profits, neither productive nor allocative efficiency is achieved.

A moot point is whether the threat of entry will in fact persuade firms that they cannot set a price above average cost. If entry and exit are so rapid, perhaps the firms can risk making some profit above normal profits and then respond to entry very aggressively if and when it happens. After all, it is difficult to think of an example in which there are absolutely no sunk costs. Almost any business is going to have to advertise in order to find customers, and such advertising expenditure cannot be recovered.

This will be re-examined in the next chapter when discussing competition policy, as it is an important issue in that context, and the degree of contestability may affect the perception of how much market power is in the hands of existing firms.

Exercise 4.3

Discuss the extent to which the following markets may be considered to be contestable — or to have become more so in recent years:

a Opticians

b Travel agents

c Financial services

d The postal service

e Aircraft manufacture

Other entry deterrence strategies

Pricing is not the only strategy that firms adopt in order to deter entry by new firms. Another approach that has been used over a wide range of economic activities is to raise the fixed costs of being in the industry.

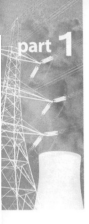

Advertising and publicity

Advertising can be regarded as a component of fixed costs, because expenditure on it does not vary directly with the volume of output. If the firms in an industry typically spend heavily on advertising, it will be more difficult for new firms to become established, as they too will need to advertise widely in order to attract customers.

Similarly, firms may spend heavily on achieving a well-known brand image that will ensure customer loyalty. Hence they may invest a lot in the design and packaging of their merchandise. One such example was the high-profile TV campaign run by Sunny Delight when trying to gain entry into the soft drinks market in the early part of the twenty-first century.

Notice that such costs are also sunk costs, and cannot be recovered if the new firm fails to gain a foothold. It has sometimes been suggested that the cost of excessive advertising should be included in calculations of the social cost of monopoly.

Research and development

A characteristic of some industries is the heavy expenditure undertaken on research and development (R&D). A prominent example is the pharmaceutical industry, which spends large amounts on researching new drugs — and new cosmetics.

This is another component of fixed costs, as it does not vary with the volume of production. Again, new firms wanting to break into the market know that they will need to invest heavily in R&D if they are going to keep up with the new and better drugs and cosmetics always coming on to the market.

Exercise 4.4

For each of the following, explain under what circumstances the action of the firm constitutes a barrier to entry and discuss whether there is a strategic element to it, or whether it might be regarded as a 'natural' or 'innocent' barrier.

a A firm takes advantage of economies of scale to reduce its average costs of production.

b A firm holds a patent on the sale of a product.

c A firm engages in widespread advertising of its product.

d A firm installs surplus capacity relative to normal production levels.

e A firm produces a range of very similar products under different brand names.

f A firm chooses not to set price at the profit-maximising level.

g A firm spends extensively on research and development in order to produce a better product.

Market structure and competitiveness: a case study

A good way of gaining insight into the way in which market structure can affect the intensity of competitiveness in a market is to look at examples of markets that have experienced a change in market conditions that has induced a change in market structure. The process of deregulation affords such an opportunity, and there have been several examples of this in recent years. The low-cost airlines have transformed the face of air travel. They show some of the effects of changing market structure, and how firms are able to become profitable by understanding some economic analysis.

The low-cost airlines appeared on the scene as long ago as 1971, with the advent of Southwestern in the USA, followed by Ryanair in 1985 and easyJet in 1995. The model has now been copied by Air Asia and other airlines operating in southeast Asia.

This market provides an illustration of how intensified competition can affect the operation of markets. Before the advent of the low-cost airlines, the market for air travel was dominated by large national carriers, in many cases either state-run or heavily subsidised by governments. As time went by, these large airlines began to join together in strategic alliances that enabled them to work together yet maintain their individual characters. The market seemed to be consolidating and was effectively becoming more concentrated.

Deregulation provided an opening for changes in the market structure, by reducing the barriers to entry of new firms. However, in order to exploit that opening, the budget airlines needed a good understanding of economic analysis. Their success has been built on a thorough understanding of cost structures and a recognition of the contestability of airlines, together with the judicious use of price discrimination.

Profits depend upon costs as well as revenue. EasyJet (not to mention other budget airlines, such as Ryanair and Flybe) have taken a close look at the structure of costs. Figure 4.4 shows a detailed breakdown of the costs of a typical easyJet flight. By focusing on each individual item of costs and looking for ways of cutting costs to a minimum, the budget airlines have been able to achieve profitability.

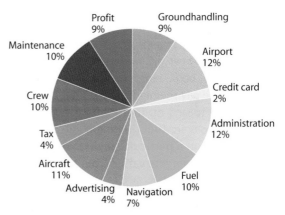

Figure 4.4 *The cost of an easyJet flight*
Source: *Guardian*, 20 August 2003.

In part, this has been connected with the understanding of demand. The budget airlines offer a 'no frills' approach, doing away with pre-assigned seats and pre-issued tickets, free in-flight catering, a separate business class and so on. They also use more remote airports, where charges are relatively low. But the savings go way beyond these conspicuous items.

In particular, the budget airlines have followed a pattern established by the Texas-based airline Southwestern, which sets out four key rules.

First, only fly one type of plane. This reduces maintenance costs and avoids the need to hold a wide range of spare parts. This is one source of potential economies of scale.

Second, drive down costs every year. This may be achieved while the airline is still expanding if there are economies of scale to be reaped. For example, it may be achieved by negotiating improved deals from suppliers – of fuel, insurance etc.

Third, minimise the time that aircraft spend parked on the tarmac. The no frills and no tickets approach enables a much quicker turn-round of aircraft – which, after all, only earn money for the company when they are in the air. For example, an easyJet plane flying between Luton and Nice can make four round-trips per day – by spending only about half-an-hour on the tarmac at each end.

Fourth, do not try to sell anything except seats. Schemes that offer loyalty bonuses or air miles cost money to administer, and are more complicated than they are worth.

Following these rules, and paying careful attention to the various forms of costs identified in Figure 4.4 has enabled the budget airlines to expand, to make profits (9% in the diagram), and to transform air travel.

As far as price discrimination is concerned, easyJet says on its website that it 'operates a very simple fare structure...based on supply and demand'. The nature of the price structure is that passengers who book early pay the lowest prices, whereas those who book close to their travel time pay the highest prices. Figure 4.5 (based on information in an article in the *Guardian*) shows

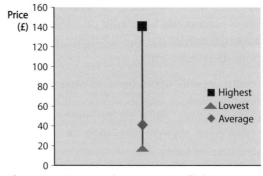

Figure 4.5 *Prices paid on an easyJet flight*

that on a particular flight from Luton to Nice on 20 August 2003, the prices paid by passengers varied from just £20 to about £140.

You might expect that in a competitive market, the price structure would be the opposite. If prices follow costs, the marginal cost to easyJet of carrying an extra passenger is likely to be pretty low, so the flight could be filled up by offering last-minute deals, with the price being driven close to marginal cost. But this is clearly not happening at easyJet, as the later a passenger books, the higher the price that they face.

This suggests that easyJet understands enough about the nature of demand to use price discrimination on its flights. People who book at the last minute are likely to be business travellers who need to fly urgently, perhaps for a business meeting or to clinch a deal. Such customers are likely to have low elasticity of demand, and thus be prepared to pay a higher price for their ticket. This is in contrast to those who can book well in advance, who are more likely to be people travelling for pleasure – visiting relatives or going on holiday. For these travellers, the choice of when to fly is more flexible. This means there are more possible flights from which they can choose. And we know that when there are substitutes for a commodity, the price elasticity of demand is high. It is for these customers that easyJet can offer the low prices that we see being advertised. After all, at £20, it probably costs some customers more to get to the airport than it costs for the flight!

So, easyJet can make use of this difference in demand elasticity to charge different prices to different customers, even if the product (the flight from London to Nice) is the same for all of them. Thus an understanding of demand is important for easyJet.

The entry of the budget airlines also caused the existing firms to reconsider the way in which they operate. Some reacted by setting up their own budget subsidiaries, with varying degrees of success. Others have had to accept that they need to focus on longer-haul flights.

The budget airlines case therefore provides another example of how competition can transform a market, and how contestability can affect firms' behaviour. Why can the airline business be regarded as contestable? After all, it might be argued that the set-up costs of establishing an airline are likely to be high, so it is difficult to claim that there are no sunk costs faced by firms. However, the key issue is that market conditions on particular routes may well encourage contestability. Once the airline is estab-

Andrew Harrison, chief executive of easyJet.

lished, the costs of flying a new route are relatively low. There are bound to be some advertising costs, but otherwise an airline can switch aircraft to new routes quite quickly. It could then switch to other routes if profits were disappointing. In other words, hit-and-run entry is possible on particular routes. This may mean that existing airlines will not set prices at such levels that entry is attracted.

It is also worth noting that the low-cost airlines have flourished not only by taking customers away from the existing airlines, but also by tapping a new customer base. By offering low fares and easy accessibility, they have attracted passengers who would not otherwise have dreamed of flying.

Summary

➤ Although price wars are expected to be damaging for the firms involved, they do break out from time to time.

➤ This may occur when firms wish to increase their market shares, or when existing firms wish to deter the entry of new firms into the market.

➤ Predatory pricing is an extreme strategy that forces all firms to endure losses. It is normally invoked in an attempt to eliminate a competitor, and is illegal in many countries.

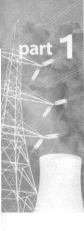
➤ Limit pricing occurs when a firm or firms choose to set price below the profit-maximising level in order to prevent entry. The limit price is the highest price that an existing firm can set without allowing entry.

➤ In some cases the limit price may enable the incumbent firm or firms to make only normal profit. Such a market is said to be contestable.

➤ Contestability requires that there are no barriers to entry or exit and no sunk costs — and that the incumbent firm/s have no cost advantage over hit-and-run entrants.

➤ Firms have adopted other strategies designed to deter entry, such as using advertising or R&D spending to raise the cost of entry by adding to required fixed costs.

Government intervention to promote competition

If resources are going to be allocated efficiently within a society, it is crucial that business organisations make the appropriate economic decisions. Previous chapters have shown that firms may sometimes be able to gain market dominance, giving them sufficient market power to take decisions that cause a distortion in resource allocation. This chapter explores the major policy areas in which authorities attempt to influence firms' economic decision making. It looks first at competition policy, through which the authorities attempt to encourage competition in markets and protect the interests of consumers. It then examines measures introduced to regulate privatised industries, most of which are natural monopolies posing particular problems for resource allocation. There is also discussion of ways in which the private sector has become involved in public sector organisations.

Learning outcomes

After studying this chapter, you should:
➤ understand the economic underpinnings of competition policy
➤ appreciate that there may be situations in which unremitting competition may not be in the best interests of society
➤ be familiar with the roles of the Office of Fair Trading and the Competition Commission
➤ be aware of the issues that may affect their judgements of a market under investigation
➤ be familiar with the general institutional background of competition policy in the UK and the EU
➤ be familiar with some examples of investigations of mergers
➤ appreciate the arguments for and against privatisation
➤ understand the need to regulate natural monopolies and some of the problems that may arise in attempting to do so
➤ be familiar with ways in which private sector involvement in public sector organisations has been encouraged

Competition and the government

An awareness of the market failure that can arise from imperfect competition has led governments to introduce measures designed to promote competition and protect consumers. Such measures are known as **competition policy**.

A key focus of such legislation in the past has been monopoly, as economic analysis highlighted the allocative inefficiency that can arise in a monopoly market if the firm sets out to maximise profit. More recently however, the scope of legislation has widened, and since 1997 competition policy has been toughened significantly.

Key term

competition policy: a set of measures designed to promote competition in markets and protect consumers in order to enhance the efficiency of markets

Underlying this aspect of government policy has been the growing belief that competition induces firms to eliminate X-inefficiency as well as encouraging better resource allocation. However, this must always be balanced against the possible sacrifice of economies of scale if competition can only be enabled by fragmentation of the production process. The question of contestability is also important, as it is possible that the very threat of competition may be sufficient to affect firms' behaviour.

X-inefficiency does not only occur in the private sector, and a further set of measures has tried to address the question of efficiency in the provision of public sector services by encouraging the private sector to be involved in partnership with the public sector in its economic activities.

Economic analysis and competition policy

The final section of Chapter 2 undertook a comparison of perfect competition and monopoly, and it is this analysis that lies at the heart of competition policy. Figure 5.1 should remind you of the discussion.

Here it is assumed there is an industry that can operate either under perfect competition, with a large number of small firms, or as a multi-plant monopolist. For simplicity, it is also assumed that there is no cost difference between the two forms of market structure, so that the long-run

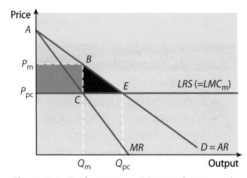

Figure 5.1 *Perfect competition and monopoly compared*

supply schedule (LRS) under perfect competition is perceived by the monopolist as its long-run marginal cost curve. In other words, in long-run equilibrium the monopoly varies output by varying the number of plants it is operating.

Under perfect competition, output would be set at Q_{pc} and market price would be P_{pc}. However, a monopolist will choose to restrict output to Q_m and raise price to

P_m. Consumer surplus will be reduced by this process, partly by a transfer of the blue rectangle to the monopoly as profits, and partly by the red triangle of dead-weight loss. It is this deadweight loss that imposes a cost on society that competition policy is intended to alleviate.

Indeed, this analysis led to a belief in what became known in the economics literature as the *structure–conduct–performance paradigm*. At the core of this belief, illustrated in Figure 5.2, is the simple idea that the structure of a market, in terms of the number of firms, determines how firms in the market conduct themselves, which in turn determines how well the market performs in achieving productive and allocative efficiency.

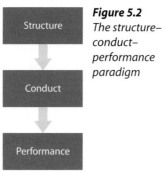

Figure 5.2
The structure–
conduct–
performance
paradigm

Thus, under perfect competition firms cannot influence price, and all firms act competitively to maximise profits, thereby producing good overall performance of the market in allocating resources. On the other hand, under monopoly the single firm finds that it can extract consumer surplus by using its market power, and as a result the market performs less well.

This point of view leads to a distrust of monopoly – or, indeed, of any market structure in which firms might be seen to be conducting themselves in an anti-competitive manner. Moreover, it is the structure of the market itself that leads to this anti-competitive behaviour.

If this line of reasoning is accepted, then monopoly is always bad, and mergers that lead to higher concentration in a market will always lead to allocative inefficiency in the market's performance. Thus, legislation in the USA tends to presume that a monopoly will work against the interests of society. However, there are some important issues to consider before pinning too much faith on this assumption.

Cost conditions

The first issue concerns the assumption that cost conditions will be the same under perfect competition as under monopoly. This simplifies the analysis, but there are many reasons to expect economies of scale in a number of economic activities. If this assumption is correct, then a monopoly firm will face lower cost conditions than would apply under perfect competition.

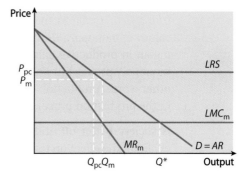

Figure 5.3 *Suppose that monopoly offers much better cost conditions*

In Figure 5.3, *LRS* represents the long-run supply schedule if an industry is operating under perfect competition. The perfectly competitive equilibrium would be at output level with the price at P_{pc}. However, suppose that a monopolist had a strong cost advantage, and was able to produce at constant long-

run marginal cost LMC_m. It would then maximise profit by choosing the output Q_m, where MR_m is equal to LMC_m, and would sell at a price P_m. In this situation the monopolist could actually produce more output at a lower price than a firm operating under perfect competition.

Notice that in the monopoly situation the market does not achieve allocative efficiency, because with these cost conditions, setting price equal to marginal cost would require the firm to produce Q^* output. However, this loss of allocative efficiency is offset by the improvements in productive efficiency that are achieved by the monopoly firm.

It could be argued that the monopolist should be regulated, and forced to produce at Q^*. However, what incentives would this establish for the firm? If a monopolist knows that whenever it makes supernormal profits the regulator will step in and take them away, it will have no incentive to operate efficiently. Indeed, Joseph Schumpeter argued that monopoly profits were an incentive for innovation, and would benefit society, because only with monopoly profits would firms be able to engage in research and development (R&D). In other words, it is only when firms are relatively large, and when they are able to make supernormal profits, that they are able to devote resources to R&D. Small firms operating in a perfectly competitive market do not have the resources or the incentive to be innovative.

Figure 5.4 illustrates a less extreme case. As before, equilibrium under perfect competition produces output at Q_{pc} and price at P_{pc}. The monopoly alternative faces lower long-run marginal cost, although with a less marked difference than before: here the firm produces Q_m output in order to maximise profits, and sets price at P_m.

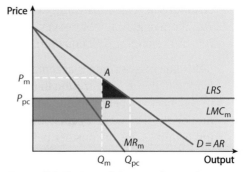

Figure 5.4 *Cost conditions again — a less extreme example*

Analysis of this situation reveals that there is a deadweight loss given by the red triangle; this reflects the allocative inefficiency of monopoly. However, there is also a gain in productive efficiency represented by the green rectangle. This is part of monopoly profits, but under perfect competition it was part of production costs. In other words, production under the monopoly is less wasteful in its use of resources in the production process.

Is society better off under monopoly or under perfect competition? In order to evaluate the effect on total welfare, it is necessary to balance the loss of allocative efficiency (the red triangle) against the gain in productive efficiency (the green rectangle). In Figure 5.4 it would seem that the rectangle is larger than the triangle, so society overall is better off with the monopoly. Of course, there is also the distribution of income to take into account — the area P_mABP_{pc} would be part of consumer surplus under perfect competition, but under monopoly becomes part of the firm's profits.

Contestability

A second important issue concerns contestability, which was introduced in Chapter 4. If barriers to entry into the market are weak, and if the sunk costs of entry and exit are low, the monopoly firm will need to temper its actions to avoid potential entry.

Thus, in judging a market situation, the degree of contestability is important. If the market is perfectly contestable, then the monopoly firm cannot set a price that is above average cost without allowing hit-and-run entry. In this case, the regulator does not need to intervene. Even without perfect contestability, the firm may need to set a price that is not so high as to induce entry. In other words, it may choose not to produce at the profit-maximising level of output, and to set a price below that level.

Concentration and collusion

The structure–conduct–performance argument suggests that it is not only monopolies that should be the subject of competition policy, but any market in which firms have some influence over price. In other words, oligopolies also need careful attention, because of the danger that they will collude, and act *as if* they were a joint monopoly. After all, it was argued that where a market has just a small number of sellers there may be a temptation to collude, either in a cartel or tacitly. For this reason, government authorities may be wary of markets in which concentration ratios are simply high, even if not 100%.

For this reason, it is important to examine whether a concentrated market is *always* and *necessarily* an anti-competitive market. This is tantamount to asking whether structure necessarily determines conduct. A high concentration ratio may mean that there is a small number of firms of more or less equal size, or it could mean that there is one large firm and a number of smaller competitors. In the latter case you might expect the dominant firm to have sufficient market power to control price.

With a small number of equally sized firms it is by no means certain that they will agree to collude. They may be very conscious of their respective market shares, and so act in an aggressively competitive way in order to defend them. This may be especially true where the market is not expanding, so that a firm can grow only at the expense of the other firms. Such a market could well display intense competition, causing it to drift towards the competitive end of the scale. This would suggest that the authorities should not presume guilt in a merger investigation, since the pattern of market shares may prove significant in determining the firms' conduct, and hence the performance of the market. An example of this appears later in this chapter in the context of the battle for Safeway.

Globalisation

Another significant issue is that a firm that comes to dominate a domestic market may still face competition in the broader global market. This may be especially significant within the European single market.

In this regard, there has been a longstanding debate about how a domestic government should behave towards its large firms. Some economists believe that the government should allow such firms to dominate the domestic market in order that they can become 'national champions' in the global market. This has been especially apparent in the airline industry, where some national airlines are heavily subsidised by their national governments in order to allow them to compete internationally. Others have argued that if a large firm faces competition within the domestic market this should help to encourage its productive efficiency, enabling it to become more capable of coping with international competition.

Exercise 5.1

Discuss whether a concentrated market is necessarily anti-competitive.

Summary

> Competition policy refers to a range of measures designed to promote competition in markets and to protect consumers in order to enhance the efficiency of markets in resource allocation.

> One view is that market structure determines the conduct of firms within a market, and this conduct then determines the performance of the market in terms of allocative efficiency.

> A profit-maximising monopolist will produce less output at a higher price than a perfectly competitive market, causing allocative inefficiency.

> However, there may be situations in which the monopolist can enjoy economies of scale, and thereby gain in productive efficiency.

> In the presence of contestability, a monopolist may not be able to charge a price above average cost without encouraging hit-and-run entry.

> In a concentrated market, the pattern of market shares may influence the intensity of competition between firms.

> A firm that is a monopoly in its own country may be exposed to competition in the international markets in which it operates.

Competition policy in the UK

In the UK, competition policy has tended to be less rigid than in the USA, where there seems to be a natural tendency to distrust monopoly. Policy has therefore been conducted in such a way as to take account of the issues discussed above. This has meant that cases of monopoly or concentrated markets have been judged on their individual merits on a case-by-case basis.

This pragmatic approach was embedded in UK legislation from the start — which was the 1948 Monopolies and Restrictive Practices (Inquiry and Control) Act. This

Act set up the Monopolies and Restrictive Practices Commission to investigate markets in which a single firm (or a group of firms in collusion) supplied more than one-third of a market. The Commission was asked to decide whether such a market was operating in the public interest, although at that stage the legislation was not very precisely defined.

Since then the legislation has been steadily tightened through a sequence of Acts, the most recent of which are the Competition Act of 1998 and the Enterprise Act of 2002. The Competition Act is in two sections ('chapters'), one dealing with anti-competitive agreements between parties (e.g. firms) and the other dealing with anti-competitive practices by one or more parties — that is, the abuse of a dominant position in a market.

Cartels are covered by Chapter 1 of the 1998 Act, but less formal agreements between firms are also within the scope of the Act, for example price-fixing, agreements to restrict output or agreements to share a market. The Enterprise Act elevated the operation of a cartel to a criminal offence (as opposed to a civil offence).

The conduct of the policy is entrusted to two agencies: the Office of Fair Trading (OFT) and the Competition Commission. The OFT has the preliminary responsibility for investigating a proposed merger, and then has the power either to impose sanctions directly or to refer the market to the Competition Commission for a full investigation.

The OFT has the power to enforce competition and consumer regulation.

A merger is subject to OFT investigation if the firms involved in the proposed merger or acquisition have a combined market share in the UK of more than 25% and if the combined assets of the firms exceed £70 million worldwide. The mission statement of the OFT states:

> The OFT is responsible for making markets work well for consumers. We achieve this by promoting and protecting consumer interests throughout the UK, while ensuring that businesses are fair and competitive. (**www.oft.gov.uk**)

The possible results of an OFT investigation are:

➤ enforcement action by the OFT's competition and consumer regulation divisions

➤ referral of the market to the Competition Commission

➤ recommendations for changes in laws and regulations

➤ recommendations to regulators, self-regulatory bodies and others to consider changes to their rules

➤ campaigns to promote consumer education and awareness

➤ a clean bill of health

The last of these indicates that there is no presumption that the OFT will find anything wrong with a market. Indeed, on a number of occasions the OFT has launched a consumer awareness campaign, having found that the problem with the market lay in the way consumers understood its workings, and not with the market itself.

Probably the best way of understanding how competition policy operates is by exploring some examples of how it has worked in practice. First, however, there is a very important issue to be examined.

Relevant markets

The first step in any investigation is to identify the **relevant market**. Until the scope of the market has been defined, it is not possible to calculate market shares or concentration ratios.

How should the market be defined in this context? In other words, which products should be included? Or over which region should the market be defined? Take the market for sugar — is this defined as the market for all sugar, or just for granulated sugar? Is organic sugar a separate product? Or, regarding the market for rail travel in Scotland, do bus services need to be considered as part of the Scottish market for travel?

 Key *term*

relevant market: a market to be investigated under competition law, defined in such a way that no major substitutes are omitted but no non-substitutes are included

One way of addressing this question is to apply the *hypothetical monopoly test*. Under this approach, the product market is defined as the smallest set of products and producers in which a hypothetical monopolist controlling all such products could raise profits by a small increase in price above the competitive level.

Extension material

The hypothetical monopoly test is effectively a question about substitution. If in a hypothetical market an increase in price will induce consumers to switch to a substitute product, then the market has not been defined sufficiently widely for it to be regarded as a monopoly. This is demand-side substitutability. One way of evaluating it would be to consult the cross-price elasticity of demand — if it could be measured. This would determine which products were perceived as substitutes for each other by consumers.

For example, in 2003 a number of supermarkets put in bids to take over the Safeway chain. The first step in the investigation was to define the relevant market. One issue that was raised was whether discount stores such as Lidl and Aldi, which sell a limited range of groceries, should be considered part of the same market as supermarkets selling a wide range of grocery products. In the south of the country, the cross-price elasticity of Sainsbury's demand was 0.05 with respect to Lidl's price, but 1.48 with respect to Tesco's price. This suggested that Sainsbury and Tesco were in the same market, but Lidl was not.

It is also important to consider the question of substitutes on the supply side, i.e. whether an increase in price may induce suppliers to join the market. Supply-side substitutability is related to the notion of contestability, in the sense that one way a market can be seen to be contestable is if other firms can switch readily into it, i.e. if there are potential substitutes.

In the following case studies, more detailed material can be gathered from the websites of the OFT (**www.oft.gov.uk**) and the Competition Commission (**www.competition-commission.org.uk**).

Case study 1 Stena and P&O in the Irish Sea

Stena and P&O are two ferry companies providing ferry services across the Irish Sea. In 2003 the OFT reported on an investigation that it had undertaken into a proposed acquisition by Stena of 'certain assets' (five vessels, related staff, port leases and agreements) used by P&O in its ferry operations on the Irish Sea between Liverpool and Dublin and between Fleetwood and Larne.

The OFT began by considering the relevant market; it decided to separate the markets for freight and passengers, and to focus on the ferry services on two of the main routes across the Irish Sea. In terms of the freight market, there were also seen to be two segments, lorry trailers and containers. The OFT chose to focus on the lorry trailer segment.

The OFT found that after such a merger, Stena would have a market share of between 35% and 45%, and that the other three firms operating the route would act as only a weak constraint on Stena's activities. In trying to apply the hypothetical monopoly test, customers were asked whether they would switch their custom to another route if the price were to rise by between 5% and 10%. Many indicated that they would.

The OFT found that in theory there were low barriers to entry into the market, but that in practice the limited availability of berths in the key ports would make entry by a new firm difficult.

In consequence of these investigations, the OFT found that:

The merger does…appear to result in a substantial lessening of competition within a market or markets in the UK for goods or services.

The merger was thus referred to the Competition Commission for further investigation. The Commission accepted that the merger should be investigated under the share of supply test; in other words, Stena would have more than 25% of the market (as defined) after the merger. The Commission decided that the impact on the tourist market would be small and focused on the market for freight, but it did not accept that the market should be segmented between the lorry trailer and container traffic.

The Commission found that pricing for freight was opaque, and was based on individual negotiations between the ferry company concerned and individual customers. This would allow for price discrimination to take place.

The outcome of the investigation was that the Commission decided that Stena would gain significant market power on the Liverpool–Dublin route, and would have scope to exercise price discrimination on that route, raising prices to some customers in particular. It was felt that the shortage of berths would discourage entry into this market, but that removing that barrier would not be sufficient to attract new firms. The Commission thus prohibited the acquisition by Stena of P&O's assets relating to the Liverpool–Dublin route.

Notice the key steps in the investigation. First, the authorities had to define the market carefully in order to set the context for the investigation. Once that was done, it was not just a question of checking the market shares — although this is important in determining whether the merger qualifies for investigation.

The next step was to investigate the extent to which the merged firm would be able to operate without competitive constraint; in other words, how dynamic is the competition from other existing firms, and how likely is it that new firms could gain entry into the market?

Case study 2 Railways in Scotland

The second case study involves FirstGroup plc (First), a UK-based transport company operating a wide range of bus services in Scotland. First put in a bid for the ScotRail franchise, which was due to come into operation in October 2004. The franchise related to the operation of approximately 95% of the passenger rail services in Scotland, together with sleeper services between Scotland and London and through services to Newcastle.

One key issue here is the extent to which bus and rail services were in competition with each other, and the extent to which the combined group would face effective competition.

The OFT collected evidence, some of which suggested that there would be a significant lessening of competition, in particular on 'over lapping routes', i.e. routes in which bus and rail services were both offered. However, First responded that, given that many of its bus services were already subject to price and frequency regulation, it would have no incentive or ability to give poorer value for money to bus passengers as a result of becoming the rail franchise operator.

The OFT concluded that it could not confidently reject the view that the merger would result in a lessening of competition, and thus referred the proposed acquisition to the Competition Commission.

The Commission's report pointed out that First was the leading supplier of bus travel in the UK, accounting for about 22% of turnover

of local bus services in 2003. It was also estimated to operate about 35% of the total route mileage of all bus services in Scotland. As mentioned, the Scottish rail franchise accounts for 95% of railway services in Scotland. So, again, there was no question that the combined group would have a major market share for passenger transport in Scotland were it allowed to go ahead.

In evaluating the likely extent of competition, it was also recognised that the role of private transport could not be ignored in considering the extent of competition.

Of particular concern was the extent to which consumers would be sensitive to changes in the price of bus and rail travel. One source of evidence related to the price elasticities of demand for rail and bus services, and the Commission commissioned a study to collect evidence. The conclusion of this was that the price elasticities of demand for both rail and bus services were significantly inelastic, especially in the short term. In other words, an increase in fares would lead to an increase in revenues of the service operators. This seems to suggest a relatively low degree of competition. However, on overlapping routes bus and rail services were likely to be substitutable.

The Commission then looked in detail at 55 individual routes, focusing on overlapping routes. On 46 of those routes, it concluded that there was a possibility of adverse effects arising from the loss of competition. The expectation was that First would find it profitable to

increase fares on the bus services and thus encourage passengers to switch to rail services. This could be reinforced by actions to reduce frequency, re-route services or reconfigure routes. The Commission thus concluded that there would be a substantial lessening of competition on overlapping routes.

There would also be scope for First to introduce multi-modal ticketing, under which passengers could hold tickets that would allow them to use either rail or First bus services. This could be to the detriment of other bus operators.

In this instance, however, the Commission did not prohibit the merger. Instead, it allowed the bid for the franchise to go ahead, on condition that First agree to undertakings related to fares, frequencies and other aspects of services on the affected routes. It was also required to provide information at stations about other operators' bus services.

Thus, a substantial lessening of competition is not always dealt with by prohibiting the merger. After all, if the merger creates economies of scale or economies of scope (as might be available in this instance), then prohibiting the merger prevents those gains in productive efficiency from being achieved.

Case study 3 Biscuits

The third case study involves a proposed acquisition of Jacobs Bakery Ltd (Jacobs) by United Biscuits (UK) Ltd (UB). UB is active mainly in the manufacture and sale of biscuits, cakes and savoury snacks. The OFT investigated the market situation of the firms.

The merger qualified under the turnover test, as the UK turnover of Jacobs alone exceeded £70 million. In addition, the two firms overlapped in the supply of biscuits in the UK, such that the combined firm would together account for a relatively high post-merger share of UK biscuit manufacturing. For these reasons, the merger qualified as a relevant merger situation — hence the OFT involvement.

When the OFT examined the market, it found that there would still be significant competition from other producers across a wide range of biscuit products, from strong retailer own-label products and also from what the OFT referred to as 'non-biscuit snacking products'. In addition, there was evidence of recent new entry from 'non-core' biscuit manufacturers which were successfully gaining market share.

Furthermore, there was some evidence that the manufacturers faced significant buyer power in the form of the supermarkets. Finally, there were a number of alternative biscuit manufacturers that could supply the retailers, not only within the UK but abroad.

Putting all these arguments together, the OFT concluded that the merger would not result in a substantial lessening of competition in the UK biscuit market, and did not refer it for further investigation by the Competition Commission.

Case study 4 Supermarkets

In January 2003 the supermarket group Morrison's made an offer for the Safeway group. In the following 3 weeks, five other groups expressed an interest in buying Safeway — the rival supermarket groups Sainsbury, Asda and Tesco, plus Philip Green (owner of BHS) and a US venture capital firm Kohlberg Kravis Roberts (KKR).

The Competition Commission had investigated British supermarkets in 1999–2000, and

concluded that overall the market was 'generally competitive'. It did however highlight some practices that it considered to be against the public interest; in particular, it investigated the way in which the main super-markets tended to compete very intensively on a narrow range of products, selling some frequently purchased products below cost, and thereby inhibiting competition in other products. It also investigated the practice of varying prices in different geographic locations in the light of local competitive conditions, i.e. varying prices in ways that did not reflect variations in costs. This implies that the supermarkets were ready to exploit their position in markets where competition was weak. Nonetheless, the Commission concluded that measures to remedy these practices would not be likely to improve overall competitiveness.

So, would changes to the structure of the sector significantly affect these general conclusions in 2003? In other words, would an increase in concentration among British super-markets be good or bad for consumers?

As usual, any investigation of a market begins by defining the relevant market. In the Competition Commission's earlier investiga-tion, it defined the market as:

> …the supply in Great Britain of groceries from multiple stores, that is, supermarkets with 600 sq metres or more of grocery sales area, where the space devoted to the retail sale of food and non-alcoholic drinks exceeds 300 sq metres and which are controlled by a person who controls ten or more such stores.

The scope of the inquiry was later extended to the UK (i.e. Northern Ireland was added). 'Groceries' were to include food and drink, cleaning products, toiletries and household goods. This definition then set the context for a discussion of market shares.

Figure 5.5 shows estimated market shares in British supermarkets in January 2003. The

issue now begins to become clearer. If Morrison's were to take over Safeway, their combined market share would be 15.9%, which is well below the threshold at which the OFT or Competition Commission would investigate. However, if Tesco, Sainsbury or Asda were to merge with Safeway the combined market share would go through the 25% level, and thus would trigger an investigation.

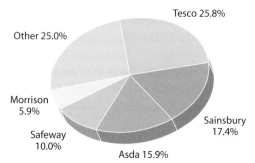

Figure 5.5 *Market shares among British supermarkets, January 2003*

One reason why supermarkets may be looking for merger deals is that planning permission for new stores is increasingly difficult to obtain, so that expansion by buying existing stores is an attractive option.

In analysing this market, a number of issues needed to be weighed carefully before concluding that a merger between Safeway and Morrison's, or Safeway and some other firm, would have costly consequences for consumers or for society as a whole.

It is clear that there are economies of scale in grocery retailing. The corner shop cannot compete on price or on range of produce with the supermarkets, and even specialist quality fish mongers and butchers have a struggle to survive. So perfect competition is not a realistic alternative market structure, and cannot be seen as the reference point for an evaluation of supermarket consolidation.

In any case, in considering a merger involving Safeway, the reference point was the pre-merger market structure. Figure 5.5 shows that the market was already dominated by a few players, so that it was the *marginal* effect on market power that would be important in an investigation.

The relative market shares of firms in the market may be significant. A Morrison's–Safeway merger would create a firm with a 15.9% market share — the same as Asda, and a little smaller than Sainsbury. Morrison's/Safeway might argue that such a merger would enable it to compete more effectively with the other firms in the group, since the result would be to equalise market shares; on the other hand, a move by Tesco for Safeway would create a firm with 35.8% of the market, almost double the size of the second-largest firm. It might be thought that the scope for exploiting market power would be much greater in such a context. Thus, the *pattern* of market shares could be another important consideration.

In its earlier investigation, the Competition Commission was concerned to ensure that consumer choice was protected. In particular, it took steps to guard against the possibility that one of the major players in the market might dominate in particular locations, effectively becoming a local monopoly. It thus recommended that:

> …if Asda, Morrison, Safeway, Sainsbury or Tesco wish to acquire an existing store, or build a new store, having over 1000 sq metres of grocery retail sales area within a 15-minute drive time of one of its existing stores, or significantly to extend the grocery retailing area of an existing store, it should be required to apply to the Director General of Fair Trading for consent.

In any acquisition of Safeway, analysis would be needed to ensure that such local monopoly situations did not arise. For example, one estimate (*The Financial Times*, 28 January 2003) suggested that Morrison would have to sell 41 stores if it were to acquire Safeway — although the group's own estimate

was that it had competition issues in fewer than 10 stores.

Another potentially significant issue arose in the case of Asda, which was bought by the US-based firm Wal-Mart in 1999. Wal-Mart is the world's biggest retailer, and its global *weekly* takings would have sufficed to buy out Safeway. It had expanded at a rapid rate in recent years, with a strong focus on driving down costs to deliver price and value — and to wipe out the competition. Wal-Mart has aspirations to expand in Europe, and thus could be keen to acquire Safeway. However, one stumbling block was that an Asda–Safeway merger would go through the 25% combined market share barrier, and thus threaten to trigger a formal investigation by the OFT/Competition Commission.

Monopsony is a form of market structure that tends to attract less attention than monopoly. Pure monopsony occurs where there is a single *buyer* of a good. The buyer may then be able to exert substantial influence over the suppliers of the good when drawing up contracts on the price and quality of goods. This power may be especially strong when the sellers are relatively small and numerous.

In the context of the supermarkets, it is possible that the sheer buying power of the large chains would leave the relatively fragmented suppliers in a weak bargaining position. The supermarkets would then be able to keep their costs down by using their bargaining strength.

The eventual outcome was that the Commission ruled against all of the bids except that from Morrison's, which was allowed to go ahead — and has indeed now done so.

Key term

monopsony: a market in which there is a single buyer of a good

Case study 5 Airports

In 1987 the British Airports Authority was privatised, and BAA plc was established. The firm was responsible for the airports that had previously been under the aegis of the previous authority — namely, the three London airports (Heathrow, Gatwick and Stansted), plus airports in Scotland (Aberdeen, Edinburgh, Glasgow and Prestwick). Prestwick was sold in 1991, and Southampton was acquired in 1990. This meant that BAA plc had an effective monopoly on flights in and out of London and a stranglehold on flights in and out of Scotland.

One of the objectives in setting up BAA plc was to have a single enterprise that would be able to take strategic decisions to plan ahead, and to provide the airport capacity needed to meet the expected growth in demand. In addition, it was hoped that the provision of the infrastructure needed for air travel would help to encourage competition amongst the airlines providing the transport services.

In the event, things did not work out well, and after 20 years of operation, BAA plc was seen to have failed to provide sufficient capacity to meet demand in the South East region. There was also mounting criticism of the way that BAA was managing its airports — especially Heathrow. In March 2007, the OFT referred the case to the CC for investigation under the Enterprise Act 2002. The brief for the investigation was '…to investigate whether any feature, or combination of features, of the market or markets for airport services in the UK as exist in connection with the supply of airport services by BAA Limited prevents, restricts or distorts competition in connection with the supply or acquisition of any goods or services in the UK or a part of the UK. If so there is an "adverse effect on competition".' (Competition Commission, 2008)

In terms of market share, it was clear that BAA was in a very strong position. The CC noted that its seven airports accounted for more than 60% of all passengers using UK airports. In the South East, Heathrow, Gatwick, Stansted and Southampton between them accounted for 90% of air passengers; in Scotland, 84% of air passengers were accounted for by Edinburgh, Glasgow and Aberdeen. The key issue is whether this market position was damaging competition, and hence working against consumer interests.

An important aspect of this is whether there is scope for competition between airports, and what effect such competition would have on the nature and quality of service that would be offered. In order to approach this question, the CC looked at evidence relating to non-BAA airports that could be regarded as being in potential competition with each other — for example, Birmingham International Airport and East Midlands Airport, Cardiff International Airport and Bristol International Airport and other combinations. Some evidence was found that suggested that there could be competition between airports — in particular in relation to the low-cost airlines. However, competition is most likely where there is spare capacity — which is not the case for Heathrow and Gatwick.

Competition also requires there to be the potential for substitution in demand. In other words, there needs to be some overlap in the potential catchment area for competing airports. In relation to BAA's airports in Scotland, it was found that there was some overlap in catchment between Glasgow and Edinburgh — but not with Aberdeen. In the South East, there was little evidence of competition between BAA's London airports and non-BAA airports (apart from some competition between Southampton and Bournemouth). However, there was significant overlap in the catchment areas of these

airports, suggesting the possibility of some competition (subject to capacity constraints).

The CC came to the view that the shortage of capacity in the South East had partly arisen from the common ownership of the three BAA London airports, and that had these airports been under separate ownership, the incentives to expand capacity and improve the quality of service being offered would be higher.

Having concluded that there was evidence that the market structure was having an adverse effect on competition, the CC in its provisional findings recommended that BAA should sell two of its three airports in the South East, and should not be allowed to continue to own airports in both Glasgow and Edinburgh.

Competition policy in the European Union

With increasing integration within the European Union, it has become important to be able to investigate possible monopoly situations that arise at an EU level. Accordingly, the EU has a competition policy that enables it to investigate potential abuse of market power when such abuse transcends national borders.

The stance adopted in EU policy has been consistent with that of member countries; indeed, the structure of EU competition policy has informed recent UK legislation. With expanding globalisation, it may be important to coordinate policy still more widely, but this is likely to be problematic. For example, Microsoft went on trial in the USA for alleged predatory action in the way that it had launched its internet browser; although initially the judgement went against it, there followed a lengthy appeal. The EU then launched its own court action against Microsoft making similar allegations about the way it marketed its media player.

Summary

➤ Competition policy in the UK is implemented through the Office of Fair Trading and the Competition Commission.

➤ The main pillars of policy are legislation dealing with agreements between firms and the abuse of a dominant position.

➤ A key step in any investigation is to define the relevant market.

➤ The OFT carries out a preliminary investigation of mergers that meet the criteria in terms of market share and size of assets.

➤ It then decides whether to refer the merger to the Competition Commission for a thorough investigation.

➤ Some mergers are allowed to proceed without referral.

➤ Others are sent to the Commission, which may permit the merger to go ahead, may impose conditions on the firm, or may prohibit it.

Exercise 5.2

The following key facts relate to OFT investigations carried out in recent years. In each case:

➤ discuss the information provided

➤ identify actual or potential sources of anti-competitive behaviour

➤ make a judgement about guilt or innocence

➤ identify possible remedial action that could be taken (where appropriate)

Case 1 Banking services to small and medium-sized enterprises (SMEs)

There are over 3.5 million SMEs in the UK, accounting for some 55% of employment and 45% of turnover of businesses in the UK; that is, they are crucial to the strength of the economy, especially for their flexibility and adaptability.

There are three separate geographical markets for liquidity management services and general purpose business loans, each highly concentrated, with 90% or more of these services being supplied by four clearing groups.

SMEs are reluctant to switch, and have limited price sensitivity.

A lack of transparency has been observed in the determination of availability and price of overdrafts and general purpose loans.

The main clearing banks show similarities of pricing structure, including in general no payment of interest on current accounts.

There are significant barriers to entry and expansion in the markets for liquidity and general purpose business loans.

Case 2 Veterinary medicines (prescription only medicines (POMs))

Most POMs are supplied by manufacturers to veterinary surgeries via veterinary wholesalers, and are sold by veterinary surgeons to animal owners. Pharmacies also supply to animal owners.

One firm supplies more than a quarter of POMs at the wholesale level.

Veterinary surgeons have been slow to inform animal owners that they can ask for prescriptions; they also tend not to inform clients of the prices prior to dispensing them and not to provide itemised bills. Pricing of POMs does not always reflect the cost of supply, in that prices may not take manufacturers' discounts into account, or may be used to subsidise professional fees.

A group of eight manufacturers has failed to allow pharmacies to obtain supplies of POMs on terms that would enable them to compete with veterinary surgeons. A similar situation exists with all the wholesalers in the market.

Most best-selling POMs in the UK are substantially more expensive in the UK than in Europe, and the price differential is greater for POMs than for other veterinary medicines.

Ex-manufacturer's prices are lowest in countries where pharmacies play a larger role in their supply.

Case 3 Interbrew SA and Bass plc

Interbrew (a quoted Belgian company) acquired Bass plc in May 2000. This merger would have made Interbrew the largest brewer in Great Britain, with an overall market share of between 33% and 38% and a portfolio of leading beer brands. The market would have effectively become a duopoly between Interbrew and Scottish & Newcastle.

The two firms have a common interest in raising operating margins.

Consumers are not price-sensitive in choice of brand.

Interbrew charges different prices according to the type of customer. Discounts are offered to multiple retailers.

It is thought that an increase in non-price competition (advertising and marketing) is likely to follow the merger.

Interbrew argued that the merger would bring synergy benefits and cost savings.

Case 4 Consumer IT goods and services

Around £2 billion is spent on personal computers each year, with the average consumer spending around £1000. In addition, around £250 million is spent by consumers on inkjet printers and £315 million on inkjet cartridges. Over 40% of consumers are first-time buyers.

Overall consumer satisfaction rates are high, and in general consumers can find information enabling them to compare products and prices. However, first-time or inexperienced buyers tend to carry out the least research, placing a premium on point-of-sale information.

Support services are vital for many consumers, but information provided was found to be poor, and the quality of support services often unsatisfactory.

Consumer spending on ink over the lifetime of a printer can amount to more than twice the cost of the inkjet printer, but little information is made available to consumers on the cost per printed page at the point of sale.

Warranty terms tended to be buried in small print.

Regulation of privatised industries

Chapter 2 noted the case of the natural monopoly, and hinted that this poses particular problems with regard to allocative efficiency. Figure 5.6 involves an industry with substantial economies of scale relative to market demand – indeed, the minimum efficient scale is beyond the market demand curve. (In other words, long-run average cost is still falling beyond market demand.)

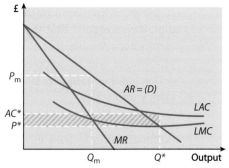

Figure 5.6 *A natural monopoly*

This market is almost bound to end up as a monopoly, because the largest firm is always able to dominate the market and undercut smaller competitors, as it has a natural cost leadership position. If the monopoly chooses to maximise profits, it will set marginal revenue equal to marginal cost, choose output Q_m and set price at P_m.

Such industries tend to have large fixed costs relative to marginal costs. Railway systems, water or gas supply and electricity generation are all examples of natural monopolies.

The key problem is that, if such firms were forced to set a price equal to marginal cost, they would make a loss. If the firm in Figure 5.6 were required to set price equal to marginal cost, i.e. at P^*, then it would not be viable: average cost would be AC^*, with losses represented by the shaded area on the diagram.

In the past, one response to this situation would have been to nationalise the industry, i.e. take it into state ownership, since no private-sector firm would be prepared to operate at a loss, and the government would not allow firms running such natural monopolies to act as profit-maximising monopolists making super-normal profits.

In order to prevent the losses from becoming too substantial, many utilities such as gas and electricity supply adopted a pricing system known as a *two-part tariff system*, under which all consumers paid a monthly charge for being connected to the supply, and on top of that a variable amount based on usage. In terms of Figure 5.6, the connection charge would cover the difference between AC^* and P^*, spread across all consumers, and the variable charge would reflect marginal cost.

Electricity generation is an example of a natural monopoly.

However, as time went by this sort of system came to be heavily criticised. In partic-ular, it was argued that the managers of the nationalised industries were insuffi-ciently accountable. It could be regarded as an extreme form of the principal–agent problem, in which the consumers (the principals) had very little control over the actions of the managers (their agents), a situation leading to widespread X-ineffi-ciency and waste.

In the 1980s such criticism led to widespread privatisation, i.e. the transfer of nationalised industries into private ownership, one central argument being that now at least the managers would have to be accountable to their shareholders, which would encourage an increase in efficiency.

However, this did not remove the original problem: that they were natural monopolies. So privatisation was accompanied by the imposition of a regulatory system, to ensure that the newly privatised firms did not abuse their monopoly situations.

Wherever possible, privatisation was also accompanied by measures to encourage competition, which was seen as an even better way to ensure efficiency improvements. This proved to be more feasible in some industries than in others, because of the nature of economies of scale — there is little to be gained by requiring that there must be several firms in a market where the economies of scale can be reaped only by one large firm. However, the changing technology in some of the industries did allow some competition to be encouraged, especially in telecommunications.

Where it was not possible, or feasible, to encourage competition, regulation was seen as the solution. Attention of the regulatory bodies focused on price, and the key control method was to allow price increases each year at a rate that was a set amount below changes in the retail price index (RPI). This became known as the (RPI − X) rule, and was widely used, the idea being that it would force companies to look for productivity gains to eliminate the X-inefficiency that had built up. The 'X' refers to the amount of productivity gain that the regulator believes can be achieved, expressed in terms of the change in average costs. For example, if the regulator believed that it was possible to achieve productivity gains of 5% per year, and if the RPI was increasing at a rate of 10% per year, then the maximum price increase that would be allowed in a year would be 10% − 5% = 5%.

There are problems inherent in this approach. For example, how does the regulator set 'X'? This is problematic in a situation where the company has better information about costs than the regulator — another instance of the problems caused by the existence of asymmetric information. There is also the possibility that the firm will achieve its productivity gains by reducing the quality of the product, or by neglecting long-term investment for the future and allowing maintenance standards to lapse.

It is also important to realise that as time goes by, if the (RPI − X) system is effective, the X-inefficiency will be gradually squeezed out, and the 'X' will have to be reduced as it becomes ever more difficult to achieve productivity gains.

In some cases **regulatory capture** is a further problem. This occurs when the regulator becomes so closely involved with the firm it is supposed to be regulating that it begins to champion its cause rather than imposing tough rules where they are needed.

 Key *term*

regulatory capture: a situation in which the regulator of an industry comes to represent its interests rather than regulating it

An alternative method of regulation would be to place a limit on the rate of return the firm is permitted to make, thereby preventing it from making supernormal

profits. This too may affect the incentive mechanism: the firm may not feel the need to be as efficient as possible, or may fritter away some of the profits in managerial perks to avoid declaring too high a rate of return.

Case study 5 Gas and electricity supply

British Gas was privatised in 1986, and the electricity sector followed in 1989. These industries have a joint regulator known as Ofgem. They have a joint regulator because together they comprise the energy market.

The energy market in the early twenty-first century is structured as three sub-markets: the wholesale markets, the delivery system and the retail markets.

The delivery sector, which is sometimes referred to as the 'pipes and wires' business, remains a monopoly — or, rather, a sequence of geographical monopolies. These companies run the gas and electricity transportation networks. They are subject to price control using the (RPI — X) rule, and the value of 'X' is reviewed every 5 years.

In the wholesale and retail segments competition has been encouraged. The retail gas market was opened fully to competition in 1998, and the electricity market followed in 1999 — to the extent that price regulation ended in 2002. The wholesale market is now going through a process of reform.

Ofgem claims that the best way to protect customers' interests is through the promotion of competition between suppliers. A review published in 2004 estimated that around 50% of customers had switched their supplier of gas or electricity. The ease of switching supplier is of course crucial if effective competition is to be a way of holding prices at a competitive level. High switching costs are a disincentive to switching.

Research quoted by Ofgem indicates that suppliers lose customers when they increase their prices, and Ofgem claims that this is evidence that competition is working.

A cautionary note is struck by the observation that non-price factors such as brand and marketing methods are increasing in importance, and there have been occasional items on programmes such as BBC's *Watchdog* about high-pressure door-to-door sales methods used to try to get customers to change supplier. Indeed, Ofgem imposed a £2 million penalty on London Electricity (now EDF Energy) for mis-selling, after which complaints about high-pressure sales methods fell by 60%.

Thus, Ofgem's current strategy is to monitor the energy market and find ways of stimulating greater competition among suppliers. The focus is especially on facilitating switching between suppliers and lowering barriers to the entry of new suppliers.

Public Private Partnerships (PPP)

It has been recognised that the same arguments that apply to the impact of competition on private sector efficiency are also relevant for public sector activity. In the case of public goods, there has to be some sort of government involvement as a free market will not ensure the provision of these goods. However, this does not necessarily mean that the public sector has to provide these goods directly. A number of ways in which the public sector can ensure provision through some sort of engagement with the private sector have been developed.

The simplest form of this is through **contracting out**. Under such an arrangement, the public sector issues a contract to a private firm for the supply of some good or service. One example would be waste disposal, where a local authority may issue a contract for a firm to provide the necessary waste disposal service. Competition between firms can be encouraged by a **competitive tendering** process. In other words, the contract would be announced and firms invited to put in bids specifying the quality of service they are prepared to provide, and at what price. The local authority would then be in a position to look for efficiency in choosing the most competitive bid.

More complex models of cooperation between public and private sectors have been developed, involving various kinds of **Public Private Partnership** (PPP). A PPP is 'an arrangement by which a government service or private business venture is funded and operated through a partnership of government and the private sector' (National Audit Office). The most common partnership model is the **Private Finance Initiative** (PFI).

The Private Finance Initiative (PFI)

The PFI was launched in 1992 as a way of trying to increase the involvement of the private sector in the provision of public services. This established a partnership between the public and private sectors. The public sector specifies, perhaps in broad terms, the services that it requires, and then invites tenders from the private sector to design, build, finance and operate the scheme. In some cases, it may be that the project would be entirely free-standing – for example, the government may initiate a project such as a new bridge that is then taken up by a private firm that will recover its costs entirely through user charges such as tolls. In some other cases, the project may be a joint venture between the public and private sectors. The public sector could get involved with such a venture in order to secure wider social benefits, perhaps through reductions in traffic congestion that would not be reflected in market prices, and thus would not be fully taken into account by the private sector. In other cases, it may be that the private sector undertakes a project and then sells the services to the public sector, often over a period of 25 or 30 years.

> **Key terms**
>
> **contracting out:** a situation in which the public sector places activities in the hands of a private firm and pays for the provision
>
> **competitive tendering:** a process by which the public sector calls for private firms to bid for a contract for provision of a good or service
>
> **Public Private Partnership (PPP):** an arrangement by which a government service or private business venture is funded and operated through a partnership of government and the private sector
>
> **Private Finance Initiative (PFI):** a funding arrangement under which the private sector designs, builds, finances and operates an asset and associated services for the public sector in return for an annual payment linked to its performance in delivering the service

Former deputy prime minister John Prescott signed the agreement to secure the completion of the Channel Tunnel Rail Link.

Figure 5.7 shows the range of PFI deals that were signed during the first 10 years of the scheme: you can see that a sizeable proportion of these were in transport. This covered projects involving road construction, street lighting, bridges and rail projects. The largest project in this period was the Channel Tunnel Rail Link (£4,178 million),

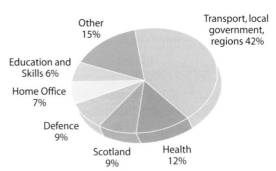

Figure 5.7 *PFI signed deals as at September 2001*

signed in 2000. Subsequently, projects involving the London Underground were signed in 2003, totalling £10,695 million. By March 2008 more than 600 projects had been signed, with a total capital value of almost £60 billion.

The aim of the PFI is to improve the financing of public sector projects. This is partly achieved by introducing a competitive element into the tendering process, but in addition it enables the risk of a project to be shared between the public and private sectors. This should enable efficiency gains to be made.

The PFI has been much debated — and much criticised. One effect of the PFI is to reduce the pressures on public finances by enabling greater private sector involvement in funding. However, it might be argued that this may in fact raise the cost of borrowing, if the public sector would have been able to borrow on more favourable terms than commercial firms. The introduction of a competitive element in the tendering process may be beneficial, but on the other hand it could be argued that the private sector may have less incentive to give due attention to health and safety issues as compared with the public sector. In other words, there may be a concern that private firms will be tempted to sacrifice safety or service standards in the quest for profit. Achieving the appropriate balance between

efficiency and quality of service is an inevitable problem to be faced in whatever way transport is financed and provided, but becomes a more critical issue to the extent that use of the PFI switches the focus more towards efficiency and lower costs.

Summary

➤ Natural monopolies pose particular problems for policy, as setting price equal to marginal cost forces such firms to make a loss.

➤ In the past, many such industries were run by the state as nationalised industries.

➤ However, this led to widespread X-inefficiency.

➤ Many of these industries were privatised after 1979.

➤ Regulation was put into place to ensure that the newly privatised firms did not abuse their market positions.

➤ Prices were controlled through the application of the (RPI — X) rule.

➤ In some cases regulatory capture was a problem, whereby the regulators became too close to their industries.

➤ The authorities have also attempted to encourage efficiency through the establishment of Public Private Partnerships, such as the Private Finance Initiative.

The global economy

Part 2

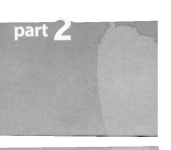

Chapter 6

Globalisation and trade

The world economy is becoming increasingly integrated, and it is no longer possible to think of any single economy in isolation. The UK economy is no exception. It relies on international trade, engaging in exporting and importing activity, and many UK firms are increasingly active in global markets. This situation has created opportunities for British firms to expand and become global players, and for British consumers to have access to a wider range of goods and services. However, there is also a downside: global shocks, whether caused by oil prices, financial crises or the emergence of China as a world economic force, can reverberate throughout economies in all parts of the world. These are some of the issues that will be explored in this chapter.

Learning outcomes

After studying this chapter, you should:
- ➤ understand what is meant by globalisation, and be aware of the factors that have given rise to this phenomenon
- ➤ appreciate the importance of trade and exchange between nations
- ➤ be familiar with the arguments for trade liberalisation as opposed to protectionism
- ➤ be aware of the role and workings of the World Trade Organisation
- ➤ understand the importance of foreign direct investment and the role of multinational corporations
- ➤ be aware of the impact that external shocks can have within the global economy

Globalisation

The term 'globalisation' has been much used in recent years, not the least by the protest groups that have demonstrated against it. It is therefore important to be clear about what the term means before seeking to evaluate the strengths and weaknesses of the phenomenon.

Ann Krueger, the first deputy managing director of the IMF, defined globalisation as 'a phenomenon by which economic agents in any given part of the world are

much more affected by events elsewhere in the world' than before. Joseph Stiglitz, the Nobel Laureate and former Chief Economist at the World Bank, defined it as follows:

> Fundamentally, [globalisation] is the closer integration of countries and peoples of the world which has been brought about by the enormous reduction of costs of transportation and communication, and the breaking down of artificial barriers to the flows of goods, services, capital, knowledge, and (to a lesser extent) people across borders.

(*Globalization and its Discontents*, Penguin, 2004)

On this basis, globalisation is crucially about the closer integration of the world's economies. Critics have focused partly on the environmental effects of rapid global economic growth, and partly on the opportunities that powerful nations and large corporations have for exploiting the weak. Some of these arguments will be evaluated after a more careful exploration of the topic.

 Key term

globalisation: a process by which the world's economies are becoming more closely integrated

The quotation from the book by Joseph Stiglitz not only defines what is meant by globalisation, but also offers some reasons for its occurrence.

Transportation costs

One of the contributory factors to the spread of globalisation has undoubtedly been the rapid advances in the technology of transportation and communications.

Improvements in transport have been partly responsible for increasing international trade.

Improvements in transportation have enabled firms to fragment their production process to take advantage of varying cost conditions in different parts of the world. For example, it is now possible to site labour-intensive parts of a production process in parts of the world where labour is relatively plentiful, and thus relatively cheap. This is one way in which **multinational corporations** (MNCs) arise, in some cases operating across a wide range of countries.

 Key term

multinational corporation (MNC): a company whose production activities are carried out in a number of countries

Furthermore, communications technology has developed rapidly with the growth of the internet and e-commerce, enabling firms to compete more easily in global markets.

These technological changes have augmented the existing economies of scale and scope, enabling firms to grow. If the size of firms were measured by their gross

The Sheffield College
Hillsborough LRC
Telephone: 0114 260 2254

turnover, many of them would be found to be larger in size than a lot of the countries in which they operate (when size is measured by GDP), for example, on this basis General Motors is bigger than Hong Kong or Norway.

Reduction of trade barriers

A second factor that has contributed to globalisation has been the successive reduction in trade barriers during the period since the Second World War, first under the auspices of the **General Agreement on Tariffs and Trade (GATT)**, and later under the **World Trade Organisation (WTO)** which replaced it.

In addition to these trade-liberalising measures, there has been a trend towards the establishment of free trade areas and customs unions in various parts of the world, with the European Union being just one example.

Key terms

General Agreement on Tariffs and Trade (GATT): the precursor of the WTO, which organised a series of 'Rounds' of tariff reductions

World Trade Organisation (WTO): a multilateral body responsible for overseeing the conduct of international trade

By facilitating the process of international trade, such developments have encouraged firms to become more active in trade, and thus have added to the impetus towards globalisation.

Deregulation of financial markets

Hand in hand with these developments, there have been moves towards removing restrictions on the movement of financial capital between countries. Many countries have removed capital controls, thereby making it much easier for firms to operate globally. This has been reinforced by developments in technology that enable financial transactions to be undertaken more quickly and efficiently.

Globalisation and sustainability

Critics of globalisation have pointed to the impact that the increase in trade associated with globalisation may be having on the environment, especially in the context of climate change and global warming. This is bound up with the notion of **sustainable development**, which refers to the effect that economic growth and increased trade may have on future generations.

Key term

sustainable development: 'development which meets the needs of the present without compromising the ability of future generations to meet their own needs' (Brundtland Commission, 1987)

The core of the argument is that increased trade means increased emissions of greenhouse gases because of the need to transport goods over long distances. For example, if you check the country of origin of the fruit and vegetables in your local supermarket you will find that these are imported from far and wide. This is the case even for some produce that can be grown in the UK. On this basis it is argued that increasing such trade damages the environment. However, the case is not fully accepted by everyone. For example, a study by DEFRA showed that importing tomatoes from Spain into the UK (especially if transported by sea) causes less environmental damage than growing them at home, because of the difference in climate that enables tomatoes to be grown in a more environmentally friendly manner in Spain where no heat is needed to encourage growth and ripening. Nonetheless, this is an aspect of globalisation that needs to be considered and taken into account.

The pattern of world trade

In order to provide the context for a discussion of the effect of globalisation on trade, and the place of the UK economy in the global economy, it is helpful to examine the pattern of world trade.

Table 6.1 presents some data on this pattern. It shows the size of trade flows between regions. The rows of the table show the exports from each of the regions to each other region, while the columns show the pattern of imports from each region. The numbers on the 'diagonal' of the table (in bold type) show the trade flows *within* regions. One remarkable feature of the table is the high involvement of Europe in world trade, accounting for 44% of imports and 42% of the exports. Of course, this includes substantial flows within Europe. In contrast, Africa shows very little involvement in world trade, in spite of the fact that, in population terms, it is far larger.

				Destination				
Origin	North America	South & Central America	Europe	CIS	Africa	Middle East	Asia	World
North America	**905**	107	279	8	22	42	314	1678
S & C America	135	**112**	86	6	11	8	62	420
Europe	431	67	**3652**	142	120	129	366	4906
CIS	24	8	247	**80**	6	13	46	423
Africa	80	11	148	1	**33**	6	73	352
Middle East	72	4	103	3	21	**72**	340	615
Asia	708	70	604	50	70	111	**1639**	3251
World	2356	378	5118	290	283	381	2839	11644

Note: world totals have been calculated from the table. Data for China are included in the Asia total.

Source: World Trade Organisation.

Table 6.1 *Intra- and interregional merchandise trade, 2006 (US$bn)*

Indeed, trade flows between the developed countries — and with the more advanced developing countries — have tended to dominate world trade, with the flows between developing countries being relatively minor. This is not surprising, given that by definition the richer countries have greater purchasing power. However, the degree of openness to trade of economies around the world varies also as a result of conscious policy decisions. Some countries, especially in East Asia, have adopted very open policies towards trade, promoting exports in order

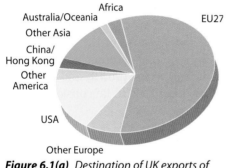

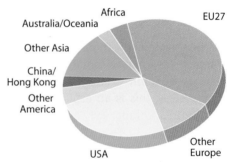

Figure 6.1(a) *Destination of UK exports of goods, 2007*

Figure 6.1(b) *Destination of UK exports of services, 2007*

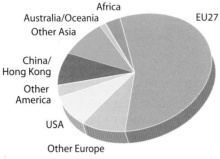

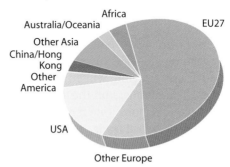

Figure 6.2(a) *Source of UK imports of goods, 2007*

Figure 6.2(b) *Source of UK imports of services, 2007*

Source: Pink Book.

to achieve export-led growth. In contrast, countries such as India and a number of Latin American countries have been much more reluctant to become dependent on international trade, and have adopted a more closed attitude towards trade. In more recent years, both China and India have been experiencing economic growth at a very high rate indeed, and have become significant trading nations. This has had repercussions on other countries around the world, especially in the case of China.

The pattern of UK trade

Figures 6.1(a) and (b) show the destination of UK exports of goods and services to major regional groupings in the world. The most striking feature of this graph is the extent to which the UK relies on Europe and the USA for more than three-quarters of its exports. Figures 6.2(a) and (b) reveal a similar pattern for the UK's imports of goods and services. Notice also that imports of goods from China and Hong Kong have become significant — and comprise a much larger share in imports than in exports.

The proportion of UK trade (both exports and imports) that is with Europe has undergone substantial change over the past 50 years. In 1960, when the Commonwealth was still thriving and the UK was ambivalent about the idea of European integration, less than a quarter of UK exports went to other European countries (23% of exports of goods in 1960). However, this has changed as the UK has grown closer to Europe, reaching 57% in 1990. Figure 6.3 shows that exports to the 15 members of the European Union prior to the expansion of the EU in 2004 have continued to be of high importance in terms of their share of UK exports.

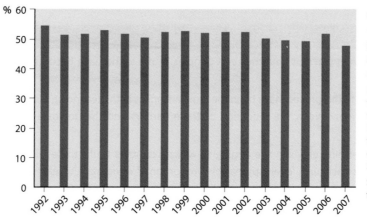

Figure 6.3
UK exports of goods and services going to EU15 (%)

Note:'EU15' refers to the 15 countries that were members of the European Union prior to the most recent expansion in May 2004.

Source: calculated from ONS data.

Table 6.2 shows the top 10 countries that make up the UK's export markets and import sources in 2007. This again shows the importance of UK trade with European countries in the twenty-first century, although the USA remains an important trading partner, ranked first among the UK's export markets, and the second largest source of imports into the UK.

	Export markets			Import sources	
	Country	% of total UK exports		Country	% of total UK imports
1	USA	14.6	1	Germany	13.5
2	Germany	11.2	2	USA	7.8
3	France	8.2	3	China (inc. Hong Kong)	7.8
4	Ireland	8.1	4	Netherlands	7.0
5	Netherlands	6.8	5	France	6.6
6	Belgium-Luxembourg	5.4	6	Belgium-Luxembourg	4.6
7	Spain	4.5	7	Norway	4.3
8	Italy	4.2	8	Italy	4.0
9	China (inc. Hong Kong)	3.0	9	Ireland	3.4
10	Sweden	2.2	10	Spain	3.2

Table 6.2 *The UK's top 10 export markets and import sources, 2007*

Exercise 6.1

a Using the data provided in Table 6.1, calculate the share of each region of world exports and imports. Think about the factors that might influence the contrasting performance of Western Europe and Africa. Also, for each region calculate the share of exports and imports that are within the region and comment on any significant differences that you find.

b Using Table 6.2, calculate the cumulative percentage of exports and imports in the UK's top 10 export markets and import sources. Discuss the extent to which this suggests that the UK concentrates on trading with a relatively small number of partners.

c Are there any aspects of the pattern of world trade that took you by surprise? Can you find reasons for these?

Summary

➤ Globalisation has taken place as countries and peoples of the world have become more closely integrated.

➤ Factors contributing to this process have been the rapid advances in the technology of transportation and communications, the reduction of trade barriers and the deregulation of financial markets.

➤ There are substantial differences in the degree to which countries trade: trade with and within Western Europe accounts for an appreciable proportion of world trade, whereas Africa shows very little involvement.

➤ More than three-quarters of UK exports go to Europe and the USA.

➤ The share of UK trade with the rest of Europe has increased substantially over the past 40 years.

The importance of international trade

The central importance of international trade for growth and development has been recognised since the days of Adam Smith and David Ricardo. For example, during the Industrial Revolution a key factor was that Britain could bring in raw materials from its colonies for use in manufacturing activity. Today, consumers in the UK are able to buy and consume many goods that simply could not be produced within the domestic economy. From the point of view of economic analysis, Ricardo showed that countries could gain from trade through a process of *specialisation*.

Absolute and comparative advantage

The notion of specialisation was introduced in *AS Economics, Chapter 1*, where you were introduced to Colin and Debbie, who produced pots and bracelets with varying levels of effectiveness. Colin and Debbie's relative skill levels in producing these two goods can now be extended. Table 6.3 reminds you of Colin and Debbie's production possibilities.

Colin		Debbie	
Pots	**Bracelets**	**Pots**	**Bracelets**
12	0	18	0
9	3	12	12
6	6	6	24
3	9	3	30
0	12	0	36

Table 6.3 Colin and Debbie's production

You may remember that Debbie was much better at both activities than Colin. If they each devote all their time to producing pots, Colin produces only 12 to Debbie's 18. If they each produce only bracelets, Colin produces 12 and Debbie, 36.

This illustrates **absolute advantage**. Debbie is simply better than Colin at both activities. Another way of looking at this is that, in order to produce a given quantity of a good, Debbie needs less labour time than Colin.

There is another significant feature of this table. Although Debbie is better at producing both goods, the difference is much more marked in the case of bracelet production than for pot production. So Debbie is relatively more proficient in bracelet production: in other words, she has a **comparative advantage** in making bracelets. This is reflected in differences in opportunity cost. If Debbie switches from producing pots to producing bracelets, she gives up 6 pots for every 12 additional bracelets that she makes. The opportunity cost of an additional bracelet is thus 6/12 = 0.5 pots. For Colin, there is a one-to-one trade-off between the two, so his opportunity cost of a bracelet is 1 pot.

More interesting is what happens if the same calculation is made for Colin and pot making. Although Debbie is absolutely better at making pots, if Colin increases his production of pots, his opportunity cost in terms of bracelets is still 1. But for Debbie the opportunity cost of making pots in terms of bracelets is 12/6 = 2, so Colin has the lower opportunity cost. Although Debbie has an *absolute* advantage in pot making, Colin has a *comparative* advantage. It was this difference in comparative advantage that gave rise to the gains from specialisation that were set out in *AS Economics, Chapter 1*.

> **Key terms**
>
> **absolute advantage:** the ability to produce a good more efficiently (e.g. with less labour)
>
> **comparative advantage:** the ability to produce a good *relatively* more efficiently (i.e. at lower opportunity cost)
>
> **law of comparative advantage:** a theory arguing that there may be gains from trade arising when countries (or individuals) specialise in the production of goods or services in which they have a comparative advantage

The **law of comparative advantage** states that overall output can be increased if all individuals specialise in producing the goods in which they have a comparative advantage.

Gains from international trade

This same principle can be applied in the context of international trade. Suppose there are two countries — call them Anywhere and Somewhere. Each country can produce combinations of agricultural goods and manufactures. However, Anywhere has a comparative advantage in producing manufactured goods, and Somewhere has a comparative advantage in agricultural goods. Their respective production possibility frontiers (*PPFs*) are shown in Figure 6.4.

You can see the pattern of comparative advantage reflected in the different slopes of the countries' *PPFs*. If the countries each produce some of each of the goods, one possibility (chosen for

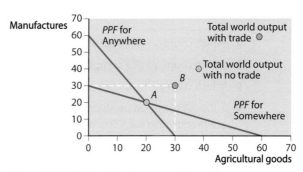

Figure 6.4 *PPFs for Anywhere and Somewhere*

simplicity) is that they produce at point *A*, which is the intersection of the two *PPFs*. At this point each country produces 20 units of manufactures and 20 units of agricultural goods. Total world output is thus 40 units of manufactures and 40 units of agricultural goods — this point is marked on the figure.

However, suppose each country were to specialise in the product in which it has a comparative advantage. Anywhere could produce 60 units of manufactured products, and Somewhere could produce 60 units of agricultural goods. This point is marked on the figure. Trade could take place such that each country had 30 units of each good (point B), leaving them both unequivocally better off: they would each have more of both commodities. The figure shows that total world output of each type of good has increased by 20 units.

It can be seen that in this situation trade may be mutually beneficial. Notice that this particular result of trading has assumed that the countries exchange the goods on a one-to-one basis. Although this exchange rate makes both better off, it is not the only possibility. It is possible that exchange will take place at different prices for the goods, and clearly, the prices at which exchange takes place will determine which of the countries gains most from the trade that occurs.

Exercise 6.2

Figure 6.5 shows production possibility frontiers for two countries, each of which produces both bales of cotton and cars. The countries are called 'West' and 'East'.

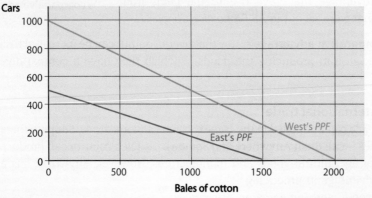

Figure 6.5
PPFs for East and West

a Which country has an absolute advantage in the production of both commodities?

b Which country has a comparative advantage in the production of bales of cotton?

c Which country has a comparative advantage in the production of cars?

d Suppose that West produces 500 cars and East produces 300. How many bales of cotton are produced in each country?

e Now suppose that 800 cars and 400 bales of cotton are produced by West, and that East produces only bales of cotton. What has happened to total production of bales of cotton and cars?

In the above examples and exercises, specialisation and trade are seen to lead to higher overall production of goods. Although the examples have related to goods, you should be equally aware that services too may be a source of specialisation and trade. This is potentially important for an economy like that of the UK, where there is a comparative advantage in the provision of financial services.

When you think about the global economy, it should be clear that comparative advantage will vary according to the very different balance of conditions around the world, not only in terms of climate (which may be important in agricultural production), but also in terms of the relative balance of factors of production (labour, capital, land, entrepreneurship etc.) and the skills of the workforce. This helps to explain why MNCs may choose to locate capital-intensive parts of their production process in one location and labour-intensive activities elsewhere, reflecting different relative prices in different countries.

It may also help to explain some of the patterns of trade. At first glance, it may seem curious that the UK both exports and imports cars, as initially this may seem to contradict comparative advantage. However, if British and (say) German cars have different characteristics, then each country may choose to specialise in certain segments of the market, taking advantage of the economies of scale that are so crucial in car production. Consumers benefit from this, as they then have a wider range of products to choose from.

Trade liberalisation or protectionism?

In spite of the well-known gains from trade, countries often seem reluctant to open their economies fully to international trade, and tend to intervene in various ways to protect their domestic producers.

Tariffs

A policy instrument commonly used in the past to give protection to domestic producers is the imposition of a **tariff**. Tariff rates in the developed countries have been considerably reduced in the period since the Second World War, but nonetheless are still in place.

Key term

tariff: a tax imposed on imported goods

Figure 6.6 shows how a tariff is expected to operate. D represents the domestic demand for a commodity, and S_{dom} shows how much domestic producers are prepared to supply at any given price. The price at which the good can be imported from world markets is given by P_w. If dealing with a global market, it is reasonable to assume that the supply at the world price is perfectly elastic. So in the absence of a tariff domestic demand is given by D_0, of which S_0 is supplied within

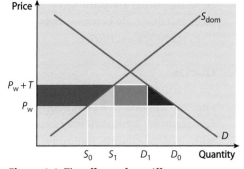

Figure 6.6 The effects of a tariff

the domestic economy and the remainder $(D_0 - S_0)$ is imported. If the government wishes to protect this industry within the domestic economy, it needs to find a way of restricting imports and encouraging home producers to expand their capacity.

By imposing a tariff, the domestic price rises to $P_w + T$, where T is the amount of the tariff. This has two key effects. One is to reduce the demand for the good from D_0 to D_1; the second is to encourage domestic producers to expand their output of this good from S_0 to S_1. As a consequence imports fall substantially, to $(D_1 - S_1)$. On the face of it, the policy has achieved its objective. Furthermore, the government has been able to raise some tax revenue (given by the green rectangle).

However, not all the effects of the tariff are favourable for the economy. Consumers are certainly worse off, as they have to pay a higher price for the good; they therefore consume less, and there is a loss of consumer surplus. Some of what was formerly consumer surplus has been redistributed to others in society. The government has gained the tariff revenue, as mentioned. In addition, producers gain economic rent, shown by the dark blue coloured area. There is also a deadweight loss to society, represented by the red and pale blue triangles. In other words, overall the society is worse off as a result of the imposition of the tariff.

Effectively, the government is subsidising inefficient local producers, and forcing domestic consumers to pay a price that is above that of similar goods imported from abroad.

Some would try to defend this policy on the grounds that it allows the country to protect an industry, thus saving jobs that would otherwise be lost. However, this goes against comparative advantage, and forces society to incur the deadweight loss. In the longer term it may delay structural change. For an economy to develop new specialisations and new sources of comparative advantage, there needs to be a transitional process in which old industries contract and new ones emerge. Although this process may be painful, it is necessary in the long run if the economy is to remain competitive. Furthermore, the protection that firms enjoy that allows them to reap economic rents from the tariff may foster complacency and an inward-looking attitude. This is likely to lead to X-inefficiency, and an inability to compete in the global market.

Even worse is the situation that develops where nations respond to tariffs raised by competitors by putting up tariffs of their own. This has the effect of further reducing the trade between countries, and everyone ends up worse off, as the gains from trade are sacrificed.

Quotas

An alternative policy that a country may adopt is to limit the imports of a commodity to a given volume. For example, a country may come to an agreement with another country that only a certain quantity of imports will be accepted by the importing country. Such arrangements are sometimes known as **voluntary export restraints (VERs)** or as **quotas**.

Key term

voluntary export restraint (VER): an agreement by a country to limit its exports to another country to a given quantity or **quota**

Figure 6.7 illustrates the effects of such a quota. D represents the domestic demand for this commodity, and S_{dom} is the quantity that domestic producers are prepared to supply at any given price. Suppose that without any agreement producers from country A would be prepared to supply any amount of the product at a price P_a. If the product is sold at this price, D_0 represents domestic demand, of which S_0 is supplied by domestic producers and the remainder $(D_0 - S_0)$ is imported from country A.

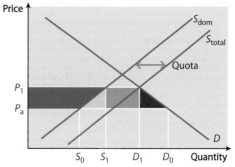

Figure 6.7 *The effects of a quota*

By imposing a quota, total supply is now given by S_{total}, which is domestic supply plus the quota of imports allowed into the economy from country A. The market equilibrium price rises to P_1 and demand falls to D_1, of which S_1 is supplied by domestic producers and the remainder is the agreed quota of imports.

Figure 6.7 shows who gains and who loses by this policy. Domestic producers gain by being able to sell at the higher price, so (as in the case of the tariff) they receive additional economic rent given by the dark blue area. Furthermore, the producers exporting from country A also gain, receiving the green rectangle (which, in the case of the tariff, was tax revenue received by the government). As in the case of the tariff, the two triangles (red and pale blue) represent the deadweight loss of welfare suffered by the importing country. Such an arrangement effectively subsidises the foreign producers by allowing them to charge a higher price than they would have been prepared to accept. Furthermore, although domestic producers are encouraged to produce more, the protection offered to them is likely to lead to X-inefficiency and weak attitudes towards competition.

There are a number of examples of such agreements, especially in the textile industry. For example, the USA and China have long-standing agreements on quotas for a range of textile products. Ninety-one such quotas expired at the end of 2004 as part of China's accession to the World Trade Organisation (WTO). As you might expect, this led to extensive lobbying by producers in the USA, especially during the run-up to the 2004 presidential election. Trade unions in the USA supported the producers, using the argument that 350,000 jobs had been lost since the expiry

The USA has tried to curtail growth of the highly competitive Chinese textile industry through the use of import quotas.

of earlier quota agreements in 2002. In the case of three of these earlier agreements, some restraint had been reinstated for bras, dressing gowns and knitted fabrics.

Producers in other countries, such as Sri Lanka, Bangladesh, Nepal, Indonesia, Morocco, Tunisia and Turkey, were lobbying for the quotas to remain, regarding China as a major potential competitor. However, for the USA at least, it can be argued that the removal of the quotas would allow domestic consumers to benefit from lower prices, and would allow American textile workers to be released for employment in higher-productivity sectors, where the USA maintains a competitive advantage.

Non-tariff barriers

There are other ways in which trade can be hampered, one example being the use of what are known as **non-tariff barriers**. These often comprise rules and regulations that control the standard of products that can be sold in a country.

Key term

non-tariff barriers: measures imposed by a government that have the effect of inhibiting international trade

This is a grey area, as some of the rules and regulations may seem entirely sensible and apply equally to domestic and foreign producers. For example, laws that prohibit the sale of refrigerators that contain CFCs are designed to protect the ozone layer, and may be seen to be wholly appropriate. In this case, the regulation is for purposes other than trade restriction.

However, there may be other situations in which a regulation is more clearly designed to limit trade. For example, the USA specifies a larger minimum size for vine-ripened tomatoes than for green tomatoes, thereby raising costs for the former. This has to do with trade, because vine-ripened tomatoes are mainly imported from Mexico, but green tomatoes are mainly grown in Florida. Thus, the regulation gives Florida producers an advantage.

Such rules and regulations may operate especially against producers in less-developed countries, who may find it especially difficult to meet demanding standards of production. This applies in particular where such countries are trying to develop new skills and specialisations to enable them to diversify their exports and engage more actively in international trade.

The European Common Agricultural Policy

Another source of contention in the trade arena has been the operation of the EU's Common Agricultural Policy (CAP). This has been in operation since the creation of the European Union (initially known as the European Economic Community) in 1957. The policy is a set of measures that guarantees farmers a price for their products that is set above the market equilibrium rate.

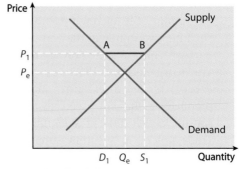

Figure 6.8 The CAP

For example, Figure 6.8 shows the demand and supply for a particular crop within the CAP. If the market were allowed to be in equilibrium, the price would be P_e and quantity traded would be Q_e. If, however, farmers are guaranteed a price of at least P_1, then they will plant more of the crop in order to supply the quantity S_1. However, consumers will then demand only D_1 of this product, and the remainder ($S_1 - D_1$: the distance AB) will need to be bought up by the authorities in order to maintain the price. If the guaranteed price is consistently above the equilibrium, the result is a build-up of surplus production — hence the notorious wine 'lakes' and butter 'mountains'.

Furthermore, consumers must pay the higher price for the product, and there is a deadweight loss imposed on society — not to mention the cost to the taxpayer of purchasing and storing the surplus. Farmers in the EU are then protected from external competition by the Common External Tariff.

The strategic arguments for protecting agriculture (that food supplies need to be assured in case of war) are less telling now than they were in 1957, and there have been many complaints from countries outside Europe that the CAP represents unfair subsidisation of EU farmers that inhibits trade and competition.

Exercise 6.3

Figure 6.9 illustrates the impact of a tariff. S_{dom} represents the quantity supplied by domestic producers, and D_{dom} shows the demand curve of domestic consumers. The world price is OE, and the country can import as much of the good at that price as it wishes.

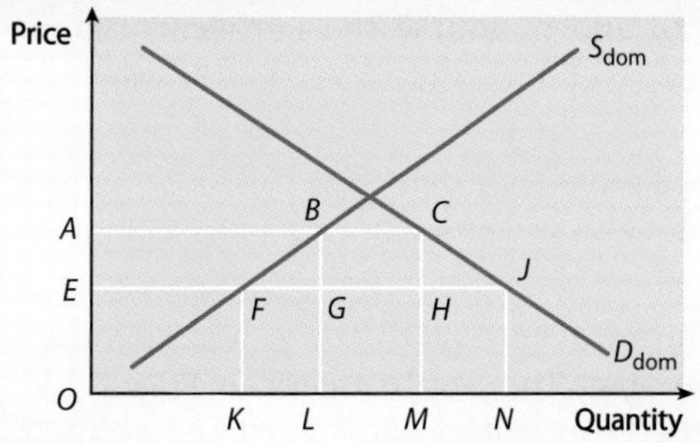

Figure 6.9
A tariff

a   In the absence of government intervention, identify domestic demand and supply, and the quantity of imports.

b   Suppose now that a tariff is imposed on imports of this product. Identify the price that will be charged in the domestic market.

c   What will be the quantity demanded, the quantity supplied by home producers, and the quantity imported?

d   Which area represents government revenue from the tariff?

e   Identify the additional economic rent received by domestic producers.

f   Identify and explain the deadweight loss of the tariff.

g   Discuss whether a tariff can be beneficial for society.

h   Suppose that a tariff has been in place on this commodity, but that the government proposes to remove it. Discuss the effects that the removal of the tariff will have, and the difficulties a government might face in removing it.

Summary

➤ The law of comparative advantage shows that countries can gain from international trade by specialising in the production of goods or services in which they have a lower opportunity cost of production.

➤ In spite of these possible gains, countries have often introduced protectionist measures to restrict trade, including tariffs, quotas and non-tariff barriers.

➤ The price guarantee system of the EU's Common Agricultural Policy has been much criticised as inhibiting trade, and reforms have been introduced.

Trade groupings

Despite the tendency towards protectionism, there are also trends in the opposite direction, with countries in various parts of the world coming together to form trade groupings of varying degrees of formality. These are intended to encourage trade among a group of nations, normally on a regional basis, in order to tap the gains from trade. Examples are ASEAN (an organisation of 10 countries in South East Asia), MERCOSUR (four countries in Latin America), NAFTA (Canada, the USA and Mexico) and of course the European Union. These groupings are at very different stages of integration and cooperation.

Free trade areas

A **free trade area** is a group of countries that agree to trade without barriers between themselves, but maintain their own individual barriers with countries outside the area. The North American Free Trade Area (NAFTA) is one such grouping. The Association of South East Asian Nations (ASEAN) has the aim of establishing a free trade area by the year 2020.

Customs unions

A **customs union** goes further than a free trade area, not only eliminating barriers to trade between the member countries, but also having a common tariff barrier against the rest of the world. The European Single Market is such an agreement. A customs union does not need to have a common currency, so for example, the UK is a member of the Single Market even though it has not yet adopted the euro. European integration will be discussed further in Chapter 7.

 Key terms

free trade area: a group of countries that agree to trade without barriers between themselves, but having their own individual barriers with countries outside the area

customs union: a group of countries that agree to trade without barriers between them, and with a common tariff barrier against the rest of the world

Evaluation

An important question in evaluating both free trade areas and customs unions is the extent to which they are able to generate increased trade and improved efficiency in production.

By creating a free trade area or customs union (i.e. without or with common barriers against the rest of the world), it is possible that the member nations will trade with each other instead of with the rest of the world; in other words, it is possible that trade will simply be diverted from the rest of the world to the partners in the agreement. Such **trade diversion** does not necessarily mean that gains from trade are being fully exploited, as ideally there should be **trade creation** as well as trade diversion. These terms are discussed in more detail in Chapter 8.

However, it is to be hoped that a trading agreement such as a free trade area or customs union would generate efficiency gains. If firms are able to service a larger overall market, it should be possible to exploit economies of scale and scope, which would reduce average production costs. This may require countries to alter their pattern of specialisation to take full advantage of the enlarged market. For example, within the European Union there is a wide range of countries having different patterns of comparative advantage, ranging from countries like the UK, France or Germany to the new members from Eastern Europe and the Baltic. The relative endowment of labour and capital among the member states can be expected to be very different.

This diversity is important for the success of a trade grouping. Remember that it is the *difference* in relative opportunity costs of production that drives the comparative advantage process and creates the potential gains from trade. However, it is clear that there also tends to be a strong political dimension affecting the outcome of such trade agreements.

The World Trade Organisation

A famous conference was held at Bretton Woods in the USA at the end of the Second World War to agree on a set of rules under which international trade would be conducted. This conference established an exchange rate system under which countries agreed to set the price of their currencies relative to the US dollar (see Chapter 7). In addition, the conference set up three institutions to oversee matters. The International Monetary Fund (IMF) would provide assistance (and advice) to countries experiencing balance of payments difficulties and the World Bank would provide assistance (and advice) on long-term development issues. However, it was also recognised that the conduct of trade would need some oversight. Initially, this role was fulfilled by the General Agreement on Tariffs and Trade (GATT), under the auspices of which there was a sequence of 'Rounds' of reductions in tariffs, together with a significant reduction in quotas and voluntary export restraints. The last of these was the Uruguay Round, which covered the period 1986–94 and led to the formation of the World Trade Organisation (WTO), which replaced the GATT in 1995.

> ### Key terms
>
> **trade creation:** the replacement of more expensive domestic production or imports with cheaper output from a partner within the trading bloc
>
> **trade diversion:** the replacement of cheaper imported goods by goods from a less efficient trading partner within a bloc

While continuing to pursue reductions in barriers to trade, the WTO has also taken on the role of providing a framework for the settlement of trade disputes. You will appreciate that, with all the moves towards regional integration and protectionism, such a role is very important. Indeed, the WTO reports that around 300 cases for settlement of disputes were brought to the WTO in its first 8 years — about the same number that were dealt with over the entire life of the GATT, i.e. 1947–94.

In 2000 new talks started covering agriculture and services. The fourth WTO Ministerial Conference in Doha in November 2001 incorporated these discussions into a broader work programme, the Doha Development Agenda. According to the WTO website, this agenda includes:

> ...work on non-agricultural tariffs, trade and environment, WTO rules such as anti-dumping and subsidies, investment, competition policy, trade facilitation, transparency in government procurement, intellectual property, and a range of issues raised by developing countries.

Progress on the Doha agenda has not been smooth. This is partly because agriculture is an especially contentious area, with the USA, the EU and Japan having large-scale policies in place to support their agricultural sectors. In the case of the EU's Single Market, some moves have been made towards reforming the Common Agricultural Policy, but progress has not been as rapid as developing countries would like — remembering that agriculture is especially important for many of the less-developed countries. *The Economist* in 2003 drew attention to the fact that 'the rich world spends over $300 billion a year supporting its farmers, more than six times the amount it spends on foreign aid.'

Trading blocs and the WTO

There has been a proliferation of regional trade agreements in recent years, and the WTO has estimated that there are some 400 agreements that are scheduled to be implemented by 2010. This may partly reflect the slow progress made in the Doha negotiations. There has been much debate as to whether these agreements are stepping stones to further global cooperation, or whether they may turn out to be obstacles to that process. If nations establish individual agreements with other nations or groups of nations, this may militate against reaching agreement on a more global scale, especially if the groupings of nations establish stronger barriers against trade with nations that are not part of the blocs. In other words, such regional agreements may be divisive rather than advancing globally freer trade.

Summary

> Regional groupings of countries have been formed to promote trade between neighbours; examples include ASEAN, MERCOSUR, NAFTA and the EU's Single Market.

> A free trade area is a group of countries that agree to trade between themselves without barriers.

> A customs union not only eliminates barriers to trade between member countries, but also imposes a common tariff against the rest of the world.

➤ A key factor influencing the success of such arrangements is the degree to which there is trade creation as well as trade diversion.

➤ The World Trade Organisation (WTO) has a responsibility to promote trade by pursuing reductions in tariffs and other barriers to trade, and also discharges a role in dispute settlement between nations.

Foreign direct investment

An important aspect of globalisation has been the spread of **foreign direct investment (FDI)** by MNCs. UNCTAD has identified three main reasons for such activity:

1 market-seeking

2 resource-seeking

3 efficiency-seeking

> **Key term**
>
> **foreign direct investment (FDI):** investment undertaken in one country by companies based in other countries

Some MNCs may engage in FDI because they want to sell their products within a particular market, and find it preferable to produce within the market rather than elsewhere: such FDI is *market-seeking*. Second, MNCs may undertake investment in a country in order to take advantage of some key resource. This might be a natural resource such as oil or natural gas, or a labour force with certain skills, or simply be cheap unskilled labour: such FDI is *resource-seeking*. Third, MNCs may simply review their options globally, and decide that they can produce most efficiently in a particular location. This might entail locating just part of their production chain in a certain country. Such FDI is *efficiency-seeking*.

Market-seeking FDI has been important in some regions in particular. The opening up of China to foreign investment has proved a magnet for MNCs wanting to gain access to this large and growing market. In addition, non-European firms have been keen to gain entry to the EU's Single Market, which has encouraged substantial flows of FDI into Europe.

For the UK, there has been a two-way flow of direct investment. In other words, foreign investors have invested in the UK, and UK investors have invested abroad. Figure 6.10 shows the inward and outward flows, expressed as a percentage of GDP.

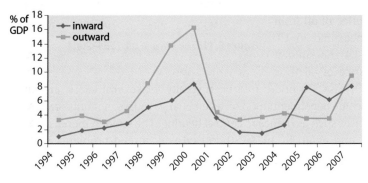

Figure 6.10 *UK foreign direct investment, 1994–2007*

Source: Pink Book.

Both inward and outward flows peaked in 2000, a year in which outward direct investment reached more than 16% of GDP. This reflected intense merger and acquisition activity at that time. The largest outward acquisitions were by Vodafone Airtouch, which invested in Mannesmann AG to the tune of £100 billion, and BP Amoco plc, which purchased the Atlantic Richfield Company for a reported £18 billion. After 2000, merger and acquisition activity slowed down, partly following the terrorist attacks in September 2001. Figure 6.10 shows that it was some time before FDI activity began to pick up again.

Summary

➤ An important part of globalisation has been the spread of foreign direct investment (FDI) by multinational corporations.

➤ Motivations for FDI include market-seeking, resource-seeking and efficiency-seeking reasons.

➤ Cross-border mergers and acquisitions have tended to follow a cyclical pattern over time, with a peak in 2000.

External shocks

One of the issues concerning a more closely integrated global economy is the question of how robust the global economy will be to shocks. In other words, globalisation may be fine when the world economy is booming, as all nations may be able to share in the success. But if the global economy goes into recession, will all nations suffer the consequences? There are a number of situations that might cause the global economy to take a downturn.

Oil prices

Oil prices seem to provide one possible threat. In the past, sudden changes in oil prices have caused widespread disruption — for example, in 1973–74 and in 1979–80.

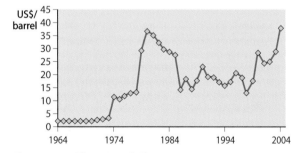

Figure 6.11 shows the historical time path of the price of oil from 1964 to 2004, measured in US dollars. In 1973–74 the sudden increase in the price of oil took

Figure 6.11 The price of oil, 1964–2004

Source: IMF.

most people by surprise. Oil prices had been steady for several years, and many economies had become dependent upon oil as an energy source, not only for running cars but for other uses such as domestic central heating. The sudden increases in the price in 1973–74 and again in 1979–80 caused widespread problems, because demand in the short run was highly inelastic, and oil-importing countries faced

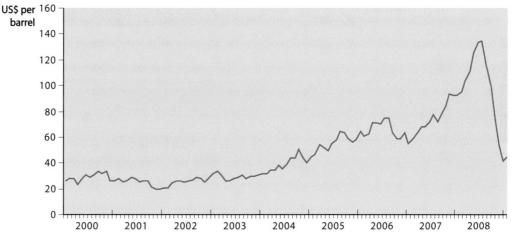

Figure 6.12 *The price of oil since 2000*
Source: IMF.

sudden deficits on their balance of payments current accounts. However, in time people switched away from oil for heating, firms developed more energy-efficient cars, and demand was able to adjust. Arguably, national economies in the 2000s are less vulnerable to changes in the price of oil than they were in 1973.

Figure 6.12 shows how the price of oil changed on a monthly basis after 2000, showing how the market again began to cause concern in late 2004 when prices again began to rise. Notice that the scale of the vertical axis has had to be changed in order to accommodate the rise in price, which became even more severe in 2007/08. When the price of oil began to fall again, OPEC met to discuss whether to reduce supply in order to maintain the oil price at its high level. In the event, the pressures of falling demand as the global recession began to unfold brought the price of oil tumbling.

Arguably, economies were better equipped to withstand the increase than they had been in the 1970s. The UK was partly able to weather the storm because of its position as an oil producer, although by this time, reserves were becoming depleted.

Another difference was that the price rises in 1973–74 and 1979–80 had been primarily supply-side changes, caused by disruptions to

China's demand for oil has been strong, contributing to the upward pressure on oil prices.

supply following the actions of the OPEC cartel. In the 2000s part of the upward pressure on price was coming from demand, with China's demand for oil being especially strong.

Financial crises

Given the increasing integration of financial markets, a further concern is whether globalisation increases the chances that a financial crisis will spread rapidly between countries, rather than being contained within a country or region. The 1997 Asian financial crisis provides some evidence on this issue.

This crisis began in Thailand and South Korea. Both countries had been the recipients of large flows of FDI. In the case of Thailand, a significant part of this had been investment in property, rather than in productive investment. The Thai currency (the baht) came under speculative pressure early in 1997, and eventually the authorities had to allow a devaluation. This sparked a crisis of confidence in the region, and foreign investors began to withdraw funds, not only from Thailand but from other countries too. As far as globalisation was concerned, the key questions were how far the crisis would spread, and how long it would last.

In the event, five countries bore the main burden of the crisis: Indonesia, Malaysia, the Philippines, South Korea and Thailand. Beyond this grouping there were some knock-on effects because of the trade linkages, but arguably these were not too severe, and were probably dominated by other events taking place in the period. At the time of the crisis, Indonesia and the Philippines had been at a somewhat lower stage of development than the other countries involved, and thus suffered more deeply in terms of recession. However, with the benefit of hindsight, it seems that the region showed resilience in recovering from the crisis. Indeed, it can be argued that South Korea and Thailand especially emerged as stronger economies after the crisis, through the weeding out of some relatively inefficient firms and institutions and through a heightened awareness of the importance of sound financial regulation.

China and the USA

An important question in the early to mid-2000s was how the global economy would cope with two seemingly distant but related phenomena: the rapid growth of the Chinese economy, and the deficit on the US current account of the balance of payments. The US current account deficit arose partly from the heavy public expenditure programme of the Bush Administration. However, the deficit grew to unprecedented levels partly through the actions of China and other East Asian economies that had chosen to peg their currencies to the US dollar. Effectively, this meant that those economies were buying US government securities as a way of maintaining their currencies against the dollar, thereby keeping US interest rates relatively low and allowing the American public to borrow to finance high consumer spending.

Who gains from this situation? The USA is able to spend, and China is able to sell, fuelling its rapid rate of economic growth. For how long the situation can be sustained remains to be seen.

The credit crunch

Another significant financial crisis afflicted the global economy in the late 2000s, known as the credit crunch. The focus of this problem was the banking system, and governments in many of the developed countries were forced to intervene to prevent banks from failing. Several factors contributed to the build-up of the crisis. It became clear that many banks had over-extended themselves by excessive lending. House prices had also risen to high levels in many countries, and when this bubble burst, some borrowers found difficulty in maintaining their payments, and the banks found themselves facing liquidity problems. The governments of several countries took steps to safeguard the banks, but by this time the real economy was being affected, and the UK and other nations found themselves heading into recession. The banks became highly risk averse and were reluctant to lend. However, without lending, aggregate demand remained weak, thus deepening the recession. In the UK, the Bank of England reduced interest rates to unprecedented low levels, but the response in terms of lending was sluggish.

Globalisation evaluated

The economic arguments in favour of allowing freer trade are strong, in the sense that there are potential gains to be made from countries specialising in the production of goods and services in which they have a comparative advantage. Globalisation facilitates and accelerates this process. And yet, there have sometimes been violent protests against globalisation, directed in particular at the WTO, whose meeting at Seattle in 1999 ended in chaos following demonstrations in the streets.

Tension has always been present during moves towards freer trade. Even if the economic arguments appear to be compelling, nations are cautious about opening up to free trade. In particular, there has been concern about jobs in the domestic economy. This is partly because there are transitional costs involved in liberalising trade, as some economic activities must contract to allow others to expand. Vested interests can then lead to lobbying and political pressure, as was apparent in the USA in the early part of the twenty-first century. There is also the question of whether globalisation will allow recession to spread more quickly between countries.

In many ways, the WTO gets caught in the middle. The WTO has the responsibility of encouraging moves towards free trade, and thus comes under pressure from nations that want to keep some degree of protection because they are unwilling to undergo the transitional costs of structural change. The WTO thus has the unpalatable job of protecting countries from themselves, enforcing short-term costs in the interests of long-term gains.

However, the anti-globalisation protests are based on rather different arguments. One concern is that economic growth can proceed only at some cost to the environment. It has been argued that, by fragmenting the production process, the cost to the environment is high. This is partly because the need to transport goods around the world uses up valuable resources. It is also argued that nations have an incentive to lower their environmental standards in order to attract MNCs by enabling low-cost production. This is not so much an argument against globalisation as an argument that an international agency is required to monitor global environmental standards.

It has also been suggested that it is the rich countries of the world that stand to gain most from increasing global trade, as they have the market power to ensure that trading conditions work in their favour. Again, the WTO may have a role here in monitoring the conditions under which trade takes place. At the end of the day, trade allows an overall increase in global production and more choice for consumers. The challenge is to ensure that these gains are equitably distributed, and that the environment can be conserved.

Summary

➤ Although closer integration may bring benefits in terms of increased global production and trade, it may also create a vulnerability by allowing adverse shocks to spread more rapidly between countries.

➤ Such shocks would include oil price changes or financial crises. However, the integrated global economy may turn out to be more resilient in reacting to adverse circumstances.

➤ Globalisation facilitates and accelerates the process by which gains from trade may be tapped.

➤ However, the transitional costs for individual economies in terms of the need for structural change have encouraged politicians to turn to protectionist measures.

➤ Critics of globalisation have pointed to the environmental costs of rapid global economic growth and the expansion of trade, and have argued that it is the rich countries and the multinational corporations that gain the most, rather than the less-developed countries.

Exercise 6.5

Examine the economic arguments for and against globalisation.

The balance of payments and exchange rates

For an individual economy, the potential gains from international trade in a globalised economy depend on the pattern of comparative advantage and on the competitiveness of domestic economic activity compared with the rest of the world. The ultimate health of the economy also requires long-term external balance. This chapter explores these issues. For any economy that is open to international trade, the exchange rate is a crucial variable, as it influences the competitiveness of domestic firms in international markets. The way in which the exchange rate is determined has wide-reaching effects on the conduct and effectiveness of macroeconomic policy. From the end of the Second World War until the early 1970s, a system of fixed exchange rates was in operation, whereby economies set the value of their currency relative to the US dollar. After this system broke down, most developed countries allowed their currencies to 'float', finding their own market levels, although at times governments have been tempted to intervene in this market. Some countries continue to peg their exchange rates to the US dollar. This chapter thus also investigates why the exchange rate is so important, and how the various systems for determining its value work.

Learning outcomes

After studying this chapter, you should:
- ➤ understand the role and significance of the balance of payments and the need to maintain external balance in the long run
- ➤ be familiar with the use of alternative policy measures to manage the balance of payments
- ➤ understand what is meant by the market for foreign exchange
- ➤ understand the operation of a fixed exchange rate system
- ➤ be familiar with a floating exchange rate system
- ➤ be aware of the major determinants of exchange rates within a floating exchange rate system
- ➤ understand the way in which macroeconomic policy influences the exchange rate, and vice versa

The balance of payments

For an economy like the UK that is open to international trade, it is important to monitor the trade that takes place. *AS Economics, Chapter 10* introduced the balance of payments, a set of accounts that monitors the transactions that take place between UK residents and the rest of the world. For an individual household it is important to monitor incomings and outgoings, as items purchased must be paid for in some way — either by using income or savings, or by borrowing. In a similar way, a country has to pay for goods, services or assets that are bought from other countries. The balance of payments accounts enable the analysis of such international transactions.

As with the household, transactions can be categorised as being either incoming or outgoing items. For example, if a car made in the UK is exported (i.e. purchased by a non-resident of the UK), this is an 'incoming' item, as the payment for the car is a credit to the UK. On the other hand, the purchase of a bottle of Italian wine (an import) is a debit item.

Similarly, all other transactions entered into the balance of payments accounts can be identified as credit or debit items, depending upon the direction of the payment. In other words, when money flows into the country as the result of a transaction, that is a credit; if money flows out, it is a debit. As all items have to be paid for in some way, the overall balance of payments when everything is added together must be zero. However, individual components can be positive or negative.

In line with international standards, the accounts are divided into three categories. The **current account** identifies transactions in goods and services, together with income payments and international transfers. Income payments here include the earnings of UK nationals from employment abroad and payments of investment income. Transfers are mainly transactions between governments, for example between the British government and EU institutions, which makes up the largest component. Also included here are flows of bilateral aid and social security payments abroad.

The **financial account** measures transactions in financial assets, including investment flows and central government transactions in foreign exchange reserves.

 Key terms

current account of the balance of payments: account identifying transactions in goods and services between the residents of a country and the rest of the world

financial account of the balance of payments: account identifying transactions in financial assets between the residents of a country and the rest of the world

capital account of the balance of payments: account identifying transactions in (physical) capital between the residents of a country and the rest of the world

The **capital account** is relatively small. It contains capital transfers, the largest item of which is associated with migrants. When a person changes status from non-resident to resident of the UK, then any assets owned by that person are transferred to being British-owned.

Figure 7.1 shows the relative size of the main accounts since 1970. Notice that these data are in current prices, so no account has been taken of changing prices during the period. This has the effect of compressing the apparent magnitude of the variables in the early part of the period (when prices were relatively low), and exaggerating the size towards the end of the period. Expressing these nominal values as a percentage of nominal GDP (as in Figure 7.2 for a longer period) provides a less misleading picture.

As the total balance of payments must always be zero, the surplus (positive) components above the line must always exactly match the deficit (negative) items below the line. However, both figures indicate that the relative magnitudes of the three major accounts vary through time.

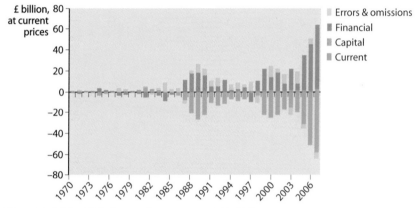

Figure 7.1 *The UK balance of payments, 1970–2007*

Source: ONS.

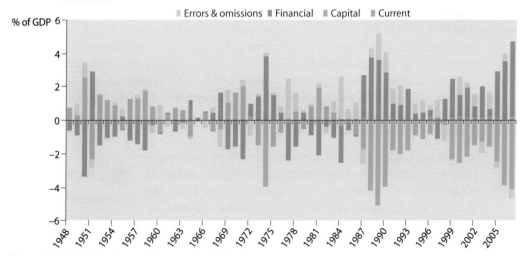

Figure 7.2 *The UK balance of payments, 1948–2007*

Source: ONS.

The current account

The current account has been in deficit every year since 1984. The recorded current account surpluses in 1980–83 were associated with North Sea oil, which was then just coming on stream. There followed a phase in which the deficit grew to record levels, peaking in 1989. During the 1990s, the deficit fell until 1999, at which time the UK economy entered into a period in which the current account has been consistently in substantial deficit, and the financial account in surplus.

Figure 7.3 shows the components of the current account. You can see that until the early 1990s the overall balance on the current account (CBAL) tracked closely the trade in goods. More recently, however, the trade in goods has moved further into deficit, although this has been partially offset by a gradual increase in the trade in services and (except in 1999) by an increase in income – which is made up mainly of investment income.

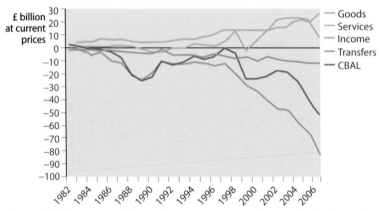

Figure 7.3 *The composition of the current account, 1982–2007 (balances)*
Source: ONS.

Trade in goods (sometimes known as **visible trade**) has traditionally shown a deficit for the UK – it has shown a surplus in only 6 years since 1900. As reserves of oil in the North Sea run down, the UK has become a net importer of oil, although up to 2004 the UK had been a net exporter of oil; in other words, the oil part of the trade in goods was in surplus. However, imports of cars and other consumer goods have persistently exceeded exports. A summary for 2007 is presented in Table 7.1, with data for 1997 as well to show how the pattern has changed. You should be aware that these data are in current prices, so you need to focus on the relative sizes rather than the absolute values.

In contrast, trade in services has recorded a surplus in every year since 1966. This is sometimes referred to as **invisible trade**. Table 7.2 shows the component items in 1997 and 2007 – again, measured in current prices, so that no allowance has been made for the effects of inflation.

As you can see, the largest deficit items in trade in services are transportation (especially air transport services, which

Key terms

visible trade:
trade in goods

invisible trade:
trade in services

Item	1997	2007
Food, beverages and tobacco	−5,808	−15,018
Basic materials	−3,520	−4,052
Oil	4,560	−4,047
Coal, gas and electricity	−368	−3,202
Semi-manufactured goods:		
Chemicals	4,496	4,180
Precious stones and silver	−318	−406
Other	−5,014	−10,069
Finished manufactured goods:		
Motor cars	−4,465	−7,230
Other consumer goods	−6,683	−24,734
Intermediate goods	−625	−11,112
Capital goods	3,753	−11,563
Ships and aircraft	1,646	−894
Commodities not classified	184	−1,105
Total	**−12,342**	**−89,252**

Table 7.1 UK trade in goods (balances), 1997 and 2007 (£m in current prices)

Source: Pink Book.

Item	1997	2007
Transportation	−2,092	−2,189
Travel	−3,638	−17,332
Communications	−185	346
Construction	98	154
Insurance	2,597	4,513
Financial	11,145	31,045
Computer and information	952	4,009
Royalties and licence fees	503	1,539
Other business	8,018	18,859
Personal cultural and recreational	274	1,128
Government	−769	−1,013
Total	**16,801**	**41,772**

Table 7.2 UK trade in services (balances), 1997 and 2007 (£m in current prices)

Source: Pink Book.

has shown a deficit every year since the mid-1980s) and travel, where again the deficit has grown significantly since the late 1980s. The main reason for this is the increasing number of UK residents travelling aboard. However, these negative items are more than compensated by the surplus components, especially financial services, which has grown steadily, as have computer and information services. You can see that 'Other business' also makes a significant contribution. This category includes trade-related services such as merchanting, consultancy services such as advertising, engineering and legal services, and operational leasing.

An important item on the current account is investment income, which represents earnings on past investment abroad. This item has shown strong growth since 1999 (when there was a deficit). The largest item in this part of the account is earnings from direct investment, although there is also an element of portfolio investment — earnings from holdings of bonds and other securities. The final category is current transfers. This includes taxes and social contributions received from non-resident workers and businesses, bilateral aid flows and military grants. However, the largest item is transfers with EU institutions, which has been in persistent deficit.

The financial account

The trend towards globalisation means that both inward and outward investment increased substantially during the 1990s, although there was a dip after 2000. However, Figure 7.1 shows that the financial account has been in strong surplus in the early part of the twenty-first century. This is in part forced by the deficit on the current account. In other words, if an economy runs a current account deficit, it can do so only by running a surplus on the financial account. Effectively, what is happening is that, in order to fund the current account deficit, the UK is selling assets to foreign investors and borrowing abroad.

An important question is whether this practice is sustainable in the long run. Selling assets or borrowing abroad has future implications for the current account, as there will be outflows of investment income, and debt repayments in the future following today's financial surplus. It also has implications for interest rate policy. If the authorities hold interest rates high relative to the rest of the world, this will tend to attract inflows of investment, again with future implications for the current account.

The capital account

The capital account is relatively small. The largest item relates to the flows of capital associated with migration. If someone migrates to the UK, that person's status changes from being a non-resident to being a resident. His or her property then becomes part of the UK's assets, and a transaction has to be entered in the balance of payments accounts. There are also some items relating to various EU transactions. This account has been in surplus for 20 years.

Summary

> The balance of payments is a set of accounts that contains details of the transactions that take place between the residents of an economy and the rest of the world.

> The accounts are divided into three sections: the current, financial and capital accounts.

> The current account identifies transactions in goods and services, together with some income payments and international transfers.

> The financial account measures transactions in financial assets, including investment flows and central government transactions in foreign reserves.

> The capital account, which is relatively small, contains capital transfers.

> The overall balance of payments must always be zero.

> The current account has been in persistent deficit since 1984, reflecting a deficit in trade in goods that is partly offset by a surplus in invisible trade.

> The financial account has been in strong surplus — as is required to balance the current account deficit.

Exercise 7.1

Allocate each of the following items to either the current, financial or capital accounts, and calculate the balances for each account. Check that (together with errors and omissions) the total is zero. All data refer to 2007, at current prices in £ billion.

a	Trade in goods	−89.25	g	Trade in services	+41.77
b	Migrants' transfers	+ 2.26	h	Other capital transfers	+ 0.39
c	Total net direct investment	−18.99	i	Compensation of employees	−0.67
d	Investment income	+ 9.27	j	Total net portfolio investment	+78.22
e	Current transfers	−13.69	k	Other transactions in financial assets	−18.20
f	Transactions in reserve assets	−1.19	l	Errors and omissions	+10.10

The foreign exchange market

AS Economics, Chapter 5 introduced the foreign exchange market, and argued that it could be regarded as involving demand and supply, just like any normal market. A foreign exchange transaction is needed whenever trade takes place. If, as a UK resident, you buy goods from abroad, you need to purchase foreign exchange – say, euros – and you will have to supply pounds in order to buy euros. Similarly, if a French tourist in the UK buys UK goods or services, the transaction needs to be carried out in pounds, so there is a demand for pounds.

This market is shown in Figure 7.4. The demand curve is downward sloping because when the €/£ rate is low British goods, services and assets are relatively cheap in terms of euros, so demand is relatively high. On the other hand, when the €/£ rate is relatively high, Europeans receive fewer euros for their pounds, so the demand will be relatively low.

The supply curve of pounds is upward sloping. When the €/£ rate is relatively high, the supply of pounds will be relatively strong, as UK residents will get plenty of euros for their pounds and thus will demand European goods, services and assets, supplying pounds in order to buy the foreign exchange needed for the transactions. When the €/£ rate is low, European goods, services and assets will be relatively expensive for UK residents, so fewer pounds will be supplied.

The market is in equilibrium at e^*, where the demand for pounds is just matched by the supply of pounds. This position has a direct connection with the balance of payments. If the demand for pounds exactly matches the supply

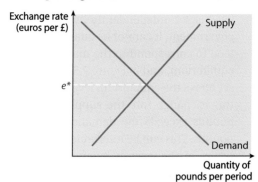

Figure 7.4 *The market for pounds*

of pounds, this implies that there is a balance between the demand from Europeans for UK goods, services and assets and the demand by UK residents for European goods, services and assets. In other words, the balance of payments is in overall balance. The key question for consideration is how the market reaches e^* — in particular, do the authorities allow the exchange rate to find its own way to e^*, or do they intervene to ensure that it gets there?

Summary

➤ The foreign exchange market can be seen as operating according to the laws of demand and supply.

➤ The demand for pounds arises when non-residents want to buy British goods, services or assets.

➤ The supply of pounds arises when UK residents wish to buy foreign goods, services or assets.

➤ When the exchange rate is at its equilibrium level, this automatically ensures that the overall balance of payments is zero.

A fixed exchange rate system

In the Bretton Woods conference at the end of the Second World War, it was agreed to establish a fixed exchange rate system, under which countries would commit to maintaining the price of their currencies in terms of the US dollar. This system remained in place until the early 1970s. For example, from 1950 until 1967 the sterling exchange rate was set at $2.80, and the British government was committed to making sure that it stayed at this rate. This system became known as the Dollar Standard. Occasional changes in exchange rates were permitted after consultation if a currency was seen to be substantially out of line — as happened for the UK in 1967.

Figure 7.5 illustrates how this works. Suppose the authorities announce that the exchange rate will be set at e_f. Given that this level is set independently by the government, it cannot be guaranteed to correspond to the market equilibrium, and in Figure 7.5 it is set above the equilibrium level. At this exchange rate the supply of pounds exceeds the demand for pounds. This can be interpreted in terms of the overall balance of payments. If there is an excess supply of pounds, the implication is that UK residents are trying to buy more American goods, services and assets than Americans are

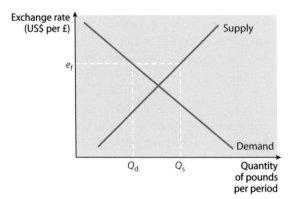

Figure 7.5 Maintaining a fixed exchange rate

trying to buy British; in other words, there is an overall deficit on the balance of payments.

In a free market, you would expect the exchange rate to adjust until the demand and supply of pounds came back into equilibrium. However, with the authorities committed to maintaining the exchange rate at e_f, such adjustment cannot take place. However, the UK owes the USA for the excess goods, services and assets that its residents have purchased, so the authorities then have to sell **foreign exchange reserves** in order to make the books balance.

Key term

foreign exchange reserves: stocks of foreign currency and gold owned by the central bank of a country to enable it to meet any mismatch between the demand and supply of the country's currency

In terms of Figure 7.5, Q_d represents the demand for pounds at e_f and Q_s represents the supply. The difference represents the amount of foreign exchange reserves that the authorities have to sell to preserve the balance of payments. Such transactions were known as 'official financing', and are incorporated into the financial account of the balance of payments.

Notice that the *position* of the demand and supply curves depends on factors other than the exchange rate that can affect the demand for British and American goods, services and assets in the respective countries. It is likely that through time these will shift in position. For example, if the preference of Americans for British goods changes through time, this would affect the demand for pounds.

Consider Figure 7.6. For simplicity, suppose that the supply curve remains fixed but demand shifts through time. Let e_f be the value of the exchange rate that the UK monetary authorities have undertaken to maintain. If the demand for pounds is at D_1, the chosen exchange rate corresponds to the market equilibrium, and no action by the authorities is needed. If demand is at D_0, then with the exchange rate at e_f there is an excess supply of pounds (as shown in Figure 7.5). The monetary authorities in the UK need to buy up the

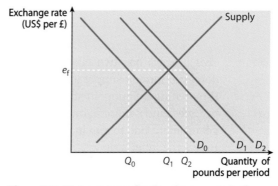

Figure 7.6 *Maintaining a fixed exchange rate in the face of changing demand for pounds*

excess supply by selling foreign exchange reserves. Conversely, if the demand for pounds is strong, say because Americans have developed a preference for Scotch whisky, then demand could be at D_2. There is now excess demand for pounds, and the British monetary authorities supply additional pounds in return for US dollars. Foreign exchange reserves thus accumulate.

In the long term, the system will operate successfully for the country so long as the chosen exchange rate is close to the average equilibrium value over time, so that the central bank is neither running down its foreign exchange reserves nor accumulating them.

A country that tries to hold its currency away from equilibrium indefinitely will find this problematic in the long run. For example, in the early years of the twenty-first century China and some other Asian economies were pegging their currencies against the US dollar at such a low level that they were accumulating foreign exchange. In the case of China, it was accumulating substantial amounts of US government stock. The low exchange rate had the effect of keeping the exports of these countries highly competitive in world markets. However, such a strategy relies on being able to continue to expand domestic production to meet the high demand; otherwise inflationary pressure will begin to build.

During the period of the Dollar Standard, the pound was probably set at too high a level, which meant that British exports were relatively uncompetitive, and in 1967 the British government announced a **devaluation** of the pound from $2.80 to $2.40.

During the Dollar Standard period, the British economy went through what became known as a 'stop–go' cycle of growth. When the government tried to stimulate economic growth, the effect was to suck in imports, as the marginal propensity to import was high. The effect of this was to generate a deficit on the current account of the balance of payments, which then needed to be financed by selling foreign exchange reserves.

 Key terms

devaluation: process whereby a government reduces the price of its currency relative to an agreed rate in terms of foreign currency

revaluation: process whereby a government raises the price of domestic currency in terms of foreign currency

This process has two effects. First of all, in selling foreign exchange reserves, domestic money supply increases, which then puts upward pressure on prices, threatening inflation. In addition, the Bank of England has finite foreign exchange reserves, and cannot allow them to be run down indefinitely. This meant that the government had to rein in the economy, thereby slowing the rate of growth again. Hence the label 'stop–go'.

An important point emerges from this discussion. The fact that intervention to maintain the exchange rate affects domestic money supply means that under a fixed exchange rate regime the monetary authorities are unable to pursue an independent monetary policy. In other words, money supply and the exchange rate cannot be controlled independently of one another. Effectively, the money supply has to be targeted to maintain the value of the currency. Governments may be tempted to use tariffs or non-tariff barriers to reduce a current account deficit, but this has been shown to be distortionary.

The effects of devaluation

During the stop–go period there were many debates about whether there should be a devaluation. The effect of devaluation is to improve competitiveness. At a lower value of the pound, you would expect an increase in the demand for exports and a fall in the demand for imports, *ceteris paribus.*

However, this does not necessarily mean that there will be an improvement in the current account. One reason for this concerns the elasticity of supply of exports and import substitutes. If domestic producers do not have spare capacity, or if there are time lags before production for export can be increased, then exports will not expand quickly in the short run, and so the impact of this action on exports will be limited. Furthermore, similar arguments apply to producers of goods that are potential substitutes for imported products, which reinforces the sluggishness of adjustment. In the short run, therefore, it may be that the current account will worsen rather than improve, in spite of the change in the competitiveness of domestic firms.

This is known as the *J-curve effect*, and is shown in Figure 7.7. Time is measured on the horizontal axis, and the current account is initially in deficit. A devaluation at time *A* initially pushes the current account further into deficit, because of the inelasticity of domestic supply. Only after time *B*, when domestic firms have had time to expand their output to meet the demand for exports, does the current account move into surplus.

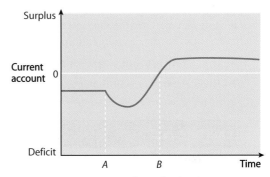

Figure 7.7 *The J-curve effect of a devaluation*

A second consideration relates to the elasticity of demand for exports and imports. Again, if competitiveness improves but demand does not respond strongly, there may be a negative impact on the current account. If the demand for exports is price-inelastic, a fall in price will lead to a fall in revenue. Indeed, the *Marshall–Lerner condition* states that a devaluation will have a positive effect on the current account only if the sum of the elasticities of demand for exports and imports is negative and numerically greater than 1.

The Bretton Woods Dollar Standard broke down in the early 1970s. Part of the reason for this was that such a system depends critically on the stability of the base currency (i.e. the US dollar). During the 1960s the US need to finance the Vietnam War meant that the supply of dollar currency began to expand, one result of which was accelerating inflation in the countries that were fixing their currency in terms of the US dollar. It then became increasingly difficult to sustain

In order to finance the Vietnam War, the USA had to increase the supply of dollars.

exchange rates at fixed levels. Britain withdrew from the Dollar Standard in June 1972. Following this, the pound fell steadily for the next 5 years or so, as is shown in Figure 8.11 in the next chapter.

Summary

➤ After the Bretton Woods conference at the end of the Second World War, the Dollar Standard was established, under which countries agreed to maintain the value of their currencies in terms of US dollars.

➤ In order to achieve this, the monetary authorities engaged in foreign currency transactions to ensure that the exchange rate was maintained at the agreed level, accumulating foreign exchange reserves to accommodate a balance of payments surplus and running down the reserves to fund a deficit.

➤ Occasional realignments were permitted, such as the devaluation of sterling in 1967.

➤ Under a fixed exchange rate system, monetary policy can only be used to achieve the exchange rate target.

➤ A devaluation has the effect of improving international competitiveness, but the effect on the current account depends upon the elasticity of demand for exports and imports.

➤ The current account may deteriorate in the short run if the supply response is sluggish.

➤ The Bretton Woods system broke down in the early 1970s.

Exercise 7.2

A firm wants to purchase a machine tool which is obtainable in the UK for a price of £125,000, or from a US supplier for $300,000. Suppose that the exchange rate is fixed at £1 = $3.

a What is the sterling price of the machine tool if the firm chooses to buy in the USA?

b From which supplier would the firm be likely to purchase?

c Suppose that between ordering the machine tool and its delivery the UK government announces a devaluation of sterling, so that when the time comes for the firm to pay up the exchange rate is £1 = $2. What is the sterling price of the machine tool bought from the USA?

d Comment on how the competitiveness of British goods has been affected.

e Discuss the effects that the devaluation is likely to have on the economy as a whole.

Floating exchange rates

Under a floating exchange rate system, the value of the currency is allowed to find its own way to equilibrium. This means that the overall balance of payments is automatically assured, and the monetary authorities do not need to intervene to make sure it happens. In practice, however, governments have tended to be wary of leaving the exchange rate entirely to market forces, and there have been occasional periods in which intervention has been used to affect the market rate.

An example of this was the **Exchange Rate Mechanism (ERM)**, which was set up by a group of European countries in 1979 with the objective of keeping member countries' currencies relatively stable against each other. This was part of the EMS (European Monetary System). Each member nation agreed to keep its currency within 2.25% of a weighted average of the members' currencies (known as the European Currency Unit (ECU). This was an *adjustable peg* system. Eleven realignments were permitted between 1979 and 1987.

 Key *term*

Exchange Rate Mechanism (ERM): a system that was set up by a group of European countries in 1979 with the objective of keeping member countries' currencies relatively stable against each other

The UK opted not to join the ERM when it was first set up, but started shadowing the Deutschmark in the mid-1980s, aiming to keep the rate at around DM3 to the pound, as you can see in Figure 7.8. Britain finally decided to become a full member of the ERM in September 1990. However, the rate at which sterling had been set against the Deutschmark was relatively high, and the situation was

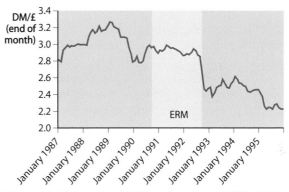

Figure 7.8 *The nominal DM/£ exchange rate, 1987–1995*
Source: Bank of England.

worsened by the effects of German reunification, which led to substantial capital flows into Germany, reinforcing the overvaluation of sterling. Once it became apparent that sterling was overvalued, speculative attacks began, and the Bank of England's foreign exchange reserves were depleted; in 1992 the pound left the ERM. You can see in Figure 7.8 that the value of the pound fell rapidly after exit.

What determines exchange rates?

If the foreign exchange market is left free to find its own way to equilibrium, it becomes important to consider what factors will influence the level of the exchange rate. In particular, will the exchange rate resulting from market equilibrium be consistent with the government's domestic policy objectives?

Exchange rate equilibrium also implies a zero overall balance of payments. If the exchange rate always adjusts to the level that ensures this, it might be argued that the long-run state of the economy is one in which the competitiveness of domestic firms remains constant over time. In other words, you would expect the exchange rate to adjust through time to offset any differences in inflation rates between countries. The **purchasing power parity theory of exchange rates** argues that this is exactly what should be expected in the long run. The nominal exchange rate should adjust in such a way as to offset changes in relative prices between countries, as will be outlined in Chapter 8.

However, in the short run the exchange rate may diverge from its long-run equilibrium. An important influence on the exchange rate in the short run is speculation. So far, the discussion of the exchange rate has stressed mainly the current account of the balance of payments. However, the financial account is also significant, especially since regulation of the movement of financial capital was removed. Some of these capital movements are associated with direct investment, which was discussed in the last chapter. However, sometimes there are also substantial movements of what has come to be known as **hot money**, i.e. stocks of funds that are moved around the globe from country to country in search of the best return. The size of the stocks of hot money is enormous, and can significantly affect exchange rates in the short run.

'Hot money' moves swiftly around the world in search of the best rate of interest.

Key terms

purchasing power parity theory of exchange rates: theory stating that in the long run exchange rates (in a floating rate system) are determined by relative inflation rates in different countries

hot money: stocks of funds that are moved around the world from country to country in search of the best return

Such movements can influence the exchange rate in the short run. The returns to be gained from such capital flows depend on the relative interest rate in the country targeted, and on the expected exchange rate in the future, which in turn may depend on expectations about inflation.

Suppose you are an investor holding assets denominated in US dollars, and the UK interest rate is 2% higher than that in the USA. You may be tempted to shift the funds into the UK in order to take advantage of the higher interest rate. However, if you believe that the exchange rate is above its long-run equilibrium, and therefore is likely to fall, this will affect your expected return on holding a British asset. Indeed, if investors holding British assets expect the exchange rate to fall, they are likely to shift their funds out of the country as soon as possible – which may then have the effect of pushing down the exchange rate. In other words, this may be a self-fulfilling prophecy. However, speculators may also react to news in an unpredictable way, so not all speculative capital movements act to influence the exchange rate towards its long-run equilibrium value.

Speculation was a key contributing factor in the unfolding of the Asian financial crisis of 1997. Substantial flows of capital had moved into Thailand in search of high returns, and speculators came to believe that the Thai currency (the baht) was overvalued. Outward capital flows put pressure on the exchange rate, and although the Thai central bank tried to resist, it eventually ran down its reserves to the point where it had to devalue. This then sparked off capital flows from other countries in the region, including South Korea.

Summary

➤ Under a floating exchange rate system, the value of a currency is allowed to find its own way to equilibrium without government intervention.

➤ This means that an overall balance of payments of zero is automatically achieved.

➤ The purchasing power parity theory argues that the exchange rate will adjust in the long run to maintain international competitiveness, by offsetting differences in inflation rates between countries.

➤ In the short run, the exchange rate may diverge from this long-run level, in particular because of speculation.

➤ The exchange rate is thus influenced by relative interest rates and expected inflation, as well as by news about the economic environment.

Fixed or floating?

In evaluating whether a fixed or a floating regime is to be preferred, there are many factors to be taken into account; this section will consider three of them. First, it is important to examine the extent to which the respective systems can accommodate and adjust to external shocks that push the economy out of equilibrium. Second, it is important to consider the stability of each of the systems. Finally, there is the question of which system best encourages governments to adopt sound macroeconomic policies.

Adjustment to shocks

Every economy has to cope with external shocks that occur for reasons outside the control of the country. A key question in evaluating exchange rate systems is whether there is an effective mechanism that allows the economy to return to equilibrium after an external shock.

Under a **floating exchange rate** system, much of the burden of adjustment is taken up by changes in the exchange rate. For example, if an economy finds itself experiencing faster inflation than other countries, perhaps because those other countries have introduced policies to reduce inflation, then the exchange rate will adjust automatically to restore competitiveness.

However, if the country is operating a **fixed exchange rate** system, the authorities are committed to maintaining

Key terms

floating exchange rate: a system in which the exchange rate is permitted to find its own level in the market

fixed exchange rate: a system in which the government of a country agrees to fix the value of its currency in terms of that of another country

the exchange rate, and this has to take precedence. Thus, the only way to restore competitiveness is by deflating the economy in order to bring inflation into line with other countries. This is likely to bring with it a transitional cost in terms of higher unemployment and slower economic growth. In other words, the burden of adjustment is on the real economy, rather than on allowing the exchange rate to adjust.

The Bretton Woods system operated for more than 20 years in a period in which many economies enjoyed steady economic growth. However, in the UK the system brought about a stop–go cycle, in which the need to maintain the exchange rate hampered economic growth, because of the tendency for growth to lead to an increase in imports and thus to a current account deficit. The increasing differences between inflation rates in different countries led to the final collapse of the system, suggesting that it was unable to cope with such variation.

Furthermore, a flexible exchange rate system allows the authorities to utilise monetary policy in order to stabilise the economy – remember that under a fixed exchange rate system monetary policy has to be devoted to the exchange rate target.

Stability

When it comes to stability, a fixed exchange rate system has much to commend it. After all, if firms know that the government is committed to maintaining the exchange rate at a given level, they can agree future contracts with some confidence. Under a floating exchange rate system, trading takes place in an environment in which the future exchange rate has to be predicted. If the exchange rate moves adversely, firms then face potential losses from trading. This foreign exchange risk is reduced under a fixed rate regime.

In a climate where speculative activity creates volatility in exchange rates, international trade may be discouraged because of the exchange rate risk. The effects of such volatility can be mitigated to some extent by the existence of **futures markets**. In such a market, it is possible to buy foreign exchange at a fixed price for delivery at a specified future date.

 Key **term**

futures market: a market in which it is possible to buy a commodity at a fixed price for delivery at a specified future date; such a market exists for foreign exchange

For example, suppose a firm is negotiating a deal to buy component parts for a manufacturing process that will be delivered in 3 months' time. The firm can buy the foreign exchange needed to close the deal in the futures market, and then knows that the contract will be viable, having negotiated a price for the components based on the known exchange rate, rather than on the unpredictable rate that will apply at that future date. The firm may of course have to pay a price for the foreign currency that is below the current (*spot*) exchange rate, but, as the future rate has been built into the terms of the contract, that will not affect the viability of the deal. The process by which a firm avoids losses by buying forward is known as *hedging*.

However, even with the use of hedging to reduce the risk, it is costly to engage in international trade when exchange rates are potentially volatile, so world trade is unlikely to be encouraged under such a system. Of course, it might be argued that the risk to firms under a fixed exchange rate system is still present, in the sense that a government may choose to realign its currency, with even greater costs to firms that are tied into contracts. However, such realignments were rare under Bretton Woods, and are more predictable than the volatility that can occur on a day-to-day basis in the foreign exchange market.

Macroeconomic policy

Critics of the flexible exchange rate system argue that it is too flexible for its own good. If governments know that the exchange rate will always adjust to maintain international competitiveness, they may have no incentive to behave responsibly in designing macroeconomic policy. Thus, they may be tempted to adopt an inflationary domestic policy, secure in the knowledge that the exchange rate will bear the burden of adjustment. In other words, a flexible exchange rate system does not impose financial discipline on individual countries.

An example of this was seen in the UK in the early 1970s when Britain first moved to a floating exchange rate regime. Money supply was allowed to expand rapidly, and inflation increased to almost 25%, aided by the oil price shock. Other examples are evident in Latin America, where hyperinflation affected many countries during the 1980s and early 1990s. For the country itself, such policies are costly in the long run, as reducing inflation under flexible exchange rates is costly. If interest rates are increased in order to reduce domestic aggregate demand and thus reduce inflationary pressure, the high return on domestic assets encourages an inflow of hot money, thereby putting upward pressure on the exchange rate. This reduces the international competitiveness of domestic goods and services, and deepens the recession.

There may also be spillover effects on other countries. Suppose that two countries have been experiencing rapid inflation, and one of them decides to tackle the problem. It raises interest rates to dampen domestic aggregate demand, which leads to an **appreciation** of its currency. For the other country, the effect is a **depreciation** of the currency. (If one currency appreciates, the other must depreciate.) The other country thus finds that its competitive position has improved, and it faces inflationary pressure in the short run. It may then also choose to tackle inflation, which in turn will affect the other country. These spillover effects could be minimised if the countries were to harmonise their policy action.

Key terms

appreciation: a rise in the exchange rate within a floating exchange rate system

depreciation: a fall in the exchange rate within a floating exchange rate system

The exchange rate and macroeconomic policy

The discussion above has shown that the relationship between the exchange rate and macroeconomic policy is an important one. Under a fixed exchange rate system, the need to maintain the value of the currency is a constraint on macroeconomic policy, and forces the economy to adjust to disequilibrium through the real economy. On the other hand, it does have the benefit of imposing financial discipline on governments.

Under floating exchange rates the relationship with policy is less obvious. With a flexible exchange rate, the authorities can use monetary policy to stabilise the economy, knowing that there will be overall balance on the balance of payments. Nonetheless, the government needs to monitor the structure of the balance of payments. When interest rates are set at a relatively high level compared with other countries, the financial account will tend to be in surplus because of capital inflows, with a corresponding deficit on the current account. This may not be sustainable in the long run.

Summary

➤ There are strengths and weaknesses with both fixed and floating exchange rate systems. A floating exchange rate system is more robust in enabling economies to adjust following external shocks, but it can lead to volatility and thus discourage international trade. A fixed rate system has the added advantage of imposing financial discipline on governments, and may allow policy harmonisation.

➤ The move towards a fixed exchange rate system within the European Union is partly in recognition that international trade is encouraged by stability in trading arrangements, and is discussed in the next chapter.

➤ Under a floating exchange rate system, much of the burden of adjustment to external shocks is borne by changes in the exchange rate, rather than by variations in the level of economic activity, which may be affected more under a fixed exchange rate system.

➤ A fixed exchange rate system offers stability, in the sense that firms know the future value of the currency, whereas under a floating rate regime there is more volatility.

➤ A fixed exchange rate system imposes discipline upon governments, and may facilitate international policy harmonisation.

Exercise 7.3

Critically evaluate the following statements, and discuss whether you regard fixed or floating exchange rates as the better system.

a A flexible exchange rate regime is better able to cope with external shocks.

b A fixed exchange rate system provides a more stable trading environment and minimises risk.

c Floating exchange rates enable individual countries to follow independent policies.

d A fixed exchange rate system may encourage governments to adopt distortionary policies such as tariffs and non-tariff barriers in order to control imports.

Monetary union and international competitiveness

The economic landscape of Europe since the Second World War has been shaped by the move towards ever-closer economic integration. The UK has been part of this, although at times a seemingly reluctant participant, choosing not to become part of the Eurozone when it was established in 2002. The economic arguments in favour of closer economic integration are partly based on notions of comparative advantage and the potential gains of allowing freer trade. However, there are other pertinent issues to be taken into consideration in evaluating the costs and benefits of closer integration. Such integration also has political ramifications that can affect an individual country's attitude towards its potential partners.

In this chapter, the history of economic integration in Europe is set out, and the nature of alternative forms of integration is highlighted. You do not need to have a detailed knowledge of the early history of economic integration in Europe. However, it is helpful to be aware of how the relationships between countries in Europe have evolved over time. Two major steps towards economic integration have taken place in the period since 1990. On 1 January 1993, the Single European Market (SEM) came into operation. Then, on 1 January 2002, 12 European countries adopted the euro as their common currency. The expansion of the SEM in 2004 to incorporate ten new members was a further significant development. This chapter highlights these developments and assesses their impact on the economic performance of the UK, referring to relevant areas of economic analysis that help in analysing the costs and benefits of closer economic integration. It also investigates steps that the UK government has taken to affect the international competitiveness of the UK economy.

After studying this chapter, you should:
➤ be aware of the different forms that economic integration may take: free trade areas, customs unions, common markets and economic and monetary union
➤ be able to explain why integration does not always operate as economic analysis suggests
➤ be familiar with the chronology of moves towards closer European integration
➤ appreciate the position of Europe in the global economy
➤ evaluate the costs and benefits of membership of a single currency area
➤ be aware of the role and effectiveness of monetary and fiscal policy within a single currency area
➤ be able to evaluate the arguments for and against the UK joining the Eurozone
➤ understand the significance of the SEM
➤ evaluate the costs and benefits of membership of a single currency area
➤ be aware of the role and effectiveness of monetary and fiscal policy within a single currency area
➤ be able to evaluate the arguments for and against the UK joining the Eurozone
➤ be familiar with the factors that influence international competitiveness
➤ be aware of the relative competitiveness of the UK in the world economy, and the changing importance of the manufacturing and service sectors
➤ appreciate the degree of openness of the UK economy
➤ understand ways in which government intervention has influenced the competitiveness of UK economic activity

Economic integration

Economies are becoming more interdependent over time. One aspect of this process deserves close attention, namely the growing formal integration of economies in regional groupings. This has been a gradual process, but it has accelerated as the technology of transport and communications has been transformed and as markets have been deregulated — especially financial markets, a process which has allowed the increased free movement of financial capital between countries.

There are many examples of such regional trade agreements. The European Union is perhaps one of the most prominent — and one of the furthest advanced, but there are also examples in the Americas (NAFTA, MERCOSUR), Asia (ASEAN, APEC), Africa (COMESA) and elsewhere. These agreements are at varying stages in the integration process. In addition, there has been a proliferation of regional trade agreements, and the World Trade Organisation has estimated that there are some 400 agreements that are scheduled to be implemented by 2010. This may partly reflect the slow progress made in the latest round of trade negotiations — the Doha Development Agenda. There has been much debate as to whether these agreements are stepping stones to further global cooperation, or whether they may turn out to be obstacles to that process.

The process of regional trade integration entails four successive stages, under which countries link their economies more closely together. The stages are as follows:

➤ free trade area

➤ customs union

➤ common market

➤ economic and monetary union

These successive stages reflect different degrees of closeness. The underlying motivation for integration is to allow trading partners to take advantage of the potential gains from international trade, as illustrated by the law of comparative advantage. This states that countries can gain from specialising in the production of goods and services in which they hold a comparative advantage, and by engaging in trade. For example, if one country has a comparative advantage in producing wine, and another has a comparative advantage in producing cars, then both countries can be made better off if they each specialise in producing what they are good at making, and then trade with each other. By reducing the barriers to trade, this specialisation can be encouraged, so there should be potential gains from the process. In practice, there may be other economic and political forces at work that affect the nature of the gains, and the extent to which integration will be possible — and beneficial.

The notion of a **free trade area** is that countries within the area agree to remove internal tariff and quota restrictions on trade between them, while still allowing member countries to impose their own pattern of tariffs and quotas on non-members.

A **customs union** is one notch up from a free trade area, in the sense that in addition to eliminating tariffs and quotas between the member nations, a common external tariff wall is set up against non-member nations. Again, the prime reason for establishing a customs union is to encourage trade between the member nations.

Such increased trade is beneficial when there is **trade creation**. This is where the formation of the customs union allows countries to specialise more, and thus to exploit their comparative advantage. The larger market for the goods means that more economies of scale may be available, and the lower prices that result generate additional trade between the member nations. These lower prices arise partly from the exploitation of comparative advantage, but

 Key *terms*

free trade area: a group of countries that agree to remove tariffs, quotas and other restrictions on trade between the member countries, but have no agreement on a common barrier against non-members

customs union: a group of countries that agree to remove restrictions on trade between the member countries, and set a common set of restrictions (including tariffs) against non-member states

trade creation: the replacement of more expensive domestic production or imports with cheaper output from a partner within the trading bloc

also from the removal of tariffs between the member nations. However, given the common external tariff, it is quite possible that members of the union are not the most efficient producers on the global stage. So there may be a situation of **trade diversion**. This occurs where a member country of a customs union imports goods from other members *instead* of from more efficient producers elsewhere in the world. This may mean that there is no net increase in trade, but simply a diversion from an external source to a new source within the union. In this situation, there are not necessarily the same gains from trade to be made.

Key term

trade diversion: the replacement of cheaper imported goods by goods from a less efficient trading partner within a bloc

A **common market** adds to the features of a customs union by harmonising some aspects of the economic environment between them. In a pure common market, this would entail adopting common tax rates across the member states, and a common framework for the laws and regulations that provide the environment for production, employment and trade. A common market would also allow for the free movement of factors of production between the member nations, especially in terms of labour and capital (land is less mobile by its nature!) Given the importance of the public sector in a modern economy, a common market would also set common procurement policies across member governments, so that individual governments did not favour their own domestic firms when purchasing goods and services. The Single European Single Market (discussed below) has encompassed most of these features, although tax rates have not been harmonised across the countries that are included.

Key term

common market: a set of trading arrangements in which a group of countries remove barriers to trade among them, adopt a common set of barriers against external trade, establish common tax rates and laws regulating economic activity, allow free movement of factors of production between members and have common public sector procurement policies

Moving beyond a common market, there is the prospect of full **economic and monetary union**. This entails taking the additional step of adopting fixed exchange rates between the member states. This in turn requires member states to follow a common monetary policy, and it is also seen as desirable to harmonise other aspects of macroeconomic policy across the union. The following discussion shows how these stages were present in the development of the European Union.

Key term

economic and monetary union: a set of trading arrangements the same as for a common market, but in addition having fixed exchange rates between the member countries and a common monetary policy

Evolution of the European Union

The European Union is one of the most prominent examples of regional trade integration, and has progressed further than most in evolving towards economic and monetary integration. It is thus instructive to examine how the process took place.

More than 50 years ago, Robert Schuman (French foreign minister at the time) proposed that France and West Germany should pool their coal and steel resources. That was the beginning of the long road towards European integration. Although integration has been primarily a question of economics, the political background cannot be ignored. To some people, integration of the countries within Europe was an attempt to avoid the conflict and wars that had afflicted Europe in the past.

The European Coal and Steel Community was established in 1951, with six participating countries: Belgium, France, West Germany, Italy, Luxembourg and the Netherlands. These same countries then formed the European Economic Community (EEC) in 1957. This became known as the *Common Market*. Since then the Community has evolved, drawing in more countries and expanding the scope of its operations. Table 8.1 sets out a chronology of the key events in the development of the present European Union (EU).

9 May 1950	Robert Schuman proposes that France and West Germany pool their coal and steel resources
1951	Treaty of Paris: European Coal and Steel Community (ECSC) is established by Belgium, France, West Germany, Italy, Luxembourg and the Netherlands
1957	Treaties of Rome: European Economic Community (EEC/'Common Market') and European Atomic Energy Community (EURATOM) are established by the six ECSC countries.
1967	Institutions of the EEC merge: a single Commission, a single Council of Ministers and a European Parliament; now known as the European Community (EC)
1970	Werner Plan proposes European monetary unity.
1973	Denmark, Ireland and the UK join the EC
1979	The European Monetary System (EMS) is launched, including the Exchange Rate Mechanism (ERM), a precursor of the single currency.
1981	Greece joins the EC
1985	Single European Market Act contains plans for completing the internal market within Europe
1986	Spain and Portugal join the EC
1989	The Delors Plan sets out proposal for creating European Economic and Monetary Union (EMU), including a single currency and European Central Bank
September 1990	The UK joins the ERM
September 1992	The UK leaves the ERM
1 January 1993	The Single Market comes into effect
November 1993	Treaty of Maastricht comes into force, creating the European Union (EU)
1995	Austria, Finland and Sweden join the EU
1 January 2002	12 EU countries adopt the euro as their currency; Denmark, Sweden and the UK are not part of this group
2004	Cyprus, the Czech Republic, Estonia, Hungary, Latvia, Lithuania, Malta, Poland, Slovakia and Slovenia join the EU

Table 8.1 *Chronology of European integration*

The 10 countries that joined in May 2004 brought the membership of the EU to 25 countries in all (the 'EU25'). Figure 8.1 shows the population size of these 25 countries in 2004, and the years in which they joined. Bulgaria and Romania were judged not to be ready to join in 2004, but were in the queue; negotiations with Turkey began in 2005, but quickly ran into problems. If Turkey were to join, this would add a massive 71.7 million citizens to the EU.

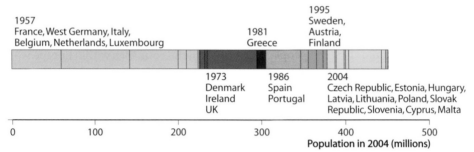

Figure 8.1 *The population of EU25*

Source: data from the World Development Report 2006.

Figure 8.2 shows how the enlarged EU would stand in the world rankings of big countries. This underlines the fact that the 15 pre-2004 member countries of the EU (the 'EU15') already contained more people than the USA; the combined population of the EU25 member states in 2004 was 455 million, compared with 293.5 million in the USA. With Bulgaria, Romania and Turkey (the EU28), the total population would be 556.8 million.

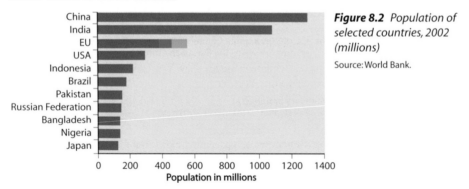

Figure 8.2 *Population of selected countries, 2002 (millions)*

Source: World Bank.

But how important is sheer size of population? After all, what matters in a market is the *effective* demand for goods and services — in other words, demand backed up by real purchasing power. So it is important to look not only at population size, but also at purchasing power. For example, average levels of GDP per capita in US dollars could be a way of trying to judge purchasing power. There will be substantial variation here, with the poorest EU acceding country, Latvia, having a GDP per capita of US$7,035 in 2005, compared with an estimated US$22,359 for Cyprus.

However, comparisons of GDP in US dollars can be quite misleading. Such measurements do not necessarily reflect local purchasing power because they are based on a conversion from local currency into US dollars using official exchange rates. This can give a distorted view of the comparison of income between countries, especially if the US dollar itself is away from its equilibrium level.

Figure 8.3 presents an alternative way of looking at the relative average income levels of the new member countries. The data here relate to GDP per capita measured in purchasing power parity dollars (PPP$), which helps to avoid the distortionary effects of official exchange rates. The data have then been converted into index number form, so that for each country the index shows GDP per capita relative to the EU27 average (the EU27 comprises the EU25, plus Romania and Bulgaria). For example, the index for the UK is 117.5, showing that the UK enjoys GDP per capita that is 17.5% higher than the average level in the EU27. For Latvia the index is 58, meaning that its average income is 58% of the EU27 average. Notice that the joining members all have lower GDP per capita than the existing members, with the sole exception of Portugal. This has implications for the size of effective demand coming from the additional consumers in the single European market, and also implications for the *pattern* of consumer demand in terms of the sorts of goods and services that are in demand.

Figure 8.4 compares the overall structure of economic activity in the EU15 and New13, as measured by the contribution of the major sectors to gross value added. The left-hand column shows how important the service sector has become in the structure of economic activity,

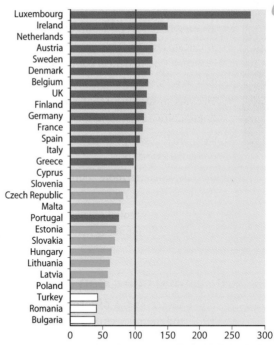

Figure 8.3 *Index of GDP per capita, 2007 (EU27 = 100)*

Source: europa.eu.nt

Note: the EU27 comprises EU25 plus Romania and Bulgaria.

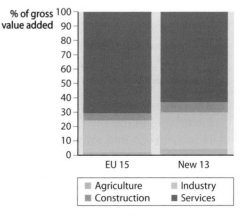

Figure 8.4 *The structure of economic activity in the EU, 2001*

Source: Eurostat.

Note: data include Bulgaria, Romania and Turkey as well as those that joined the EU in May 2004.

contributing some 71% of GDP of the EU15 on the value-added measure in 2001. In the acceding countries, agriculture, industry and construction are relatively more important than in the EU15. Thus there may be scope for gains from trade.

Summary

➤ Practical steps towards economic integration in Europe began with the formation of the European Coal and Steel Community in 1951, whereby six countries agreed to pool their coal and steel resources.

➤ This was so successful that it was replaced by the more wide-ranging European Economic Community (EEC), established in 1957.

➤ Over the following years, the EEC expanded the scope of its operations and the number of participating nations.

➤ By 2004, when ten more countries were granted membership, the combined membership in population terms represented some 455 million people.

➤ There was substantial diversity in the member countries in both living standards and the structure of economic activity.

The Single European Market (SEM)

From the moment of formation of the European Economic Community (EEC) in 1957, the member countries began working towards the creation of a single market in which there would be free movement of goods, services, people and capital. In other words, the idea was to create a *common market* in which there would be no barriers to trade. The EEC was a *customs union* in which internal tariffs and non-tariff barriers were to be removed and a common tariff was to be set against the rest of the world.

The main focus in the early years of the EEC was on coal and steel, together with the introduction of the Common Agricultural Policy (CAP). Initially, the objective of the CAP was to produce as much food as cheaply as possible, but the focus has changed in more recent years, especially since the reforms introduced in 2003.

A package of measures that came into effect in January 1993 might be seen as the final stages in the evolution of the SEM. The key measures were the removal (or reduction) of border controls and the winding down of non-tariff barriers to trade within the EU. In this way, physical, technical and fiscal barriers were removed. It has also become increasingly easy for people to move around within the EU, with passport and customs checks being abolished at most internal borders. Associated with these measures were a number of expected benefits.

Transaction costs

Tariff barriers between EU countries were abolished under the Treaty of Rome, but a range of non-tariff barriers had built up over the years as countries sought to protect domestic employment. It was expected that the removal of these obstacles to trade, combined with the removal of border controls, would reduce the costs of trade within the EU. However, it is difficult to gauge the significance of these transaction cost savings, as it is not easy to quantify them.

Economies of scale

As trade increases, firms will find that they are operating in a larger market. This should allow them to exploit more fully the economies of large-scale production. From society's point of view, this should lead to a more efficient use of resources, as long as the resulting trade creation effects are stronger than any trade diversion that may take place.

It seems that the nature of technological change in recent years has favoured the growth of large-scale enterprises. Improved transport and communications have contributed to this process. The SEM has enabled firms in Europe to take advantage of these developments.

The Common Agricultural Policy led to the creation of huge reserves of grains as well as other agricultural commodities.

Intensified competition

Firms will find that they are facing more intense competition within that larger market from firms in other parts of the EU. This then brings up the same arguments that are used to justify privatisation – that intensified competition will cause firms or their managers to seek more efficient production techniques, perhaps through the elimination of X-inefficiencies. This again is beneficial for society as a whole.

However, a note of caution needs to be sounded here. The argument that economies of scale are there to be tapped has led to the growth of some giant firms, formed through a process of merger and acquisition, often involving cross-border deals. For example, Vodafone Airtouch acquired Mannesmann AG in 2000 for a reported £100 billion, and became one of Britain's largest companies. There is a danger that these large firms will gain sufficient market power as to be in a position to make monopoly profits — at the expense of the consumer. This could occur either through a firm reaching a monopoly position, or through cooperation between a few large firms in an oligopoly market. The regulation of such large firms could be problematic, especially where they are operating on a European scale, rather than just within a domestic market. It is in this context that the European Commission has developed its own competition authority, which has the power to operate competition policy across the EU as a whole.

From the perspective of individual countries, there has been a divergence of views concerning these large firms. In some countries, large firms have been seen as 'national champions'. These have been protected (or even subsidised) by domestic governments, based on the argument that they will then be better prepared to compete in the broader European market. Elsewhere, governments have taken the view that the only way to ensure that domestic firms are lean enough to be competitive in overseas markets is to face intense competition at home, as an inducement to efficiency.

Who gains most from the SEM?

As trade within Europe becomes freer, two groups of countries stand to gain the most. First, the pattern of comparative advantage between countries will be important. Many EU countries are advanced industrial nations, where labour is expensive relative to capital. These countries tend to specialise in manufacturing or capital-intensive service activities, and already have fairly similar structures. It is thus possible that the relatively labour-abundant countries of southern Europe may gain more from closer integration and an expansion of trade. This is because they have a pattern of comparative advantage that is significantly different from existing members. This diversity was reinforced by the new entrants who joined in May 2004.

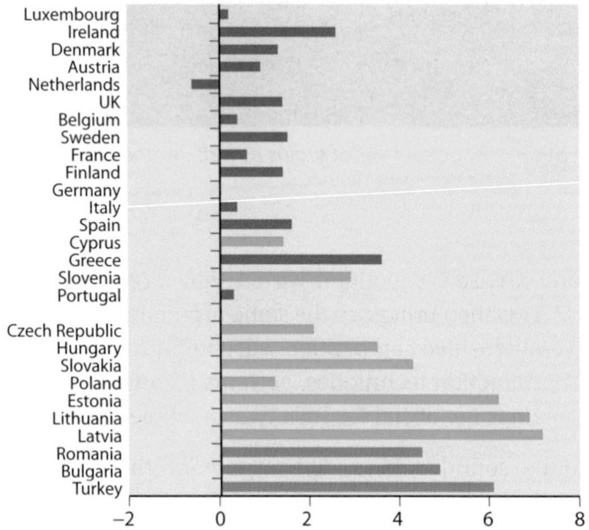

Second, if the main effect of integration is to remove barriers to trade, the countries with the most to gain may be those that begin with relatively high barriers.

Figure 8.5 shows growth rates in the countries in 2001–02, just before the enlargement of 2004. This shows that the joining members were, on the whole, enjoying more rapid economic growth than the EU15

Figure 8.5 Growth of GDP per capita, EU28, 2001–2002

Note: no data available for Malta.

Source: World Development Report 2003.

countries. The enlargement thus may have the effect of introducing new *dynamic economies*, and this may have spillover effects for the other member nations.

How important is this to the UK?

An important piece of background information is that, over the years, UK trade has become increasingly focused on Europe. This means that the UK depends heavily on trade with other countries in the EU, so successful economic performance cannot be seen in isolation from events in the broader market.

Summary

> The prime objective of the EEC was to create a single market in Europe, in which there would be free movement of goods, services, people and capital.

> The EEC was a customs union, in which internal tariffs and non-tariff barriers were to be removed and a common tariff was set against the rest of the world.

> The EEC also established the Common Agricultural Policy to protect agriculture and to produce as much food as cheaply as possible.

> The Single Market package came into effect at the beginning of 1993, freeing up trade between participating countries and winding down non-tariff barriers.

> This was expected to encourage trade by lowering transaction costs, enabling firms to reap economies of scale, and enhancing efficiency by stimulating competition between European firms.

Exercise 8.1

Explain why it might be the relatively labour-intensive countries of southern Europe — and the countries of Eastern Europe and the Baltic that joined in 2004 — that stand to gain most from the SEM.

The single currency area

The establishment of the SEM was seen by some as an end in itself, but others regarded it as a step towards full monetary integration, in which all member states would adopt a single currency, thereby reducing the transaction costs of international trade even more. However, full monetary union and the adoption of a common currency is about much more than transaction costs and has raised considerable debate, not least because of the political dimension. Critics of closer integration are concerned about the loss of sovereignty by individual countries. This concern is partly an economic one, focusing on the loss of separate currencies and (perhaps more significantly) the loss of control over national economic policy.

The European Monetary System

The foundations for monetary union began to be laid down in 1979, with the launch of the European Monetary System (EMS). One aspect of the EMS was the Exchange Rate Mechanism (ERM), which can be seen as a precursor of the single currency. As discussed in Chapter 7, those countries that chose to opt into the ERM agreed to maintain their exchange rates within a band of plus or minus 2.25% against the average of their currencies — known as the European Currency Unit (ECU). The UK remained outside the ERM except for a brief flirtation between September 1990 and September 1992. During this period, the UK was operating within a slightly wider (6%) band.

During the period of the EMS/ERM, it was recognised that occasional realignment of currencies might be needed, and in fact there were 11 realignments between 1979 and 1987. However, the conditions under which such realignments were permitted were gradually tightened, so that they became less frequent as time went by.

Another key feature of the EMS period was the removal of capital controls. During the early part of this period, most of the member nations restricted the movement of financial capital across borders. This gave them some scope for using monetary policy independently of other countries. However, it was agreed that such capital controls would be phased out.

The Delors Plan, issued in 1989, set out proposals for creating European economic and monetary union (EMU), together with plans for a single currency and a European central bank. It was crucial to establish a European central bank because, with a single currency, a central bank is needed to administer monetary policy throughout the EU.

Treaty of Maastricht

The next major step was the Maastricht Treaty, which created the European Union (EU). This treaty encompassed not only economic issues, such as the introduction of the single currency, but also aspects of social policy, steps towards creating a

The signing of the Maastricht Treaty.

common foreign, security and defence policy, and the development of a notion of European 'citizenship'.

It was considered that, if a single currency was to be established, the participating nations would need to have converged in their economic characteristics. If the countries were too diverse in their economic conditions, the transition to a single currency would be costly. For example, if they had very different inflation rates, interest rates or levels of outstanding government debt, the tensions of union might be too great to sustain. Strong countries would be dragged down, and weak countries would be unable to cope. The Maastricht Treaty therefore set out the *convergence criteria* by which countries would be eligible to join the single currency area. These criteria covered aspects of both monetary and fiscal policy.

Monetary policy

This is obviously important, as monetary union entails the centralisation of monetary policy within the EU. If there is to be a single currency and a single central bank to control interest rates or money supply, the monetary conditions of the economies concerned need to be reasonably close before union takes place. It was thus important to evaluate whether countries were sufficiently close to be able to join with minimal tension.

Inflation

Could countries with widely different inflation rates successfully join in a monetary union? One view is that it would be unreasonable to expect a country with 10% or 20% inflation to join a monetary union along with a country experiencing inflation at just 1%. An alternative view is that it is equally unreasonable to expect a country to cure its inflation before joining a union when one of the alleged benefits of joining is that it will cure inflation by enforcing financial discipline and removing discretion over monetary policy from individual states. However, the first criterion specified by the treaty was that countries joining the union should be experiencing low and similar inflation rates — defined as inflation no more than 1.5% above the average of the three countries in the EMS with the lowest rate.

Interest and exchange rates

Given that financial capital tends to follow high interest rates, it is argued that diversity of interest rates before union may be undesirable, as this would imply instability of capital movements. Similarly, it has been argued that a period of exchange rate stability before union would be some indication that countries have been following mutually consistent policies, and would indicate that union is plausible.

The criteria set out in the treaty required that long-term interest rates be no more than 2% above the average of the three EMS countries with the lowest rate, and that each joining country should have been in the narrow band of the ERM for a period of 2 years without the need for realignment.

Fiscal policy

Should there also be conformity in fiscal stance between countries? Would there be severe problems if countries embarked upon union and policy coordination in conditions in which unemployment rates differed markedly? These are separate but related questions. If unemployment is high, this will be connected (via social security payments) with the fiscal stance adopted by the government — as judged in terms of the government budget deficit.

The reason why unemployment rates are relevant is that there may need to be fiscal transfers between member states in order to reduce the differentials. This will clearly be politically significant in the context of a monetary union, and is an issue that will affect the long-term viability of the union. However, although unemployment rates are potentially important for this reason, the convergence criteria did not refer to unemployment directly. Instead, the criteria included a reference to fiscal policy. In practice, the divergence in unemployment rates was substantial.

Two areas are critical in judging the distance between countries in terms of fiscal policy. First, there is the question of the short-term fiscal stance, which can be measured by the budget deficit. Second, it is important to consider some indication of a longer-term commitment to stability in fiscal policy, in terms of achieving sustainable levels of outstanding government debt. Thus, the treaty required that the budget deficit be no larger than 3% of GDP, and that the national debt be no more than 60% of GDP.

Economic and monetary union

The final stage of the transition towards the single currency was European Economic and Monetary Union (EMU). Under EMU, exchange rates between participating countries were permanently locked together: in other words, no further realignments were allowed. Furthermore, the financial markets of the countries were integrated, with the European Central Bank setting a common interest rate across the union. This was achieved in 1999.

Formation of the euro area

In the event, 11 countries were judged to have met the Maastricht criteria (Belgium, Germany, Spain, France, Ireland, Italy, Luxembourg, the Netherlands, Austria, Portugal and Finland). Together with Greece, these countries formed the single currency area, which came into operation on 1 January 2002.

Figure 8.6 shows how interest rates in some of the Eurozone countries moved from 1977 (2 years before the formation of the EMS) until the first year of the euro. The graph shows interest rates in each country as an index, with the average of the Eurozone countries at 100. You can see that, although there is some evidence that some of the countries were converging in the run-up to monetary union, there seems to have been little historical tendency for interest rates to move together. This is especially the case for Italy, which at times seemed to have followed opposite paths to the others. Germany showed consistently lower interest rates than most other countries. From 1999, however, convergence was forced under EMU, which meant an especially rapid adjustment for Italy. The graph also reveals how a different time path of interest rates was followed by the UK.

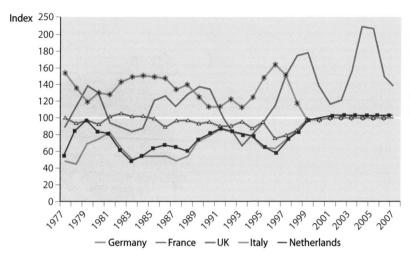

Figure 8.6
Interest rates in Europe 1977–2007 (EU12=100)

Source European Commission.

Germany — France — UK — Italy — Netherlands

Costs and benefits of a single currency

Some of the arguments for and against a single currency area such as the Eurozone are similar to those used in evaluating a fixed exchange rate system against a flexible one. This is because a common currency is effectively creating an area in which exchange rates between member nations are fixed for ever, even if that common currency varies relative to the rest of the world. The question of whether such an arrangement is beneficial overall for the member states rests on an evaluation of the benefits and costs of joining together. An *optimal currency area* occurs when a group of countries are better off with a single currency.

Benefits

The main benefits of a single currency area come in the form of a *monetary efficiency gain*, which has the effect of encouraging more trade between member countries. The hope is that this will bring further gains from exploiting comparative advantage between countries and enabling firms to reap the benefits of economies of scale.

The efficiency gain comes from two main sources. First, there are gains from reducing *transaction costs*, if there is no longer the need to convert from one currency into another. Second, there are gains from the *reduction in uncertainty*, in the sense that there is no longer a need to forecast future movements in exchange rates – at least between participating countries. This is similar to the gains from a fixed exchange rate system, but it goes further, as there is no longer a risk of occasional devaluation or revaluation of currencies.

The extent to which these gains are significant will depend upon the degree of integration between the participating nations. If most of the trade that takes place is between the participants, the gains will clearly be much more significant than if member nations are also trading extensively with countries outside the single currency area.

Costs

The costs come in the conduct and effectiveness of policy. Within the single currency area, individual countries can no longer have recourse to monetary policy in order to stabilise the macroeconomy. As with the fixed exchange rate system, one key question then is how well individual economies are able to adjust to external shocks. Thus, it is important for each economy to have flexibility.

In addition, individual countries have to be aware that, once in the single currency area, it is impossible to use monetary policy to smooth out fluctuations in output and employment.

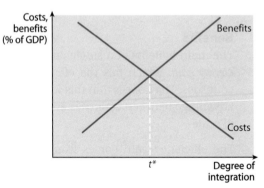

National currencies were replaced in the Eurozone from January 1999 by the euro.

In this context, it is very important that the business cycles of participating economies are well synchronised. If one economy is out of phase with the rest, it may find itself facing an inappropriate policy situation. For example, suppose that most of the countries within the Eurozone are in the boom phase of the business cycle, and are wanting to raise the interest rate in order to control aggregate demand: if one country within the zone is in recession, then the last thing it will want is rising interest rates, as this will deepen the recession and delay recovery.

Evaluation

Paul Krugman (who was awarded the Nobel Prize for Economic Science in 2008) has suggested a helpful way of using cost–benefit analysis to evaluate these aspects of a single currency area. He argues that both the costs and the benefits from a single currency area will vary with the degree to which member countries are integrated. Thus the benefits from joining such a currency area would rise as the closeness of integration increased, whereas the costs would fall.

Figure 8.7 *Costs and benefits of a single currency area*

Figure 8.7 illustrates the balance between costs and benefits. For countries that are not very closely integrated (that is, if 'integration' is less than t^*), the costs from joining the union exceed the benefits, so it would not be in the country's interest to join. However, as the degree of integration increases, so the benefits increase, and the costs decrease, so for any country beyond t^*, the benefits exceed the costs, and it is thus worth joining.

For an individual country considering whether or not to join the euro area, a first step is to reach a judgement on whether the country is to the left or to the right of t^*. There may be other issues to consider in addition to the costs and benefits, but unless the country has at least reached t^*, it could be argued that entry into the union should not be considered.

One way of viewing the situation is that the costs are mainly macroeconomic, but the benefits are microeconomic. This complicates the evaluation process. Some research published in 2006 argued that most of the boost to trade within the euro area occurred during the initial period, and would not continue to build up over time. It was also suggested that the EU countries that decided not to join the euro (Britain, Sweden and Denmark) gained almost as much as the countries that had joined. Nonetheless, it is important to view the euro area from the perspective of possible UK entry.

Exercise 8.2

Examine the problems that could arise if a country that is part of a single currency area enters a period of recession at a time when other countries in the union are in a boom.

The UK and the euro

The UK government's policy stance on membership of the euro was set out by the chancellor of the exchequer in October 1997 after only a few months of the new Labour government. This stance was essentially that, while in principle the government was in favour of UK membership, it would be prepared to enter only at a time when the economic conditions were right. Table 8.2 sets out the five economic tests that the chancellor specified as his conditions for deciding whether a case can be made for entry. You will see that these go beyond looking at the simple cost–benefit analysis, although clearly some of the criteria do relate to the closeness of integration, especially in terms of convergence.

	Test	Explanation
1	Convergence	Are business cycles and economic structures compatible so that UK citizens and others could live comfortably with euro interest rates on a permanent basis?
2	Flexibility	If problems emerge is there sufficient flexibility to deal with them?
3	Investment	Would joining EMU create better conditions for firms making long-term decisions to invest in Britain?
4	Financial services	What impact would entry into EMU have on the competitive position of the UK's financial services industry, particularly the City's wholesale markets?
5	Employment	Will joining EMU promote higher growth, stability and a lasting increase in jobs?

Table 8.2 *The chancellor's five tests*

Source: HM Treasury.

Convergence

Sustainable convergence is seen to be crucial if the UK is to be successful within the euro area. What sort of evidence should be looked for in order to judge whether the UK's business cycle is converging on Europe? The chancellor could look at fluctuations in GDP, to see whether the phase of GDP growth in the UK is in tune with the rest of Europe. However, if the concern is with interest rates because of their importance with respect to policy, it may make sense to look at interest rates directly.

Figure 8.6 showed that UK interest rates followed quite a different path to those of countries in the eurozone. Figure 8.8 shows the growth rates of GDP for France, Germany, the UK and the USA. Although there is perhaps more similarity evident towards the end of this period, there are certainly times when growth rates have diverged significantly, which would have created problems in the context of EMU. For example, look at Germany in the early 1990s.

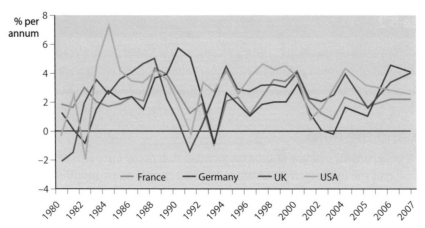

Figure 8.8 *Growth rates of GDP, selected countries, 1980–2007*
Source: OECD.

Another aspect of this issue that makes the convergence test especially important for the UK is the nature of the housing market. A larger proportion of home owners in the UK hold mortgages on a variable interest rate basis than their counterparts elsewhere in Europe, where fixed-rate mortgages are more common. This makes interest rates a particularly sensitive issue.

It is also argued that, in any approach to entry, the exchange rate is critical. The brief experience of the UK trying to tie its currency to the Exchange Rate Mechanism in the early 1990s illustrates the dangers of joining with the exchange rate at too high a level, and this is a mistake that the Treasury does not want to repeat.

Flexibility

The convergence test is concerned with whether the UK's business cycle is sufficiently synchronised with the Eurozone. The flexibility test is about what would happen if this were not the case, or if the UK fell out of line. In other words, if the UK were to be out of phase, would the economy be sufficiently flexible to be able to get back into line in the absence of an independent monetary policy? It is about resilience.

It is quite difficult to measure flexibility in this sense, and there is no simple indicator that gives a ready judgement about whether an economy is sufficiently flexible to deal with situations that may or may not occur.

The key issues here concern the flexibility of markets, and the extent to which fiscal policy can be activated in order to help stabilise the economy, should that be deemed necessary. One danger is that inflation could become more variable if the UK joins the euro, as happened to Ireland. This is because at present the exchange rate is able to fluctuate in order to accommodate differences between national economies.

In the Treasury's assessment of the tests published in June 2003, the flexibility test was said to have been failed. Although the UK labour market was found to be relatively flexible, the Treasury identified a number of areas needing improvement. In particular, it argued that regional pay differentials were insufficient to reflect differences between the regions in the demand and supply of labour, and that there was a significant skills gap between the UK and the Eurozone members. It was also difficult to judge whether the UK tax system could be sufficiently flexible to allow rapid stabilisation. In these circumstances, it is hard to say whether or not any convergence would be sustainable.

Investment

The issue for investment revolves around the incentives for firms to invest in the UK. There are two aspects to this. First, there is the question of UK-based firms, and whether they would find membership of the Eurozone conducive to investment. Second, there is the question of overseas firms, and the conditions under which they would be prepared to invest in the UK.

The question of whether firms would be prepared to invest more if the UK were part of the Eurozone depends in part on the success of the economy in meeting the convergence and flexibility tests. If firms have high expectations about the future, they will be more prepared to invest, so if they see the UK as thriving within the euro area, this will be beneficial.

An additional consideration concerns the reduction in foreign exchange risk within the single currency area. This might encourage investment by reducing the risk premium required by firms considering investment.

Inward foreign direct investment (FDI) may depend on a number of factors. In particular, there may be US or Japanese firms looking to gain a foothold in Europe – will they choose the UK? Figure 8.9 shows annual FDI into the UK between 1965 and 2007, expressed as a percentage of GDP. A striking feature of the graph is the

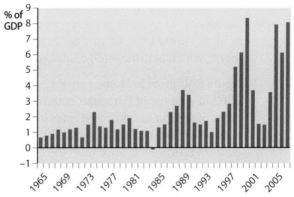

Figure 8.9 *Foreign direct investment in the UK (inward), 1965–2007*

Source: ONS.

way that FDI appeared to boom towards the end of the 1990s, only to fall back quite dramatically in 2001–03. It is important to be a little careful in interpreting this pattern. It might be tempting to argue that the launching of the euro area at the beginning of 2002 may have contributed to the fall, with the UK becoming less attractive as a destination for FDI because of its decision not to join the euro. However, it is equally likely that the fall reflected the global reduction in flows of FDI following the 9/11 terrorist attacks in the USA. The graph shows that there was a recovery of inward FDI to the UK after 2004. The fact that there are often multiple factors influencing economic decisions is a common problem in economics.

Financial services

The fourth test concerns financial services. In the June 2003 Treasury analysis, this was the only test that the UK economy was judged to have passed. The financial services sector was singled out for a special mention because of its importance in the structure of the UK economy. The UK is seen to have a significant comparative advantage in wholesale financial services, and it was accepted that the City is the pre-eminent financial centre in Europe. There was thus a concern that becoming part of the single currency area would damage the competitiveness of this sector.

The evidence here seems to suggest that the UK financial sector benefits from EMU even with the UK being outside the euro area, but that it would gain even more if the UK were to join. Financial services have become a significant item in the balance of payments, with a positive balance of more than £31 billion in 2007. This is a substantial share of the overall surplus in trade in services, which was about £41.7 billion. If the UK were a full member of the single currency area, it is likely that this balance would be even more positive.

Growth, stability and employment

The final test relates to whether becoming part of the euro zone would promote higher growth, stability and a lasting increase in jobs in the UK. This might be interpreted as an overall assessment of the potential success of the single currency in the long run. However, this test cannot be divorced from the others. In particular, sustainable convergence (i.e. convergence plus flexibility) would be expected to influence firms' expectations about the future and could affect their willingness to invest, which in turn would contribute to the rate of economic growth.

Figure 8.10 provides some context, showing rates of unemployment in 1991 and 2007 in a range of European countries. The countries are ranked in descending order of their unemployment rates in 2007. It is evident that the UK in 1991 experienced an unemployment rate that was above the average of the euro area countries. However, since then the UK rate has fallen appreciably, while the euro average rate has increased. The relativities between countries seem to have altered quite a lot over this period, with Germany showing a substantial increase and Ireland a dramatic decrease.

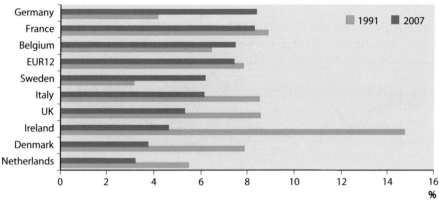

Figure 8.10 *Unemployment in Europe, 1991 and 2007*
Source: European Commission.

Exercise 8.3

Identify the costs and benefits that would be associated with the UK's entry into the euro single currency group of countries, and discuss whether you believe that the UK should join when the time is right.

International competitiveness

In analysing the UK's position within Europe, the relative competitiveness of British goods and services is an important issue. In the previous chapter, it was seen that the UK has persistently shown a deficit on the current account over a long period of time, but especially in the 2000s. Does that imply that UK goods are uncompetitive in international markets? In order to investigate this, and to evaluate its importance, it is first necessary to examine how competitiveness can be measured, and the factors that affect it.

The demand for UK exports in world markets depends upon a number of factors. In some ways, it is similar to the demand for a good. In general, the demand for a good will depend on its price, on the prices of other goods, and on consumer incomes and preferences. In a similar way, you can think of the demand for UK exports as depending on the price of UK goods, on the price of other countries' goods, and on incomes in the rest of the world and foreigners' preferences for British goods over those produced elsewhere. However, in the case of international transactions the exchange rate will also be relevant, as this determines the purchasing power of UK incomes in the rest of the world. Similarly, the demand for imports into the UK will depend upon the relative price of domestic and foreign goods, incomes in the UK, preferences for foreign and domestically produced goods and the exchange rate. These factors will all come together to determine the balance of demand for exports and imports.

The exchange rate plays a key role in influencing the levels of both imports and exports. Figure 8.11 shows the time path of the US$/£ exchange rate since 1971. It shows some fluctuations between 1971 and the late 1980s, although around a declining trend. However, since then the exchange rate seems to have remained fairly steady.

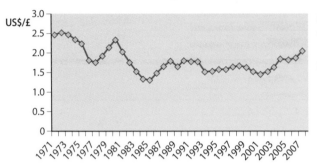

Figure 8.11 *The nominal exchange rate, US$/£, 1971–2007*

Source: ONS.

Nonetheless, there was a fall from a peak of $2.50 to the pound in 1972 to $1.50 some 30 years later. Other things being equal, this would suggest an improvement in the competitiveness of UK products. In other words, Americans wanting to buy UK goods got more pounds for their dollars in 2002 than in 1972, and thus would tend to find UK goods more attractive.

However, some care is needed, because other things do not remain equal. In particular, remember that the competitiveness of British goods in the US market depends not only on the exchange rate, but also on movements in the prices of goods over time, so this needs to be taken into account — which is why Figure 8.11 refers to the *nominal exchange rate*. In other words, if the prices of UK goods have risen more rapidly than prices in the USA, this will partly offset the downward movement in the exchange rate.

Figure 8.12 shows the nominal exchange rate again, but also the ratio of UK/US consumer prices. This reveals that between 1971 and 1977 UK prices rose much more steeply than those in the USA, and continued to rise relative to the USA until the 1990s. Thus, the early decline in the nominal exchange rate was offset by the movement in relative prices.

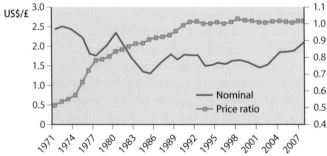

Figure 8.12 *The nominal exchange rate, US$/£, and the ratio of UK/US prices, 1971–2007*

Source: ONS, IMF.

In order to assess the overall competitiveness of UK goods compared with the USA, it is necessary to calculate the **real exchange rate**, which is defined as the nominal exchange rate multiplied by the ratio of relative prices.

The real exchange rate is shown in Figure 8.13. The real exchange rate also shows some fluctuations, especially between about 1977 and 1989. However, there does not seem to be any strong trend to the series, although the real rate was higher at the end of the period than at the beginning.

Key term

real exchange rate: the nominal exchange rate adjusted for differences in relative inflation rates between countries

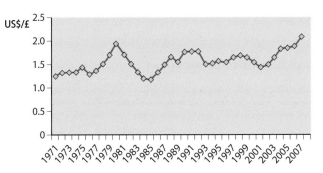

Figure 8.13 The real exchange rate. US$/£, 1971–2007

Notice that this series relates only to competitiveness relative to the USA, as it is the real US$/£ exchange rate. An alternative measure is the *sterling effective exchange rate*, shown in Figure 8.14. This shows the strength of sterling relative to a weighted average of exchange rates of the UK's trading partners.

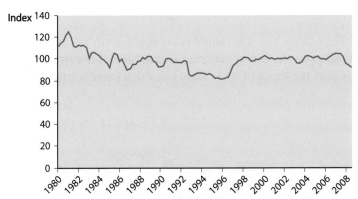

Figure 8.14 The sterling effective exchange rate, 1980–2008 (2005 = 100)

Source: Bank of Enland.

Exercise 8.4

Table 8.3 provides data for the €/£ exchange rate, together with the consumer price index for the euro area and for the UK. Use these data to calculate the real exchange rate for the period, and comment on the effect that any movement will have had on the competitive-ness of British goods and services relative to the euro area.

| | Nominal exchange rate (€/£) | Consumer price index (2000 = 100) | |
		UK	Euro area
2000	1.6422	100.0	100.0
2001	1.6087	101.8	102.4
2002	1.5909	103.5	104.7
2003	1.4456	106.5	106.9
2004	1.4739	109.7	109.2
2005	1.4629	112.8	111.6
2006	1.4670	116.4	114.0
2007	1.4619	121.3	116.4

Table 8.3 *Competitiveness of the UK compared to the euro area*
Source: OECD, IMF.

The terms of trade

A final indicator to consider is the **terms of trade**. This is defined as the ratio of export prices to import prices, and provides information about the purchasing power of exports in terms of imports.

Key term

terms of trade: the ratio of export prices to import prices

A fall in the terms of trade indicates that the same volume of exports will purchase a smaller volume of imports than before. A downward movement in the terms of trade is thus unfavourable for an economy. Figure 8.15 shows the terms of trade for the UK economy since 1970. The substantial fall that is seen in 1973 and 1974 is due to the adverse oil price shock that occurred at that time. However, it would seem from this figure that the terms of trade have remained fairly constant since the early 1980s.

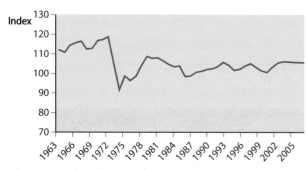

Figure 8.15 *The UK terms of trade, 1963–2007 (2001 = 100)*

Source: ONS.

The terms of trade are calculated purely with respect to prices, and take no account of changing volumes of trade. In other words, a deterioration in the terms of trade does not necessarily mean that an economy is worse off, so long as the volume of trade is increasing sufficiently rapidly.

Edexcel A2 Economics

Summary

➤ Relative prices and the exchange rate are an important influence on the competitiveness of goods and services in the international market.

➤ The real exchange rate adjusts the nominal exchange rate to allow for differing inflation rates between countries.

➤ The terms of trade are measured by the ratio of export prices to import prices.

International differences in productivity

From a different angle, competitiveness also depends upon relative costs of production in different countries, which influences the prices that firms can charge. This in turn partly reflects different levels of productivity across countries. Remember that productivity is a measure of productive efficiency; for example, labour productivity is output per unit of labour input. Different countries show appreciable differences in efficiency by this measure.

However, international comparisons of productivity are not straightforward, as measurements are subject to differences in data collection and differences in work practices. Figure 8.16 presents data for 2007 on GDP per head of population, expressed as index numbers with the USA being the reference country, and thus set to 100. On this measure, the UK performs rather better (or at least no worse) than Japan, France, Germany, Italy and Spain. As a measure of productivity levels, however, this is a misleading indicator. In particular, working hours are longer in the UK than in many other countries (especially within Europe), so in part GDP per head reflects differences in the quantity of labour input.

For this reason, GDP per hour worked is often seen as a more reliable indicator of relative productivity levels. This measure is graphed in Figure 8.17, and shows quite a different pattern. Indeed, on this basis

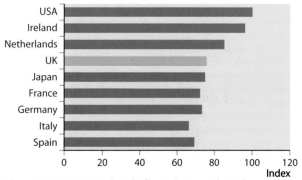

Figure 8.16 *GDP per head of population, selected countries, 2007 (USA = 100)*

Source: OECD.

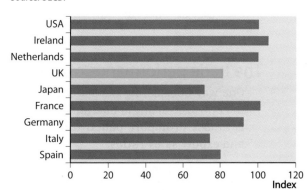

Figure 8.17 *GDP per hour worked, selected countries, 2007 (USA = 100)*

Source: OECD.

both Ireland and France show higher productivity than the USA, and the UK's performance is much more modest.

Figure 8.18 gives the time path for an index of GDP per hour worked, based this time on 1970 = 100. It shows that European countries have been experiencing stronger productivity growth than the USA over this period.

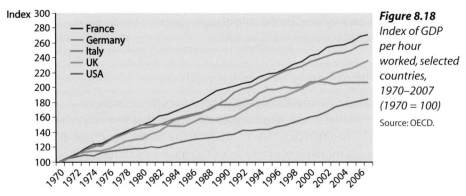

Figure 8.18
Index of GDP per hour worked, selected countries, 1970–2007 (1970 = 100)

Source: OECD.

It is also important to realise that labour productivity is not the only relevant measure, as countries may also differ in their use of capital. Total factor productivity is more difficult to measure, as the measurement of capital stock is especially prone to error and misinterpretation. However, some estimates of multifactor productivity growth are shown in Figure 8.19.

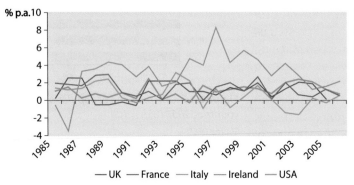

Figure 8.19
Multifactor productivity growth, selected countries, 1985–2007

Source: OECD.

The trade performance of the UK economy

One way of exploring the performance of the British economy in international trade is to look at **import penetration ratios** and **export sales ratios**.

The import penetration ratio measures the portion of home demand that is met by imports of particular commodities. As a measure, this is a little difficult to interpret where a sector is engaged in exporting as well as importing activity; for example, the

Key terms

import penetration ratio: ratio of the percentage of imports of a product to home demand

export sales ratio: ratio of the percentage of exports of a product to total manufacturers' sales

import penetration ratio (without allowing for exporting) shows that imports of office machinery and computers were 223% of home demand in 2006. It therefore is more helpful to allow for exports by measuring import penetration for a commodity as the percentage ratio of imports to (home demand + exports). Some examples for 2006 are shown in Figure 8.20.

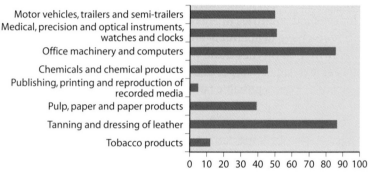

Figure 8.20 *Import penetration ratio*, selected commodities, 2006*

* Ratio of imports to [home demand + exports].

Source: ONS.

Similarly, Figure 8.21 shows export sales ratios, again allowing for the fact that trade is often two way, so that some allowance has to be made for importing activity, rather than just considering the ratio of exports to total sales.

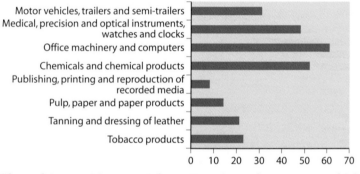

Figure 8.21 *Export sales ratio*, selected commodities 2006*

* Ratio of exports to [total sales + imports].

Source: ONS.

These data provide some information about the extent to which British firms are active in international trade. For example, the commodity group of office machinery and computers shows an import penetration ratio of 86%: in other words, imports make up 86% of home demand plus exports. However, you can also see that export sales constitute 61% of total sales plus imports. In contrast, both import penetration and export sales ratios for publishing, printing and reproduction of recorded media are relatively low, suggesting much less engagement in international trade in this activity. In the case of the tanning and dressing of leather, import penetration is relatively high but the export sales ratio is relatively low, suggesting that this is a product in which the UK does not have a comparative advantage, relying on imports and not engaging in much exporting activity.

There have been some significant changes in these ratios since 1992. Sectors in which import penetration has risen include pharmaceuticals; TV, radio and phone transmitters; jewellery and related products; coal extraction; and tobacco products. Import penetration has fallen for sports goods and toys; oil and gas extraction, 'other textiles'; and special purpose machinery. The rapid growth of output (and exports) by the UK service industries between 1992 and 2006 has meant that very few service products have high import penetration ratios.

Openness to international trade

The extent to which economies are open to international trade varies substantially. One way of measuring this is to calculate the ratio of exports plus imports to GDP, as has been done for selected countries in Figure 8.22. Countries like Hong Kong, Malaysia and South Korea have deliberately encouraged international trade as a route to economic growth, hoping that trade will give rise to economies of scale. Indeed, Hong Kong is an extreme example of this, with both exports and imports exceeding the value of GDP. This is possible because the data include re-exports — where products are imported and then exported again. For countries like Hong Kong and Singapore, where trading activity itself is part of their comparative advantage, such transactions are important. At the other extreme, Japan and the USA show a low dependence on international trade. In the case of Brazil, India, Argentina and China, trade dependence is relatively low because of a deliberate policy to limit their dependence on trade. In all of these cases, the ratio of trade to GDP has increased noticeably since 1990 — especially in the case of China, which has opened up rapidly, and is expanding both imports and exports.

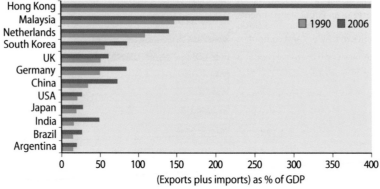

Figure 8.22 *Openness to trade, selected countries, 1990 and 2006**

*[Exports + imports] as % GDP.

Source World Bank.

Figure 8.23 presents the share of UK exports and UK imports in GDP since 1950. This shows a gradual increase in the UK's openness to trade, but conceals substantial

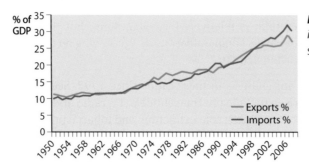

Figure 8.23 *UK exports and imports in GDP, 1950–2007*

Source: ONS.

Edexcel A2 Economics

changes in the direction of trade; these were discussed in Chapter 6, which high-lighted the increasing importance of the EU as a trading partner.

Summary

➤ Competitiveness can depend upon the relative costs of production in different countries, which in turn partly reflects differences in productivity.

➤ Data for international comparison of productivity differences need to be treated with some care, but GDP per hour worked is a helpful indicator.

➤ Labour productivity is not a sufficient measure, given that countries differ in their relative endowments of labour, capital and other factors of production.

➤ Information about the pattern of trade is provided by import penetration and export sales ratios.

➤ Import penetration ratios have been relatively low for UK service industries, which have expanded rapidly.

➤ The extent to which countries are open to international trade varies substantially around the world.

➤ In the UK exports and imports have increased as a share of GDP, but at a relatively slow pace.

Trade and the UK government

There are a number of ways in which policies adopted by governments have affected UK trade and competitiveness. Some of these policies were deliberately targeted at trade or competitiveness; others may have had different objectives.

Deregulation and privatisation

The British economy has gone through a process of deregulation and privatisation since 1980 that has had a major impact on many parts of the economy. One of the main aims of the privatisation drive that began in the 1980s was to reduce X-inefficiency by making the managers of formerly state-run enterprises more accountable. As efficiency improved, British firms experienced an improvement in their cost structures that should have improved competitiveness. For example, if the privatisation of power generation leads to productivity gains that allow electricity to be supplied at a lower price, this reduces costs for firms throughout the economy.

However, deregulation also entailed changes in many other sectors. Of particular relevance for trade and competitiveness is the liberalisation of financial markets that also took place. Such measures as the removal of restrictions on capital movements encourage trade. The advances in the technology of communications have reinforced this by enabling rapid, reliable and efficient financial transactions.

Foreign direct investment

The UK government has introduced policies to attract foreign direct investment (FDI). These may encourage trade directly. For example, if a Japanese car manufacturer chooses to build a factory in the UK in order to supply the European market, this will have an effect on UK exports. However, it will also mean an outflow of dividend payments to Japanese shareholders at a later date, so the effects on the balance of payments may not be as great as they first appear.

However, there may also be indirect effects. If a Japanese firm becomes successful operating in the UK, it is possible that working practices used by the firm may spread to other UK firms, which in turn may improve their efficiency and thereby make them more competitive internationally. Indeed, the very presence of foreign firms competing in the domestic market may be a spur for domestic firms to become more efficient.

Labour market flexibility

One of the most important policy areas as far as trade and competitiveness is concerned has been the increased flexibility in labour markets that has been encouraged by successive governments. For example, the trade union reforms that were introduced by the Thatcher government during the 1980s enabled firms to adopt more flexible working practices, and enabled labour markets to adjust more easily to changes in the pattern of consumer demand and in the UK's comparative advantage.

Furthermore, improvements in education and training have increased the skill levels of the labour force, improving productivity directly and also encouraging the growth of economic activities requiring higher skills levels. This flexibility in adjusting to a changing market environment has improved British industry and service activity and enabled firms to take advantage of new trading opportunities. In particular, the EU Single Market has encouraged British firms to compete within Europe, where labour markets tend to be less flexible. In this way, the UK has been able to maintain a competitive edge.

Moreover, these policies, which have produced a flexible labour market and a skilled workforce, have increased the attractiveness of the UK as a destination for foreign direct investment, since foreign multinationals value these characteristics.

Managing the balance of payments

It was argued earlier that, although in the short run it may be possible to balance a deficit on the current account of the balance of payments by a surplus on the financial account, in the long run this might not be sustainable. The main reason for this is that there may be a limit on foreign exchange reserves and on the extent to which it is desirable to fund the current account by borrowing or by selling UK assets.

The question then is how the government could manage the balance of payments; in other words, how is it possible to alter the structure of transactions by reducing the size of the current account deficit? There are three basic routes that could contribute to this if the government decided that it needed to do so: demand management, supply-side policies or exchange rate adjustments.

The high income elasticity of demand for imported goods has led to a deficit on the UK current account.

Demand management

One reason for a current account deficit is that, as real incomes rise in the economy, there is a tendency for UK residents to buy more imported goods or services, because the income elasticity of demand for imports tends to be relatively high. One possibility therefore would be to control the level of aggregate demand in order to limit the demand for imports; for example, the government could raise taxes, or reduce government expenditure. Whether the government would want to do this may depend upon whether such a policy would damage other aspects of the economy. For example, a reduction in aggregate demand might cause an increase in unemployment, and if the government gave a higher priority to achieving full employment it might prefer to live with the current account deficit. It is also possible that long-run economic growth could be inhibited.

The alternative would be to introduce a policy that was targeted more towards reducing the demand for imports. For example, the use of tariffs or quotas would raise the price of imports, and so reduce demand for them, and at the same time encourage domestic producers to increase their production. However, within the context of the EU it is not realistic to imagine that the UK could set its own independent tariff rates, even if it wanted to do so. In any case, it has already been explained that the use of tariffs entails a misallocation of resources in society, and a deadweight loss.

Supply-side policies

An alternative approach would be to make use of supply-side policies to influence the deficit. Many of the policies discussed earlier in this chapter that have affected trade and competitiveness fall into this category; for example, policies to improve the flexibility of the labour market would be classified as supply-side policies. If these can improve the competitiveness of British firms, they should stimulate trade.

In addition, it might be argued that steps taken to increase the productive capacity of the economy would allow an increase in exports that would (*ceteris paribus*) reduce the current account deficit.

Notice that the extent of the gain depends in part upon the import content of UK exports. Remember, from the discussion of penetration ratios and export sales ratios, that many exporting sectors also import from abroad. For example, component parts might be imported into the country, assembled and then re-exported. This may limit the gain from increasing exports.

Nonetheless, supply-side policies are an effective way of improving the competitiveness of the British economy, thereby reducing a current account deficit.

Exchange rate adjustment

The competitiveness of British exports and of domestic goods and services relative to imports both depend crucially on the exchange rate, as was mentioned earlier. Notice that it is important to note that the exchange rate will influence the size of the current account deficit. Under policy procedures in the early 2000s, the prime target of macroeconomic policy was to keep inflation at a low level. This was achieved by the Bank of England setting interest rates at the level needed to hit the inflation target. If the interest rate required for this purpose is high relative to elsewhere in the world, there will tend to be flows of financial capital into the UK. In turn, this suggests that the equilibrium for the exchange rate will be relatively high, which limits the competitiveness of British goods and services and results in a balance of payments that is achieved through a current account deficit and a financial account surplus. In this way, the government may be restricted in the extent to which it can manipulate the exchange rate to reduce the current account deficit, unless it is prepared to give a higher priority to this than to other targets of macroeconomic policy. This helps to explain why it is supply-side policies that have been at the forefront in ensuring the competitiveness of British firms in international markets.

Summary

> Trade and competitiveness have been affected by government policy, both directly and indirectly.

> Privatisation has led to productivity improvements by reducing X-inefficiency.

> Deregulation of financial markets, coupled with improved technology for undertaking financial transactions, has encouraged international trade.

> Policy measures were introduced to encourage foreign direct investment, which may have had beneficial spillover effects on domestic firms.

> Measures to improve the flexibility of labour markets have helped to make British firms competitive internationally.

> Improved education and skills training have also contributed to the competitiveness of British firms.

> Demand management could be used to reduce a deficit on the current account of the balance of payments, but governments may be reluctant to use this approach if it damages targets for full employment or economic growth.

> Supply-side policies have encouraged trade by improving the efficiency of UK industry.

chapter  8

> In principle, exchange rate adjustments could be used to influence the balance of payments, but careful attention needs to be given to the effects on other targets of macro-economic policy.

Exercise 8.5

Figure 8.24 shows the current account deficits of the UK and the USA, expressed as a percentage of GDP. Discuss the extent to which this represents a potential problem for the two countries. Does it make a difference that the US dollar plays a role as a reserve currency?

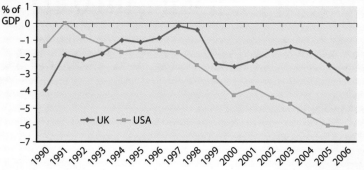

Figure 8.24
Current account deficits, UK and USA

Source: World Bank.

Chapter 9

Poverty and inequality in developed and developing countries

In all societies there is some inequality in the distribution of income and wealth, although the extent of inequality varies between countries. Indeed, one of the gravest economic challenges facing the world today is the global inequity in the distribution of resources. Worldwide, it is estimated that in 1999 more than a billion people were living in what the United Nations regard as absolute poverty. Furthermore, there were 114 million primary-age children who were not enrolled for school, more than a billion people without access to safe water, and 24 billion without access to sanitation. This chapter explores ways of measuring inequality and poverty in both developed and developing countries, looks at some of the causes of inequality and discusses some of the policies that are used to affect the distribution of income and wealth.

Learning outcomes

After studying this chapter, you should:
➤ understand what is meant by economic and human development
➤ be familiar with the most important economic and social indicators that can help to evaluate the standard of living in different societies
➤ be aware of significant differences between regions of the world in terms of their level and pace of development
➤ recognise the strengths and limitations of economic and social indicators in providing a profile of a country's stage of development
➤ be familiar with ways of identifying and monitoring inequality, including Lorenz curves and the Gini index
➤ be familiar with ways of measuring relative and absolute poverty

➤ be aware of the changing pattern of inequality in the UK
➤ understand the main causes of inequality and poverty
➤ be familiar with policies designed to affect the distribution of income and wealth

Developed and developing countries

In considering the global economy, it is apparent that there is a divide; there are some countries that have gone through a process of economic and human development to reach a high standard of living, but there are many other countries that have failed to make progress in this way. In seeking to analyse inequality, there are therefore two crucial dimensions that need to be taken into account. On the one hand, it is important to be aware of inequality between nations, and the gap in living standards that exists between different regions of the world. However, it is also important to be aware that there is inequality within societies — even within the most developed economies in the world. The first step in examining these issues is to identify the developed and developing countries in the world.

Defining development

What is meant by 'development'? You might think that it is about economic growth — if a society can expand its productive capacity, surely that is development? But development means much more than this. Economic growth may well be an *essential* ingredient, since development cannot take place without an expansion of the resources available in a society; however, it is not a *sufficient* ingredient, because those additional resources must be used wisely, and the growth that results must be the 'right' sort of growth.

Wrapped up with development are issues concerning the alleviation of poverty — no country can be considered to be 'developed' if a substantial portion of its population is living in absolute poverty. Development also requires structural change, and possibly changes in institutions and, in some cases, cultural and political attitudes.

The Millennium Development Goals

In September 2000, the 189 member states of the United Nations met at what became known as the *Millennium Summit.* They agreed the following declaration:

> We will spare no effort to free our fellow men, women and children from the abject and dehumanising conditions of extreme poverty to which more than a billion of them are currently subjected.

This was a global recognition of the extreme inequality that is a feature of the world distribution of resources. Before beginning to analyse these important questions, it is important to identify what is meant by 'development', and to recognise the symptoms of under development. Once the symptoms have been identified, explanations can be sought.

As part of the Millennium Summit, it was agreed to set quantifiable targets for a number of dimensions of development, in order to monitor progress. These are known as the **Millennium Development Goals (MDGs)**, and will be the starting point for learning to recognise the symptoms of underdevelopment.

There are eight goals, each of which has specific targets associated with it.

Key term

Millennium Development Goals (MDGs): targets set for each less-developed country, reflecting a range of development objectives to be monitored each year to evaluate progress

Goal 1: Eradicate extreme poverty and hunger

The target for goal 1 is to halve the proportion of people whose income is less than $1 per day, and to halve the proportion of people suffering from hunger, between 1990 and 2015. The alleviation of such extreme poverty is essential for development to take place. This will be monitored through the following indicators:

➤ proportion of population living on less than $1 per day

➤ poverty gap ratio (incidence × depth of poverty)

➤ share of poorest quintile in national consumption

➤ prevalence of underweight children under 5 years of age

➤ proportion of population below the minimum level of dietary energy consumption

Goal 2: Achieve universal primary education

The target here is to ensure that by 2015 all children everywhere will be able to complete a full course of primary schooling. Education is seen as an essential feature of the process of development, as it provides the knowledge that is needed for people to use resources effectively. The indicators are:

➤ net enrolment ratio in primary education

➤ proportion of pupils starting grade 1 who reach grade 5

➤ literacy rate of 15- to 24-year-olds

Goal 3: Promote gender equality and empower women

This target aims to eliminate gender disparity in primary and secondary education, preferably by 2005, and in all levels of education no later than 2015. Gender inequality is widespread in less-developed countries, and means that large numbers of women are disadvantaged. Indicators are:

➤ ratio of girls to boys in primary, secondary and tertiary education

➤ ratio of literate females to males among 15- to 24-year-olds

➤ share of women in waged employment in the non-agricultural sector

➤ proportion of seats held by women in national parliament

Goal 4: Reduce child mortality

This target is to reduce the under-5 mortality rate by two-thirds between 1990 and 2015. The indicators are:

➤ under-5 mortality rate

➤ infant mortality rate

➤ proportion of 1-year-old children immunised against measles

Goal 5: Improve maternal health

The target is to reduce the maternal mortality ratio by three-quarters between 1990 and 2015. The indicators specified to monitor this target are:

➤ maternal mortality ratio

➤ proportion of births attended by skilled health personnel

Goal 6: Combat HIV/AIDS, malaria and other diseases

The target is to have halted, and begun to reverse, the spread of HIV/AIDS and the incidence of malaria and other major diseases by 2015. The impact of HIV/AIDS and other diseases has been felt especially in sub-Saharan Africa, and is having adverse effects on the age structure of the population in many less-developed countries. Indicators will cover:

➤ HIV prevalence among 15- to 24-year-old pregnant women

➤ contraceptive prevalence rate

➤ number of children orphaned by HIV/AIDS

➤ prevalence and death rates associated with malaria

➤ proportion of population in malaria-risk areas

➤ prevalence and death rates associated with tuberculosis (TB)

➤ proportion of TB cases detected and cured under DOTS (directly observed treatment short course)

Goal 7: Ensure environmental sustainability

The targets here are to integrate the principles of sustainable development into country policies and programmes and to reverse the loss of environmental resources, to halve the proportion of people without sustainable access to safe drinking water by 2015, and to have achieved a significant improvement in the lives of at least 100 million slum dwellers by 2020. Development must be *sustainable*, in the sense that the foundations for future development need to be laid in such a way that they do not endanger the resources available for future generations. The indicators are:

➤ change in land area covered by forest

➤ extent of land area protected to maintain biological diversity

- GDP per unit of energy use

- carbon dioxide emissions (per capita)

- proportion of population with sustainable access to an improved water source

- proportion of population with access to improved sanitation

- proportion of population with access to secure tenure

Goal 8: Develop a global partnership for development

The target here is to develop further an open, rule-based, predictable, non-discrim-inatory trading and financial system, including a commitment to good governance, development and poverty reduction, both nationally and internationally. A wide range of indicators will be used to monitor this in relation to *official development assistance* (ODA), *market access*, *debt sustainability* and some other targets. The need for international cooperation in ensuring development is pressing and will be a recurring theme over the following chapters — it is crucial if globalisation is to be beneficial to all nations.

This final goal is less focused than the other seven, but no less important. There is a widespread view that less-developed countries have been disadvantaged by the international trading system, and that richer countries have been insufficiently cooperative — partly in terms of the amount of overseas assistance (ODA) that has been provided, but also in terms of a reluctance of some developed countries to open their markets to products from less-developed countries.

ODA was the subject of an earlier UN summit in the 1970s, at which the more-developed countries promised to provide overseas assistance. Indeed, there was a specific commitment that 0.7% of developed countries' GDP would be devoted to this purpose.

'Market access' refers to the difficulty experienced by developing countries seeking to increase exports to the developed world in order to earn more foreign exchange. This target is aimed especially at landlocked and small island developing states, but market access is not a problem for these countries alone.

'Debt sustainability' refers to the difficulties that many countries have experienced in paying off their accumulated debt. This has been a major problem in recent years, especially in sub-Saharan Africa, where some countries are devoting more resources to paying off debts than to providing education and healthcare for their people. The issue is being addressed by the HIPC (Heavily Indebted Poor Countries) initiative, which has made some progress.

Other targets relate to youth unemployment, access to affordable essential medical drugs and access to new technology, especially in the fields of information and communications.

These eight goals represent the key facets of development that need to be addressed, and they constitute an enormous challenge for the period up to 2015, especially as progress in the early years has been slow and uneven. In thinking

A UN summit in the 1970s led to the commitment that 0.7% of developed countries' GDP would be set aside for development aid.

about these goals, you can begin to understand the various dimensions of development, and realise that development is about much more than economic growth — although growth may be seen as a prerequisite for the achievement of the goals. At the same time, failure to achieve these goals will retard economic growth.

Summary

➤ Economic growth is one aspect of economic development, in that it provides an increase in the resources available to members of society in less-developed countries.

➤ However, in addition, development requires that the resources made available through economic growth are used appropriately to meet development objectives.

➤ The Millennium Development Goals were set by the Millennium Summit of the United Nations in September 2000.

➤ These goals comprise a set of targets for each less-developed country, to be achieved by 2015.

Exercise 9.1

Choose two or three less-developed countries in different regions of the world. Visit the Millennium Development Goals website at **www.developmentgoals.org**. Discuss the extent to which progress is being made towards the goals for your chosen countries.

Which are the less-developed countries?

In its *Human Development Report 2007/08*, the United Nations Development Programme (UNDP) identified 137 countries or areas as 'developing'. In addition, there are 28 transition economies in Central and Eastern Europe and the

Commonwealth of Independent States (CIS). However, the range of countries that fall in this definition of 'developing' is very wide, including countries such as Singapore and South Korea, which were also classified as being in the 'high-income' bracket. In the discussion that follows this wide range of countries will be referred to as *less-developed countries* (*LDCs*), and the discussion will be illustrated by examples from a selection of countries from different regions of the world.

In broad terms, the countries regarded as LDCs are concentrated in four major regions: sub-Saharan Africa, Latin America, South Asia and South East Asia. This excludes some countries in the 'less-developed' range, but relatively few. For some purposes it may be necessary to treat China separately, rather than including it as part of South East Asia, partly because of its sheer size, and partly because it has followed a rather different development path.

It is very important when discussing economic development to remember that there is wide diversity between the countries that are classified as LDCs, and although it is tempting to generalise, you need to be a little wary of doing so. Different countries have different characteristics, and face different configurations of problems and opportunities. Therefore, a policy that might work for one country may fail totally in a different part of the world.

Indicators of development

GDP per capita

One measure of the level of development is GDP per capita — the average level of income per person in the population. For reasons outlined in *AS Economics, Chapter 11*, the preferred measure is GDP per capita measured in purchasing power parity dollars (PPP$). This is important, because using official exchange rates to convert from local currency into US dollars can be misleading. The US$ measure understates the *real* purchasing power of income in LDCs, but what is of interest is exactly that, i.e. the relative command over resources that people in different countries have.

Figure 9.1 shows the relative size of GDP per capita in PPP$ for the regional groupings of countries around the world in 2005. The gap in income levels between the LDCs and the high-income OECD countries shows very clearly in the figure;

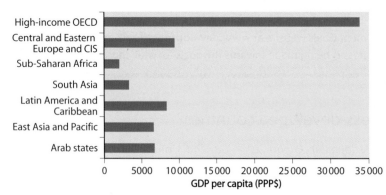

Figure 9.1
GDP per capita, regional groupings, 2005 (PPP$)

Source: Human Development Report 2007/08.

equally, the gap between the countries of sub-Saharan Africa and South Asia and those in East Asia and Latin America is apparent. The figure also puts into context the position of the transition economies of Central and Eastern Europe and the CIS and the Arab states. The Arab states are rather different in character because of the oil resources that have enabled them to increase their average income levels.

Not all data are available on a regional basis, so in discussing the developing countries, a selected group of countries has been chosen as a focus, with three countries from each of the major four groupings. The GDP per capita (PPP$) levels in 2005 are shown in Figure 9.2. Because of the diversity of countries in each of the regions, such a selection must be treated with a little caution. Singapore, South Korea and China have been chosen to represent East Asia and the Pacific in order to highlight three of the countries that have achieved rapid economic growth over a sustained period, and the following discussion will highlight some of the factors that have enabled this to take place.

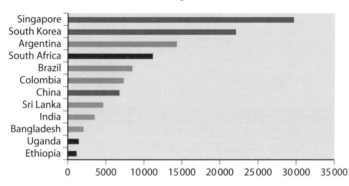

Figure 9.2 GDP per capita, selected countries, 2005 (PPP$)

Source: Human Development Report 2007/08

GDP has some limitations as a measure of living standards, even when measured in PPP$. One limitation that is especially important when considering low-income countries is that in many LDCs there is much *informal economic activity*, which may not be captured by a measure like GDP, based on monetary transactions. Such activity includes subsistence agriculture, which remains important in many countries, especially in sub-Saharan Africa. In other words, GDP may not capture production that is directly used for consumption.

However, the informal sector also encompasses many other forms of activity in both rural and urban areas, from petty traders, shoe-shiners and wayside barbers to small-scale enterprises operating in a wide range of activities. In 1999 the ILO estimated that the informal sector accounted for 50.2% of total employment in Ethiopia; in 2000 it was thought to account for 45.8% of total employment in India. This suggests the need for some caution in the use of GDP per capita data.

Income distribution and inequality

Another important limitation of GDP per capita as a measure of living standards is that it is an *average* measure, and so does not reveal information about how income is distributed among groups in society. One way of presenting data on this topic is to rank households in order of their incomes, and then calculate the share of total household income that goes to the poorest 10%, the poorest 20% and so on. When the groups are divided into tenths they are referred to as *deciles*; thus, the poorest 10% is the first decile, the next 10% is the second decile and so on. Similarly, the poorest 20% is the first *quintile*.

In Brazil, the poorest 10% of households received less than 1% of total income in the country in 1996, whereas the richest 10% received nearly half. In Belarus, on the other hand, the poorest 10% received 5% of income and the richest 10% received 20%. These are extreme examples of the degree of inequality in the distribution of income within countries.

These data are not very easy to assimilate, especially for a large number of countries, and to explore the question of income inequality, it is important to find a way of summarising the data to make it easier to interpret. Table 9.1 provides some summary data for a range of countries.

Country	Ratio of top decile to poorest decile	Ratio of top quintile to poorest quintile	Gini index
Ethiopia	6.6	4.3	30.0
Sierra Leone	87.2	57.6	62.9
Uganda	16.6	9.2	45.7
Bangladesh	7.5	4.9	33.4
India	8.6	5.6	36.8
Zimbabwe	22.0	12.0	50.1
Indonesia	7.8	5.2	34.3
China	21.6	12.2	46.9
Belarus	6.9	4.5	29.7
South Africa	33.1	17.9	57.8
Brazil	51.3	21.8	57.0
Malaysia	22.1	12.4	49.2
Hungary	5.5	3.8	26.9
Singapore	17.7	9.7	42.5
United Kingdom	13.8	7.2	36.0
United States	15.9	8.4	40.8
Japan	4.5	3.4	24.9

Table 9.1 *Inequality measures for selected countries*
Source: Human Development Report 2007/08.

By looking at the ratio of the richest decile or quintile to the poorest, it is possible to get some impression of the gap between the poorest and richest households. For example, in Sierra Leone the richest 10% of households receive 87.2 times more income than the poorest 10%, whereas in Hungary the gap is only five-fold.

One thing to notice about this table is that the countries are listed in ascending rank order of average income. If you cast your eye down the columns of the table, you will see that there is no very strong relationship between average income and the decile and quintile ratios. The contrast in the pattern of the income shares between Sierra Leone and Bangladesh is striking, but average income levels are not too different.

chapter  9

Evaluating inequality within a society

Inequality is present in all societies, and always will be. However, the degree of inequality varies from one country to another; and before exploring the causes of inequality, and the policies that might be used to influence how income and wealth are distributed within society, it is necessary to be able to characterise and measure inequality. This is important in order to be able to judge relative standards of living in different countries or different periods.

Table 9.2 presents some data for three developed countries. Notice that the unit of measurement is normally the household rather than the individual, on the presumption that members of a household tend to share their resources – a millionaire's life-partner may not earn any income, but he/she is not usually poor.

	UK, 1991	USA, 1997	Japan, 1993
First decile	2.6	1.8	4.8
First quintile	6.6	5.2	10.6
Second quintile	11.5	10.5	14.2
Third quintile	16.3	15.6	17.6
Fourth quintile	22.7	22.4	22.0
Top quintile	43.0	46.4	35.7
Top decile	27.3	30.5	21.7

Table 9.2 Distribution of income in the USA, the UK and Japan, by quintiles (%)

Source: World Development Report 2000/01.

It can be seen that in the UK households in the top decile receive ten and a half times more income than those in the poorest decile. On the basis of these data, inequality in the UK is lower than that in the USA, but higher than that in Japan.

The Lorenz curve

Although the usual types of graph are not well suited to presenting such data visually, there is a method of presenting the data visually via the Lorenz curve. Some Lorenz curves are shown in Figure 9.3.

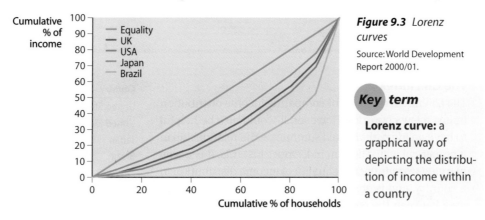

Figure 9.3 Lorenz curves

Source: World Development Report 2000/01.

Key term

Lorenz curve: a graphical way of depicting the distribution of income within a country

Lorenz curves are constructed as follows. Using the data in Table 9.2, the first step is to convert the numbers in the table into *cumulative* percentages. In other words (using the UK as an example), the data show that the poorest 20% receive 6.6% of total household income, the poorest 40% receive 6.6% + 11.5% = 18.1%, the poorest

60% receive 18.1% + 16.3% = 34.4%, and so on. It is these cumulative percentages that are plotted to produce the Lorenz curve, as in Figure 9.3. (The figure also plots the lowest and highest deciles.)

Suppose that income were perfectly equally distributed between households. In other words, suppose the poorest 10% of households received exactly 10% of income, the poorest 20% received 20% and so on. The Lorenz curve would then be a straight line going diagonally across the figure.

To interpret the country curves, the closer a country's Lorenz curve is to the diagonal equality line, the more equal is the distribution. You can see from the figure that Japan comes closest to the equality line, bearing out the earlier conclusion that income is more equally distributed in that country. The UK and the US curves are closer together, but there seems to be slightly more inequality in the USA, as its Lorenz curve is further from the equality line. Brazil has also been included on the figure, as an example of a society in which there is substantial inequality.

Exercise 9.2

Use the data provided in Table 9.3 to calculate the ratios of top decile income to bottom decile income, and of top quintile income to bottom quintile income. Then draw Lorenz curves for the two countries, and compare the inequalities shown for Belarus and South Africa with each other and with the countries already discussed.

| | Percentage share of income or consumption: | |
	South Africa	Belarus
Lowest decile	1.1	5.1
Lowest quintile	2.9	11.4
Second quintile	5.5	15.2
Third quintile	9.2	18.2
Fourth quintile	17.7	21.9
Highest quintile	64.8	33.3
Highest decile	45.9	20.0

Table 9.3 Income distribution in Belarus and South Africa

Source: World Development Report.

The Gini index

The Lorenz curve is fine for comparing income distribution in just a few countries. However, it would also be helpful to have an index that could summarise the relationship in a numerical way. The Gini index does just this. It is a way of trying to quantify the equality of income distribution in a country, and is obtained by calculating the ratio of the area between the equality line and the country's Lorenz curve to the whole area under the equality line. This is often expressed as a percentage (but sometimes as a proportion). The closer the Gini index is to 100, the further the Lorenz curve is from equality, and thus the more unequal is the income distribution. The Gini index values for the countries in Figure 9.1 are shown in Table 9.4.

Country	Gini index
United States	40.8
United Kingdom	36.1
Japan	24.9
Brazil	60.0

Table 9.4 The Gini index

Source: World Development Report.

Some measurement issues

When measuring income inequality, some important measurement issues need to be borne in mind. For example, in talking about the 'poorest' and 'richest' households, you need to be aware that absolute income levels per household may be a misleading indicator, given that households are of different sizes and compositions. Thus, when looking at the income distribution in the UK, it is important to make adjustments for this.

The way this is done is by the use of *equivalence scales*. These allow a household to be judged relative to a 'reference household' made up of a childless couple. It can then be decided that a household with a husband, wife and two young children rates as 1.18 relative to the childless couple with a rating of 1. So if the couple with two children had an income of, say, £40,000 per year, this would be the equivalent of 40,000/1.18 = £33,898. In order to examine the inequality of income, it is these equivalised incomes that need to be considered.

A further question is whether income is the most appropriate indicator. People tend to smooth their consumption over their lifetimes, and it has been argued that it is more important to look at consumption (expenditure) than income when considering inequality.

Then there is the question of housing costs. In the short run households have no control over their spending on housing. Some measures of inequality therefore choose to exclude housing costs from the calculations in order to focus on the income that households have at their disposal for other expenditures. As housing tends to constitute a higher proportion of the budgets of poor households, measures of inequality that exclude housing costs tend to show greater levels of inequality.

It is also important to bear in mind that the standard of living that households can achieve depends partly on government-provided services, such as health and education. Remember that rich as well as poor households may benefit from these.

Finally, in considering inequality in a society, it may be important to examine inequalities in the distribution of wealth as well as income. Wealth can be regarded as the accumulated stock of assets that households own, and in the UK wealth is more unequally distributed than income.

It is interesting to note that many people remain unaware of where they fit into the income distribution of their country. A survey in the USA in 2000 found that 19% of Americans believed that they were in the top 1% of earners.

The Human Development Index

Another criticism of GDP per capita as a measure of living standards is that it fails to take account of other dimensions of the quality of life. In 1990 the United Nations Development Programme (UNDP) devised an alternative indicator, known as the

Human Development Index (*HDI*), which was designed to provide a broader measure of the stage of development that a country had reached.

The basis for this measure is that there are three key aspects of human development: resources, knowledge of how to make good use of those resources, and a reasonable life span in which to make use of those resources (see Figure 9.4). The three components are measured by, respectively, GDP per capita in PPP$, indicators of education (adult literacy and school enrolment) and life expectancy. The measurements are then combined to produce a composite index ranging between 0 and 1, with higher values reflecting higher human development.

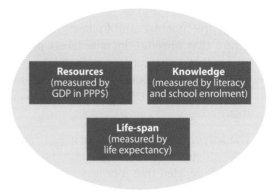

Figure 9.4 *Components of the Human Development Index*

Values of the HDI for 2005 are charted in Figure 9.5 for the selected countries. You can see that the broad ranking of the countries is preserved, but the gap between low and high human development is less marked. The exception is South Africa, which is ranked much lower on the basis of the HDI than on GDP per capita; in other words, South Africa has achieved relatively high income, but other aspects of human development have not kept pace. There are other countries in the world that share this feature. If you compare the data here with those for Figure 9.2, you will see that there are also countries that seem to perform better on HDI grounds than on GDP per capita — for example China and Sri Lanka.

Figure 9.6 shows the relative contribution of the three components of the HDI for this set of countries, and Figures 9.7 and 9.8 show the actual

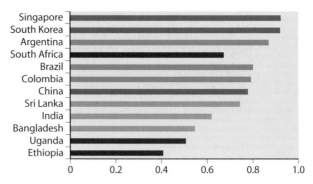

Figure 9.5 *The Human Development Index, selected countries*

Source: Human Development Report 2007/08.

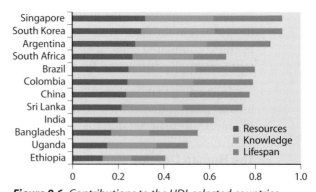

Figure 9.6 *Contributions to the HDI, selected countries*

Source: calculated from data in the Human Development Report 2007/08.

Edexcel A2 Economics

levels of two of the measures that enter into the HDI, i.e. life expectancy and adult literacy rates. It is clear that it is life expectancy that is primarily responsible for the low ranking of South Africa in the HDI, as its level of life expectancy is not very different from that of the other sub-Saharan African countries in the sample, even though its average income level is much higher. In contrast, Bangladesh performs quite well in terms of lifespan but relatively poorly in terms of education. By comparing these data, you can get some idea of the diversity between countries that was mentioned earlier.

In part, this diversity reflects differing priorities that governments have given to different aspects of development. Countries such as Brazil have aimed primarily at achieving economic growth, while those such as Sri Lanka have given greater priority to promoting education and healthcare.

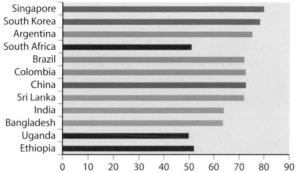

Figure 9.7 Life expectancy at birth (years), selected countries
Source: Human Development Report 2007/08.

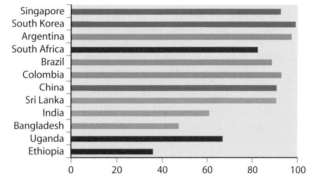

Figure 9.8 Adult literacy, selected countries (% of people aged 15 and over)
Source: Human Development Report 2007/08.

There is a view that growth should be the prime objective for development, since by expanding the resources available the benefits can begin to trickle down through the population. An opposing view claims that, by providing first for basic needs, more rapid economic growth can be facilitated. The problem in some cases is that growth has not resulted in the trickle-down effect, and inequality remains. It may be significant that countries such as Brazil and South Africa, where the GDP per capita ranking is high relative to the HDI ranking, are countries in which there remain high levels of inequality in the distribution of income.

Summary

➤ Less-developed countries (LDCs) are largely located in four major regions: sub-Saharan Africa, Latin America, South Asia and South East Asia.

➤ These regions have shown contrasting patterns of growth and development.

➤ Different countries have different characteristics, and face different configurations of problems and opportunities.

- GDP per capita is one measure of the standard of living in a country, but it has a number of shortcomings for LDCs.
- In particular, it neglects the importance of the informal sector, and fails to take into account inequality in the distribution of income.
- The Human Development Index (HDI) recognises that human development depends upon resources, knowledge and health, and therefore combines indicators of these key aspects.

Measuring poverty

One aspect of inequality is poverty. If there is a wide gap between the richest and poorest households, it is important to evaluate just how poor those poorest households are, and whether they should be regarded as being 'in poverty'. This requires a definition of poverty.

One way of defining poverty is to specify a basket of goods and services that is regarded as the minimum required to support human life. Households that are seen to have too low an income to allow them to purchase everything in that basic bundle of goods would be regarded as being in **absolute poverty**.

Key *terms*

absolute poverty: situation of a household whose income is insufficient to allow it to purchase the minimum bundle of goods and services regarded as necessary for survival

relative poverty: situation obtaining if household income falls below 50% of median adjusted household disposable income

Research published in 2008 by the World Bank claimed that new data on incomes and prices in LDCs revealed that global poverty was more widespread than had been thought previously. It was estimated that households in which people were living on less than $1.25 per person per day (in PPP$) should be regarded as being in absolute poverty. In 2005, about 1.4 billion people in the world were said to be living below this threshold. Figure 9.9 shows a regional distribution of poverty. On a more positive note, the research showed that there had been substantial progress in the preceding years in reducing the number of people in poverty, although sub-Saharan Africa had made less progress than other regions. (More discussion of this issue may be found in 'Measuring poverty', by Peter Smith in *Economic Review* February 2009.)

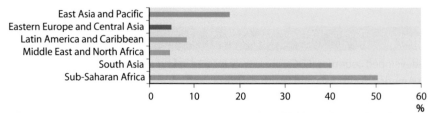

Figure 9.9 *Percentage of population living on less than $1.25 per day, regional groupings*

Source: ICP 2005.

For a country like the UK, this absolute poverty line is not helpful, as so few people fall below it. Thus poverty is defined in *relative* terms. If a household has insufficient income for its members to participate in the normal social life of the country, it is said to be in **relative poverty**. This too is defined in terms of a poverty line, set at 50% of the median adjusted household disposable income. (The median is the income of the middle-ranked household.)

Figure 9.10 presents some data for a range of developed countries. The proportion of people below the relative poverty line varies substantially across these countries, from 4.9% in the Czech Republic to 18.8% in the Russian Federation.

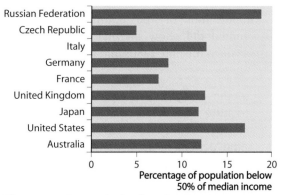

Figure 9.10 *Poverty in developed nations*
Source: Human Development Report 2007/08.

The percentage falling below the poverty line is not a totally reliable measure on its own: it is also important to know *how far* below the poverty line households are falling. The *income gap* (the distance between household income and the poverty line) is a useful measure of the intensity of poverty as well as of its incidence.

Exercise 9.3

Imagine that you are the Minister for Poverty Alleviation in a country in which the (absolute) poverty line is set at $500. Of the people living below the poverty line, you know that there are two distinct groups, each made up of 50 individuals. The people in group 1 have an income of $450, whereas those in group 2 have only $250. Suppose that your budget for poverty alleviation is $2,500.

a Your prime concern is with the most needy: how would you use your budget?

b Suppose instead that your prime minister instructs you to reduce the percentage of people living below the poverty line: do you adopt the same strategy for using the funds?

c How helpful is the poverty line as a strategic target of policy action?

Changes in inequality and poverty over time

Although the distribution of income does not change rapidly from one year to the next, there have been changes over time. Figure 9.11 graphs the Gini index, calculated for both income and expenditure in the UK over 1974–99.

Because people can be expected to smooth their consumption through time, expenditure inequality is seen to have been a little steadier than income inequality. However, both show a noticeable increase in inequality during the 1980s, since when there seems to have been no discernible trend.

It is worth noting that this has not been a general trend across all of the developed countries. A study by OECD in 2002 found no generalised trend in the distribution of household incomes since the mid-1970s, although about half of the countries studied did show an increase between the mid-1980s and mid-1990s.

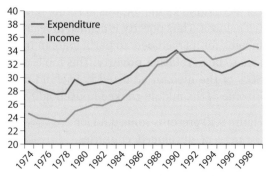

Figure 9.11 *The Gini index for income and expenditure in the UK, 1974–99*

Source: IFS in *Economic Review*, November 2003.

Another study, undertaken by the Institute for Fiscal Studies, analysed trends and noted that there were very different trends identifiable over some 'periods of political interest'. In particular, between 1979 and 1990, with Margaret Thatcher as prime minister, income growth was higher for each successive quintile.

The richest quintile saw income growth that was more than eight times that of the poorest. In other words, inequality increased during this period. Under John Major, from 1990 to 1997, growth was sluggish, but the poorest quintile gained relative to higher quintile groups. Under Tony Blair, from 1997 to 2001 income growth was more or less equally divided over the quintile groups.

However, you should not read too much into these differences. The causes of change in income distribution reflect not only the political stance of the government in power, but other changes occurring in society, and in the pattern of employment over time.

Summary

> Some degree of inequality in income and wealth is present in every society.

> Inequality is measured by ranking households in order of income, then comparing the income received by the richest decile (or quintile) with that received by the poorest.

> The Lorenz curve gives a visual impression of the income distribution; this can be quantified into the Gini index as a single statistic representing the degree of income inequality.

> Calculations of the income distribution are normally undertaken using equivalised incomes, taking into account the size and composition of households.

> In some cases consumption (expenditure) provides a more reliable measure of inequality, as people tend to smooth their consumption over time.

> Absolute poverty measures whether individuals or households have sufficient resources to maintain a reasonable life.

> Relative poverty measures whether individuals or households are able to participate in the life of the country in which they live: this is calculated as 50% of median adjusted household disposable income.

➤ Income distribution and poverty levels change relatively slowly over time.

➤ In the UK there has been little change since the mid-1990s, following a decade of increasing inequality.

Causes of inequality and poverty

Inequality arises from a variety of factors, some reflecting patterns in the ownership of assets, some relating to the operation of the labour market and some arising from the actions of governments.

Ownership of assets

Perhaps the most obvious way in which the ownership of assets influences inequality and its changes through time is through inheritance. Wealth that accumulates in a family over time and is then passed down to succeeding generations generates a source of inequality that does not arise from the current state of the economy or the operations of markets.

You need to be aware that income and wealth are not the same. Income is a 'flow' of money that households receive each period, whereas wealth is a 'stock', i.e. the accumulation of assets that a household owns. In 2003 the most wealthy 1% of households in the UK owned 21% of the marketable wealth, and the most wealthy 50% of households owned 93% of the country's marketable wealth. The Gini index for wealth in 2003 was 67, which is much higher than that for income, indicating that wealth is much less evenly distributed than income.

Figure 9.12 charts the percentage of wealth owned by the wealthiest 1% and 5% of the UK population in various years. You can see that there was an increase in the concentration of wealth between 1991 and 1999, and a levelling out since then. The distribution has been strongly influenced by rising house prices in recent years, but was also affected by the fall in share prices following the September 2001 terrorist attacks.

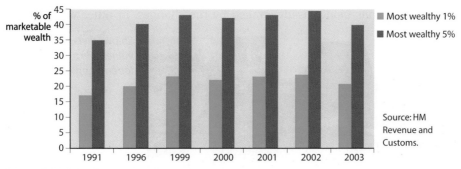

Figure 9.12 *The distribution of wealth in the UK*

Notice that, although wealth and income are not the same thing, inequality in wealth can *lead to* inequality in income, as wealth (the ownership of assets) creates an income flow — from rents and profits — which then feeds back into a household's income stream.

A significant change in the pattern of ownership of assets in recent decades has been the increase in home ownership and the rise in house prices. For those who continue to rent their homes, and in particular for those who rent council dwellings, this is a significant source of rising inequality.

For developing countries, there is also much inequality in the distribution of ownership of assets. Financial markets in developing countries are much less well developed than in the developed countries, and many people, especially in the rural areas, do not have access to the formal financial institutions. This inevitably means a concentration in the ownership of financial assets. Furthermore, the ownership of land is highly concentrated in some countries. This was notably the case in much of Latin America and contributed to the relatively high levels of inequality that have characterised that region. The situation is further complicated by the fact that property rights are weak in many developing countries, so that even if a household has farmed a piece of land for generations, it may not be able to demonstrate ownership rights over that land. Such inequality in the ownership of assets leads to inequality in income distribution also.

Labour market explanations

The labour market can be expected to give rise to inequalities in earnings in developed countries. These arise from demand and supply conditions in labour markets, which respond to changes in the pattern of consumer demand for goods and services and changes in international comparative advantage between countries. Differences in the balance between economic rent and transfer earnings between different occupations and economic sectors then reinforce income inequalities.

However, a by-product of changes in the structure of the economy may be an increase in inequality between certain groups in society. For example, a change in the structure of employment, away from unskilled jobs and towards occupations requiring a higher level of skills and qualifications, can lead to an increase in inequality, with those workers who lack the skills to adapt to changing labour market conditions being disadvantaged by the changes. In other words, if the

Shipworkers may be vulnerable to changing labour market conditions.

premium that employers are prepared to pay in order to hire skilled or well-qualified workers rises as a result of changing technology in the workplace, then those without such skills are likely to suffer.

The decline in the power of the trade unions may have contributed to this situation, as low-paid workers may find that their unions are less likely to be able to offer employment protection. It has been argued that this is a *good* thing if it increases the flexibility of the labour market. But again, a balance is needed between worker protection and free and flexible markets.

The difference in earnings between female and male workers was also highlighted. Figure 9.13 provides empirical evidence for some developed countries. In the UK, a female worker with an educational attainment below upper secondary level on average earns 55% of the average male wage. As educational attainment increases, this differential widens somewhat. The pattern varies across this group of countries. For example, in Germany education brings a marked narrowing of the earnings differential between men and women. Overall, the differentials are less for countries like Hungary or Italy than for Germany, the USA or the UK. Some of the earnings differences between men and women can be explained by the fact that when women have to take time out from working to look after children, they lose human capital by missing out on work experience. However, such market explanations may not suffice to explain all the differences in earnings that are observed.

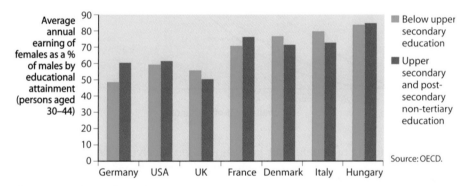

Figure 9.13 *Gender inequality in earnings, various countries*

Many LDCs are characterised by inefficient and underdeveloped labour markets, which may give rise to income inequalities. This may in particular contribute to inequality between rural and urban areas. In many countries, rural areas are still highly dependent on subsistence agriculture, with relatively little wage labour. In contrast, the modern sector, located primarily in the urban areas demonstrates higher wage levels and a more formal sector — but with limited job opportunities. This can create a situation in which there is substantial migration from the rural to the urban areas, attracted by the high wage differentials between the regions. However, given limited job opportunities in the formal urban sector, the result may be high levels of urban unemployment, together with congestion and over-crowding. The high rate of migration may also give rise to the development of an urban informal sector, so that effectively the labour market is structured in three segmented sections – rural, urban informal and urban formal. The limited linkages between them may then perpetuate inequality.

Government intervention

In the developed countries, there are a number of ways in which government intervention influences the distribution of income in a society, although not all of these interventions are expressly intended to do so. Most prominent is the range of transfer payments and taxation that has been implemented.

The overall effect of these measures has a large effect on income distribution. For example, in 2002/03 the 'original income' of the top quintile of households in the UK was about 15 times greater than that of the bottom quintile. ('Original income' is income before any adjustment is made for the effect of taxation or benefits.) After adjusting for benefits and taxes, the ratio of top to bottom quintile fell to about fourfold. Figure 9.14 shows these data in the form of Lorenz curves. Again, you can see the extent to which tax and benefit measures bring the Lorenz curve closer to the equality line.

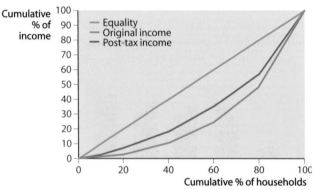

Figure 9.14 *Lorenz curves for income in the UK, 2002–03*

Source: Economics Trends, June 2004.

Benefits

There are two forms of benefit that households can receive to help equalise the income distribution. First, there are various types of cash benefit, such as Income Support, Child Benefit, Incapacity Benefit and Working Families' Tax Credit. These are designed to protect families whose income in certain circumstances would otherwise be very low. Second, there are benefits in kind, such as health and education. These accrue to individual households depending on the number of members of the household and their age and gender.

Of these, the cash benefits are far more important in influencing the distribution of income. For the lowest quintile in 2002/03 such benefits made up about three-fifths of growth in income; they were also significant for the second quintile.

Taxation

Direct taxes (taxes on incomes) tend to be progressive. In other words, higher income groups pay tax at a higher rate. In 2002/03 the top quintile paid 24% of its gross income in tax, compared with only 9% paid in the bottom quintile.

In the UK the main direct taxes are income tax, corporation tax (paid by firms on profits), capital gains tax (paid by individuals who sell assets at a profit), inheritance tax and petroleum revenue tax (paid by firms operating in the North Sea). There is also the council tax, collected by local authorities.

With a tax such as income tax, its progressive nature is reflected in the way the tax rate increases as an individual moves into a higher income range. In other words, the **marginal tax rate** increases as income increases. The **progressive** nature of the tax ensures that it does indeed help to reduce inequality in income distribution — although its effects are less than the cash benefits discussed earlier.

Key terms

direct tax: a tax levied directly on income

marginal tax rate: tax on additional income, defined as the change in tax payments due divided by the change in taxable income

progressive tax: a tax in which the marginal tax rate rises with income, i.e. a tax bearing most heavily on the relatively well-off members of society

Table 9.5 shows average tax rates for taxpayers in different income bands in 2007/08. Notice that the table shows *average* rather than *marginal* tax rates. When average rates are rising, marginal tax rates are higher than the average. Exercise 9.4 illustrates this.

Income band	Number of taxpayers (m)	Average rate of tax payable (%)	Average amount of tax payable (£)
£5,225–£7,499	2.5	1.7	107
£7,500–£9,999	3.6	4.2	365
£10,000–£14,999	6.4	8.8	1,100
£15,000–£19,999	4.9	12.4	2,150
£20,000–£29,999	6.7	14.9	3,660
£30,000–£49,999	5.2	17.1	6,460
£50,000–£99,999	1.75	24.5	16,200
£100,000–£199,999	0.4	30.8	41,200
£200,000–£499,999	0.1	34.0	98,200
All incomes	31.6	18.1	4,630

Table 9.5 *Income tax payable in the UK by annual income 2007/08*
Source: Social Trends, no. 38.

Exercise 9.4

Table 9.5 shows the amount of tax paid by an individual as income increases. Calculate the average and marginal tax rates at each of the income levels. (*Remember the definition of the marginal tax rate provided above.*)

The effect of **indirect taxes,** on the other hand, can sometimes be **regressive**; in other words, indirect taxes may impinge more heavily on lower-income households. Indirect taxes are taxes that are paid on items of expenditure, rather than on income.

Examples of indirect taxes are value added tax (VAT), which is charged on most goods and services sold in the UK, tobacco taxes, excise duties on alcohol and oil duties. These specific taxes are levied per unit sold. *AS Economics, Chapter 5* analysed how the incidence of a tax is related to the price elasticity of demand of a good or service. It explained how, where demand is price-inelastic, producers are able to pass much of an increase in the tax rate on to consumers, whereas if demand is price-elastic they have to absorb most of the increase as part of their costs.

Key terms

indirect tax: a tax on expenditure, e.g. VAT

regressive tax: a tax bearing more heavily on the relatively poorer members of society

Why should some of these taxes be regressive? Take the tobacco tax. In the first place, the number of smokers is higher among lower-income groups than among the relatively rich — research has shown that only about 10% of people in professional groups now smoke compared with nearly 40% of those in unskilled manual groups. Second, expenditure on tobacco tends to take a lower proportion of income of the rich compared with that of the poor, even for those in the former group who do smoke. Thus, the tobacco tax falls more heavily on lower-income groups than on the better-off.

The balance of taxation

Achieving a balance of taxation between direct and indirect taxes is an important aspect of the government's redistributive policy. A switch in the balance from direct to indirect taxes will tend to increase inequality in a society.

There may be reasons why such a switch is seen as desirable. When Margaret Thatcher came to power in 1979, one of the first actions of her government was to increase indirect taxes and introduce cuts in income tax. An important part of the rationale was that high marginal tax rates on income can have a disincentive effect; if people know that a large proportion of any additional work they undertake will be taxed away, they may be discouraged from providing more work. In other words, cutting income tax can encourage work effort by reducing marginal tax rates.

This is yet another reminder of the need for a balanced policy, one that recognises that while some income redistribution is needed to protect the vulnerable, disincentive effects may arise if the better-off are over-taxed.

Long-term policy

An economic analysis of the causes of inequality suggests that there are some long-term measures that can be taken to reduce future inequality, although they may take quite a while to become effective. Policies that encourage greater take-up of education, and provide skills retraining, may be important in the long run if the unskilled are not to be excluded from the benefits of economic growth.

To some extent it could be argued that some inequality is inevitable within a free market capitalist society. Indeed, it could be argued that without some inequality, capitalism could not operate, as it is the pursuit of gain that provides firms with the incentive to maximise profits, workers with the incentive to provide labour effort, and consumers to maximise their utility. It is the combination of these efforts by economic agents that leads to good resource allocation, through the working of Adam Smith's 'invisible hand' (see *AS Economics, Chapter 4*). In a world in which every individual was guaranteed the same income as everyone else, there would be no incentive for anyone to strive to do better. However, few would argue for this. More important is that there should be equality of opportunity.

Weak institutions and poor governance in developing countries mean that measures such as taxation and transfers to influence the distribution of income are largely untried or ineffective. The economist Simon Kuznets argued that there is expected to be a relationship between the degree of inequality in the income distribution and the level of development that a country has achieved. He claimed that in the early stages of economic development income is fairly equally distributed, with everyone living at a relatively low income level. However, as development begins to take off there will be some individuals at the forefront of enterprise and development, and their incomes will rise more rapidly. So in this middle phase the income distribution will tend to worsen. At a later stage of development, society will eventually be able to afford to redistribute income to protect the poor, and all will begin to share in the benefits of development.

This can be portrayed as the relationship between the Gini index and the level of development. The thrust of the Kuznets hypothesis is that this should reveal an inverted U-shaped relationship, as shown in Figure 9.15. Although the data in Table 9.1 do not strongly support this hypothesis, there is some evidence to suggest that the relationship does hold in some regions of the world.

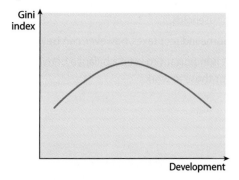

Figure 9.15 *The Kuznets curve*

Exercise 9.5

Using appropriate economic analysis, discuss the various policy measures available to a government wishing to ensure an equitable distribution of income without damaging incentives to work.

Exercise 9.6

Discuss the extent to which LDCs would benefit from introducing policies attempting to reduce income inequality.

Summary

➤ Inequality arises from a range of factors.

➤ The distribution of wealth is strongly influenced by the pattern of inheritance, but in recent years changing patterns of home ownership, coupled with rises in house prices, have also been significant.

➤ The natural operation of labour markets gives rise to some inequality in income.

➤ The skills premium resulting from technological change has widened the wage gap between skilled and educated workers on the one hand, and the unskilled on the other.

➤ Gender differences in pay persist, in spite of successive policies intended to root out discrimination.

➤ Government action influences the pattern of income distribution, with the net effect being a reduction in inequality.

➤ Most effective in this is the provision of cash benefits to low-income households.

➤ Direct taxes tend to be progressive, and help to redistribute income towards poorer households.

➤ Some indirect taxes, however, can be regressive in their impact.

➤ It is important to keep a balance between protecting the low-paid and providing incentives for those in work.

Chapter 10

Limits to growth and development

Development is not only about economic growth, but growth is of central importance as a prerequisite if progress in development is to be achieved. This chapter examines some models of economic growth that are of special significance for less-developed countries, and highlights some of their limitations. In particular, it evaluates some of the factors that may be thought to contribute to the process of economic growth – and some of the obstacles to growth that have hindered progress, especially in sub-Saharan Africa. This will be illustrated with reference to the experience of the 'tiger economies' of East Asia, which developed rapidly after the 1960s. The importance of growth for developed countries will also be examined.

Learning outcomes

After studying this chapter, you should:

➤ understand the importance of economic growth for less-developed countries
➤ be familiar with the Harrod–Domar model of economic growth, and its relevance for less-developed countries
➤ understand the importance of factors that can contribute to economic growth, such as capital, technology and human capital
➤ be aware of the World Bank model of market-friendly economic development and the role of Structural Adjustment Programmes
➤ realise the importance of sustainability in development
➤ be familiar with the contrasting patterns of development in different regions of the world
➤ be aware of important obstacles to economic growth and development
➤ understand the causes and significance of rapid population growth
➤ understand the dangers of continued dependence on primary production, especially on low productivity agriculture
➤ appreciate the importance of missing markets, especially financial markets

▶ be aware of the importance of social capital in promoting long-term development
▶ appreciate the significance of relationships with more-developed countries

Economic growth

Although development is about more than economic growth, growth is a crucial part of any process of economic and human development. It provides the necessary increase in resources to enable a country to provide for the basic needs of its citizens and to expand its choices in the future, and it lays the foundations for future development.

AS Economics, Chapter 1 interpreted economic growth in terms of a movement of the production possibility frontier (PPF). Figure 10.1 serves as a reminder. Here it is assumed that the country has a choice between producing capital goods (for investment) and producing consumer goods. In the initial period the country begins with the production possibility frontier at PPF_0 and can produce at point A, producing C_1 consumer goods and I_1 capital goods. The increase in capital goods enables an increase in the produc-

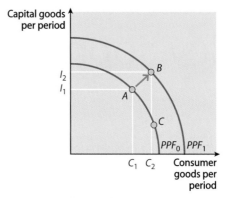

Figure 10.1 *Economic growth*

tive capacity of the economy, so that in the following period the PPF shifts to PPF_1 and the country is able to produce at point B, with C_2 consumer goods and I_2 capital goods. This in turn allows a further shift of the PPF, and so the process of economic growth has begun.

There are some important points to notice about this process. First, in order to produce more consumer goods in the future, current consumption has to be sacrificed. In other words, the country could instead have chosen to be at point C and enjoyed more consumption in the initial period; however, had it done so the opportunity cost would have been less investment, and therefore the PPF would not have moved so far in the second period. This is shown in Figure 10.2, where the choice to be at point C means

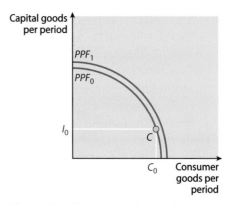

Figure 10.2 *Less economic growth*

producing only I_0 capital goods, and the PPF shifts by a very small amount in the following period. Thus, a society that chooses to use its resources for consumption in the present achieves a slower rate of economic growth.

Second, if the country has a limited capacity to produce investment goods the PPF will take on a much flatter shape, as in Figure 10.3. In this case a sacrifice of current consumption will not appreciably increase the amount of capital goods that are produced, and again, the rate of economic growth will tend to be modest.

For a less-developed country (LDC) this may well be the case. In many LDCs the capacity to produce capital goods is limited, because the countries lack the technical knowledge and resources needed to produce capital goods. Further more, a country in which there are high levels of poverty, and in which many households face low income-earning opportunities, needs to devote much of its resources to consumption. The question for LDCs is thus how to overcome this problem in order to kick-start a process of economic growth.

Figure 10.4 illustrates the problem. A shortage of capital means low per capita income, which means low savings, which in turn means low investment, limited capital, and hence low per capita incomes. In this way a country can get trapped in a *low-level equilibrium* situation.

Another view of economic growth was presented in *AS Economics, Chapter 15*, where economic growth was characterised in terms of a shift in the aggregate supply curve. Again, it was argued that investment is critical to the process of expanding the productive capacity of the economy. (This is illustrated in Figure 10.5, where the long-run aggregate supply curve shifts from AS_0 to AS_1.) It was argued that the aggregate supply curve could move to the right either following investment, which would expand the stock of capital, or following an improvement in the effectiveness of markets. All of this suggests that the first focus for LDCs must be on savings and investment.

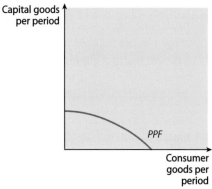

Figure 10.3 *A limited capacity to produce capital goods*

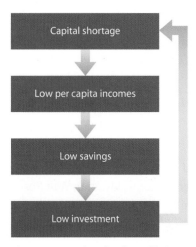

Figure 10.4 *A low-level equilibrium trap*

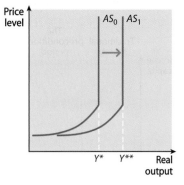

Figure 10.5 *Economic growth as a shift in aggregate supply*

For both developed and developing countries, the potential productive capacity of the economy depends fundamentally on two things: the quantity of factors of production available within the economy, and the efficiency with which they are utilised. By increasing the quantity and/or quality of the factors of production and their productivity, the aggregate supply curve can be shifted to the right. This corresponds to an outward shift of the production possibility frontier.

For the developed countries, labour is relatively scarce, and by and large the labour force only increases through migration — although the UK has enjoyed some in-migration since the expansion of the European Single Market. The quality of labour input can be increased through education and training. The quantity of capital input, and its quality, can be increased through investment, either by domestic firms, or through foreign direct investment from external sources. Encouraging competition can improve the allocative efficiency of resource allocation. Chapter 11 will discuss some ways in which macroeconomic policy can promote economic growth in the developed countries.

For the developing countries, the problem is magnified because of lack of resources. In many cases, human capital is low, and there are limited resources to devote to education, training and to improving health. Capital tends to be scarce, and the flows of foreign direct investment — especially to the poorest LDCs — are relatively low. Markets do not operate effectively to allocate resources efficiently. There are thus many obstacles to be overcome in seeking to promote growth and development.

Stages of economic growth

The economic historian Walt Rostow examined the pattern of development that had been followed in history. He argued in 1960 that all of the more developed countries could be seen to have passed through five **stages of economic growth**. Figure 10.6 gives a general impression of how income per capita changes through these stages.

Key term

stages of economic growth: a process described by economic historian Walt Rostow, which set out five stages through which he claimed that all developing countries would pass

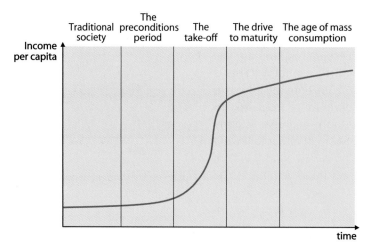

Figure 10.6 The stages of economic growth

In the first stage — the *traditional society* — land is the basis of wealth, most of the production that takes place is in agriculture, and investment is low. Some societies can remain in this stage or get trapped in it. This may correspond to the low-level equilibrium trap that was referred to above. Income per capita is static in this phase.

In order to escape from this situation, Rostow argued that a country must establish the *preconditions* for economic growth. In this period, agricultural productivity begins to increase. This enables resources to be released from the agricultural sector so that some diversification can take place: for example, into some manufacturing activity. Such changes are typically accompanied by a range of social and political changes. It is also important in this stage that some resources are devoted to the provision of the infrastructure that is needed for industrialisation to take place, especially in terms of transport and communications and market facilities.

In the *take-off* stage the economy passes through a 20–30-year period of accelerated growth, with investment rising relative to GDP. Barriers that held back economic growth are overcome. The process of growth in this period tends to be driven by a few leading sectors. A key element of this period is the emergence of entrepreneurs — people who are able to recognise opportunities for productive investment, and who are willing to accept the risk of carrying out that investment. A flow of funds for investment is also needed. Such funds may come from domestic savings, but it may also be necessary to draw in funds from external sources.

The *drive to maturity* stage is a period of self-sustaining growth. New sectors begin to emerge to complement the leading sectors that emerged during the take-off, so that the economy becomes more diversified and balanced. In this period, investment continues to take a relatively high proportion of GDP.

The final period is the *age of mass consumption*, in which the economy is now fully diversified, output per head continues to rise, but consumption now takes a higher proportion of GDP. Countries in this stage have effectively become developed.

Rostow's discussion has been much criticised. For example, it has been suggested that, as an economic historian, Rostow was more concerned with describing the way in which economies had developed in the past than with providing an explanation of *why* they had developed in this way. Nor does his approach provide much helpful guidance for designing policy that would stimulate development in those countries that are still stuck in the 'traditional society' stage, except insofar as countries could study the preconditions and try to replicate them. For example, he offers no explanation of how the barriers to growth disappear in the take-off stage, although it is helpful to be aware that there may be such barriers, and that they need to be overcome.

Dependency theory

A group of writers in the 1950s and 1960s put forward a very different view of economic history. This came to be known as **dependency theory**. The essence of the approach was to deny that the

Key term

dependency theory: the notion that the countries of the world can be divided into core and periphery, and that countries in the core developed by exploiting those in the periphery

developed countries achieved success purely by internal mechanisms or by domestic saving and investment. Instead, it was argued that the countries that first went through the process of industrialisation did so by exploiting the resources of countries elsewhere in the world.

These writers argued that the world could be seen as being divided into the *core* of countries that had developed, located in North America and Western Europe, and a *periphery* of countries in Asia, Africa and Latin America that remained reliant on primary production, and which were controlled by the countries in the core. The core used the countries in the periphery as a source of raw materials and a market for their goods, thus perpetuating the divide between them.

The triangular slave trade could be construed as an example of this. It worked as follows: a slave ship would sail from England, France or colonial North America with a cargo of manufactured goods. These would be exchanged (at a profit) in Africa for slaves, who would then be traded on the sugar or tobacco plantations in North America and the Caribbean (at another profit) in exchange for raw materials (sugar, tobacco etc.). These raw materials would then

The triangular slave trade illustrates how periphery countries were exploited.

be transported back to the factories. The British treatment of manufacturing industry in India has also come in for criticism, where (for example) the Indian cotton industry was suppressed in order to protect the cotton mills of Lancashire.

However, there is a limit to how far these arguments can be pressed. It is clear that colonial influence was not all bad, and colonies benefited from physical and social infrastructure – such as railways, roads and educational structures – provided by the colonising nations. It is also the case that a number of countries that were never colonised, such as Afghanistan, Ethiopia and Thailand, failed to develop.

In today's increasingly integrated world, the question of interdependence between countries is of great significance. It remains to be seen whether globalisation will offer further opportunities for exploitation of the poor by the rich (as some critics maintain), or whether it will offer the basis for new mutually beneficial partnerships between the countries of the world. However, it remains the case that many LDCs continue to be heavily reliant on primary production, and it is important to explore the extent to which this is an obstacle to development. Dependency theorists suggest that one possible route forward for countries in the periphery is to begin forging trading links with each other, rather than continuing to depend upon countries in the core. Indeed, some attempts have been made to establish trading agreements between LDCs, but this process has a long way to go.

Industrialisation

So what are the prospects for a country wanting to move towards **industrialisation**, and to reduce its reliance on primary production?

In an influential paper in 1954, Sir Arthur Lewis argued that agriculture in many LDCs was characterised by surplus labour. Perhaps farms were operated on a household basis, with the work and the crop being shared out between members of the household. If there was not enough work to be done by all the members of the household, then, although all seemed to be employed, there would in fact be *hidden unemployment*, or *under employment*. Given the size of the rural population and its rapid growth, there could be almost unlimited *surplus labour* existing in this way.

Lewis then pointed out that it would be possible to transfer such surplus labour into the industrial sector without a loss of agricultural output, as the remaining labour would be able to take up the slack. All that would be necessary is for the industrial sector to set a wage sufficiently higher than the rural wage to persuade workers to transfer. Industry could then reap profits that could be reinvested to allow industry to expand, without any need for the industrial wage to be pulled upwards to cause inflation.

Unfortunately, the process did not prove to be as smooth as Lewis suggested. One reason relates to *human capital* levels. Agricultural workers do not have the skills or training that prepares them for employment in the industrial sector, so it is not so straightforward to transfer them from agricultural to industrial work.

Furthermore, to the extent that they were able to transfer, the expanding industry did not always reinvest the surplus in order to enable continuous expansion of the industrial sector. Foreign firms tended to repatriate the profits (as will be seen later in this chapter), and in any case tended to use modern, relatively capital-intensive technology that did not require a large pool of unskilled labour.

Perhaps more seriously, the **Lewis model** encouraged governments to think in terms of industry-led growth, and to neglect the rural sector. This meant that agricultural productivity often remained low, and inequality between urban and rural areas grew.

The Harrod–Domar model

The idea that the initial focus for LDCs should be on savings and investment is supported by the **Harrod–Domar model** of economic growth, which first appeared in separate articles by Roy Harrod in the

> **Key term**
>
> **industrialisation:** a process of transforming an economy by expanding manufacturing and other industrial activity

> **Key terms**
>
> **Lewis model:** a model developed by Sir Arthur Lewis that argued that less-developed countries could be seen as being typified by two sectors, traditional and modern, and that labour could be transferred from the traditional to the modern sector in order to bring about growth and development
>
> **Harrod–Domar model:** a model of economic growth that emphasises the importance of savings and investment

UK and Evsey Domar in the USA in 1939. This model was to become significant in influencing LDCs' attitudes towards the process of economic growth. It was developed in an attempt to determine how equilibrium could be achieved in a growing economy.

The basic finding of this model was that an economy can remain in equilibrium through time only if it grows at a particular rate. This unique stable growth path depends on the savings ratio and the productivity of capital. Any deviation from this path will cause the economy to become unstable. This finding emphasised the importance of savings in the process of economic growth, and led to the conclusion that a country wishing for economic growth must first increase its flow of savings.

Figure 10.7 illustrates the process that leads to growth in a Harrod–Domar world. Savings are crucial in enabling investment to be undertaken — always remembering that some investment will have to be used to replace existing capital that has worn out. Investment then enables capital to accumulate and technology to be improved. The accumulation of capital leads to an increase in output and incomes, which leads to a further flow of savings, and the cycle is back where it started from.

Figure 10.7 *The Harrod–Domar process of economic development*

The key question is whether this process can allow an LDC to break out of the low-level equilibrium trap. Figure 10.7 can be used to identify a number of problems that may prevent the Harrod–Domar process from being effective for LDCs.

It has already been argued that generating a flow of savings in an LDC may be problematic. When incomes are low households may have to devote most of their resources to consumption, and so there may be a lack of savings. Nonetheless, some savings have proved possible. For example, in the early 1960s South Korea had an average income level that was not too different from that of countries like Sudan or Afghanistan, but it managed to build up the savings rate during that decade.

Setting aside the problem of low savings for the moment, what happens next?

Will savings lead to investment and the accumulation of capital?

If a flow of savings can be generated, the next important step is to transform the savings into investment. This is the process by which the sacrifice of current consumption leads to an increase in productive capacity in the future.

Some important preconditions must be met if savings are to be transformed into investment. If the funds that have been saved are to be mobilised for investment, there must be a way for potential borrowers to get access to the funds. In developed countries this takes place through the medium of financial markets. For example, it may be that households save by putting their money into a savings account at the bank; then with this money the bank can make loans to entrepreneurs, enabling them to undertake investment.

In many LDCs, however, financial markets are undeveloped, so it is much more difficult for funds to be recycled in this way. For example, a study conducted in 1997 by the Bank of Uganda found that almost 30% of households interviewed in rural Ugandan villages had undertaken savings at some time.[1] However, almost none of these had done so through formal financial institutions, which did not reach into the rural areas. Instead, the saving that took place tended to be in the form of fixed assets, or money kept under the bed. Such savings cannot readily be transformed into productive investment.

In addition, governments in some periods have made matters worse by holding down interest rates in the hope of encouraging firms to borrow. The idea here is that a low interest rate means a low cost of borrowing, which should make borrowing more attractive. However, this ignores the fact that if interest rates are very low there is little incentive to save, since the return on saving is so low. In this case, firms may wish to invest but may not be able to obtain the funds to do so.

The other prerequisite for savings to be converted into investment is that there must be entrepreneurs with the ability to identify investment possibilities, the skill to carry them through and the willingness to bear the risk. Such entrepreneurs are in limited supply in many LDCs.

This worked effectively for Hong Kong, one of the so-called tiger economies. During its period of rapid development after the 1950s Hong Kong benefited from a wave of immigrant entrepreneurs, especially from Shanghai, who provided the impetus for rapid development. In Singapore the entrepreneurship came primarily from the government, and from multinational corporations who were encouraged to become established in the country. Singapore and South Korea also adopted policies that ensured a steady flow of savings, so that, for example, in Singapore gross domestic savings amounted to 52% of GDP in 1999.

In Hong Kong, entrepreneurs mobilised funds for investment and stimulated development.

Will investment lead to higher output and income?

For investment to be productive in terms of raising output and incomes in the economy, some further conditions need to be met. In particular, it is crucial for firms to have access to physical capital, which will raise production capacity. Given the limited capability of producing capital goods in many LDCs, they have to rely on capital imported from the more-developed countries. This may be beneficial in

---

[1] Polycarp Musinguzi and Peter Smith, 'Structural adjustment and poverty: a study of rural Uganda', *Discussion Papers in Economics and Econometrics*, University of Southampton, 1998.

terms of upgrading home technology, but such equipment can be imported only if the country has earned the foreign exchange to pay for it. One of the most pressing problems for many LDCs is that they face a **foreign exchange gap** – in other words, they find it difficult to earn sufficient foreign exchange with which to purchase crucial imports required in order to allow manufacturing activity to expand. In order

Key **term**

foreign exchange gap: a situation in which an LDC is unable to import the goods that it needs for development because of a shortage of foreign exchange

to do this, physical capital is needed, together with key inputs to the production process. Indeed, many LDCs need to import food and medical supplies in order to develop their human capital. A shortage of foreign exchange therefore may make it difficult for the country to accumulate capital.

The tiger economies were all very open to international trade, and focused on promoting exports in order to earn the foreign exchange needed to import capital goods. This strategy worked very effectively, and the economies were able to widen their access to capital and move to higher value-added activities as they developed their capabilities.

The importance of human capital

If the capital *can* be obtained, there is then a need for the skilled labour with which to operate the capital goods. In other words, human capital in the form of skilled, healthy and well-trained workers is as important as physical capital if investment is to be productive.

In principle, it could be thought that today's LDCs have an advantage over the countries that developed in earlier periods. In particular, they can learn from earlier mistakes, and import technology that has already been developed, rather than having to develop it anew. This would suggest that a convergence process should be going on, whereby LDCs are able to adopt technology that has already been produced, and thereby grow more rapidly and begin to close the gap with the more-developed countries.

However, by and large this has not been happening, and a lack of human capital has been suggested as one of the key reasons for the failure. This underlines the importance of education in laying the foundations for economic growth as well as contributing directly to the quality of life.

In the case of the tiger economies, their education systems had been well estab-lished, either through the British colonial legacy (in the case of Singapore and Hong Kong) or through past Japanese occupation periods (in Taiwan and South Korea). In all of these countries, education received high priority, and cultural influences encouraged a high demand for education. The tiger economies thus benefited from having highly skilled and well-disciplined labour forces that were able to make effective use of the capital goods that had been acquired.

Harrod–Domar and external resources

Figure 10.8 extends the earlier schematic presentation of the process underlying the Harrod–Domar model of economic growth. This has been amended to underline the importance of access to technology and human capital.

The discussion above has emphasised the difficulty of mobilising domestic savings, both in generating a sufficient flow of savings and in translating such savings into productive investment.

The question arises as to whether an LDC could supplement its domestic savings with a flow of funds from abroad. Figure

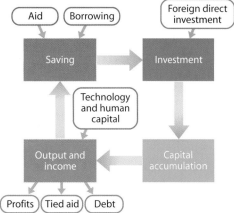

Figure 10.8 *The Harrod–Domar process of economic development augmented*

10.8 identifies three possible injections into the Harrod–Domar process. First, it might be possible to attract flows of overseas assistance from higher-income countries. Second, perhaps the amount of investment could be augmented directly by persuading multinational corporations to engage in foreign direct investment. Third, perhaps the LDC could borrow on international capital markets to finance its domestic investment. It is worth noting that the tiger economies took full advantage of these external sources of funds.

These three possibilities will be explored more fully in Chapter 12. However, it is worth noting that each of these ways of attracting external resources has a downside associated with it. As far as overseas assistance is concerned, in the past such flows have been seen by some donor countries as part of trade policy, and have brought less benefit to LDCs than had been hoped. In the case of the multi-national corporations, there is a tendency for the profits to be repatriated out of the LDC, rather than recycled into the economy. Finally, international borrowing has to be repaid at some future date, and many LDCs have found themselves burdened by debt that they can ill afford to repay.

Summary

➤ Although development is a broader concept than economic growth, growth is a key ingredient of development.

➤ Economic growth can be seen in terms of a shift in the production possibility frontier, or a shift in long-run aggregate supply.

➤ The Harrod–Domar model of economic growth highlights the importance of savings, and of transforming savings into productive investment.

➤ However, where markets are underdeveloped, this transformation may be impeded.

➤ Human capital is also a critical ingredient of economic growth.

➤ If resources cannot be generated within the domestic economy, a country may need to have recourse to external sources of funding.

Market-friendly growth

An alternative way of viewing the process of economic growth has been put forward by the World Bank. The core argument here is that markets should be allowed to work without government intervention wherever possible, and that the government should intervene only where markets cannot operate effectively. This is called a **market-friendly growth** strategy. The World Bank has argued that there are four areas that should be of high priority to LDCs looking to stimulate development; *people*, *microeconomic markets*, *macroeconomic stability*, and *global linkages*.

Key *term*

market-friendly growth: an approach to economic growth in which governments are recommended to intervene less where markets can operate effectively, but to intervene more strongly where markets are seen to fail

At the core of this approach is the argument that, if markets can be made to work effectively, this will lead to more efficient resource allocation. Furthermore, governments should intervene only where markets themselves cannot operate effectively because of some sort of market failure. If the four components can be made to work together, it will lay the foundations for economic growth and development.

The World Bank has promoted the idea of market-friendly growth.

People

The importance of human capital formation has already been stressed. The need for skilled and disciplined labour to complement capital accumulation is critical for development. However, this is an area in which market failure is widespread.

If people do not fully perceive the future benefits to be gained from educating their children, they will demand less education than is desirable for society. In the rural areas of many LDCs it is common for education to be undervalued in this way, and for drop-out rates from schooling to be high. This may arise both from a failure to perceive the potential future benefits that children will derive from education, and from the high opportunity cost of education in villages where child labour is widespread.

The situation in many LDCs has been worsened in the past by poor curriculum design, whereby the legacy of colonial rule was a school system and curriculum not well directed at providing the sort of education likely to be of most benefit within the context of an LDC. Furthermore, there tended to be a bias towards providing funds to the tertiary sector (which benefits mainly the rich elites within society) rather than trying to ensure that all children received at least primary education.

The benefits from developing people as resources may overflow into other component areas, for example through an increase in labour productivity – if healthy and educated people are able to work better – or by ensuring that products are better able to meet international standards, thereby reinforcing linkages with the rest of the world.

Microeconomic markets

The World Bank has also argued that LDCs need to encourage competitive and effective microeconomic markets in order to ensure that their resources are well allocated.

It is important that prices can act as signals to guide resource allocation. This can then create a climate for enterprise, enabling people to exploit their capabilities. In the past, many governments in LDCs have tended to intervene strongly in markets, distorting prices away from market equilibrium values – especially food prices, which were kept artificially low in urban areas, thus damaging farmers' incentives. In addition, it is important to encourage the development of financial markets that will act to channel savings into productive investment.

Again, there are likely to be overflow effects from this. First, if microeconomic markets can be made to operate effectively, this will ensure that people get a good return on the education that they undertake, which will encourage a greater demand for education in the future. Second, foreign direct investment is more likely to be attracted into a country in which there are effective operational domestic

markets. And the existence of effective financial markets creates a financial discipline that encourages stability at the macroeconomic level.

Macroeconomic stability

It is argued that stability in the macroeconomy is important in order to encourage investment. If the macroeconomic environment is unstable, firms will not be sufficiently confident of the future to want to risk investing in projects. In addition, if the government becomes over-active in the economy, this may starve the private sector of resources.

A key aim for an LDC should be to ensure that prices can act as effective signals in guiding resource allocation. If overall inflation is allowed to get out of hand, then clearly allocative efficiency cannot be expected. On the other hand, a stable macroeconomy should serve to improve the operation of microeconomic markets. An economy that is stable should also be better able to withstand external shocks.

Global linkages

The domestic markets of most LDCs are limited in terms of effective demand. For LDC producers to be able to benefit from economies of scale, they need to be exporting in sufficient quantities — which clearly means being involved in and committed to international trade. Global linkages thus become important. Furthermore, LDCs can gain access to technology only from abroad, as they do not have the capacity to produce it themselves. As mentioned above, LDCs need to find some way of closing their foreign exchange gap — which can only be achieved by developing better global linkages.

Again, there are likely to be spillover effects. The availability of physical and financial capital may help the stability of the macroeconomy; participation in world markets may help domestic markets to operate; and global linkages can provide the knowledge and technology that will improve human capital in the domestic economy.

It is important to notice that establishing global links is a two-way process. On the one hand, it is important for an LDC to be in a strong enough position to form links with more-developed countries without creating a vulnerability to outside influence that may damage it, for example in reaching trade agreements. On the other hand, the more-developed countries need to be willing to accept such linkages. This has not always been the case in the past.

So there is an interdependent system in which the four aspects of potential intervention interact. The self-reinforcing aspect of these four components not only provides a focus for analysis, but also highlights the fact that if any one of the elements is lacking, there may be problems.

Whether these aspects are sufficient to encourage development is an important issue. In most LDCs two additional matters will need to be tackled. First, there is the question of infrastructure. The *public good* aspects of some types of infrastructure need to be borne in mind. The provision of transport and communications systems,

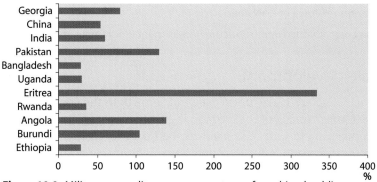

Figure 10.9 *Military expenditure as a percentage of combined public expenditure on education and health*

Source: Human Development Report 2007/08.

or the improvement of market facilities to enable trading to take place, may be crucial for the smooth development of an LDC.

Second, it is important that LDC governments maintain an appropriate balance in their spending priorities. Civil and international conflict has all too often diverted resources away from development priorities. Something of this can be seen in Figure 10.9, which shows military expenditure relative to expenditure on health and education.

The tiger economies offer a good illustration of how markets can be enabled to bring about rapid growth and development. Indeed, the World Bank model is based partly on their observation of the experience of these and some other economies. Although in some cases (especially Singapore and South Korea) the governments played an active role in encouraging economic growth and influencing the pattern of economic activity, nonetheless, markets were nurtured and encouraged to play a role in resource allocation.

Structural Adjustment Programmes (SAPs)

As the World Bank has adopted the market-friendly ideal, it has embedded its central ideas in Structural Adjustment Programmes (SAPs) that LDCs have been encouraged to follow. These will be revisited in Chapter 12, where you will see that the central policies to be adopted under SAPs relate to one of the four components outlined above.

Structural Adjustment Programme: a package of economic policy measures recommended by the World Bank

Summary

➤ The World Bank has advocated a market-friendly approach to economic growth and development.

➤ Four key elements are seen as crucial to the process: investment in people, properly functioning microeconomic markets, macroeconomic stability and international linkages.

> These elements reinforce one another.

> These ideas are embedded in the Structural Adjustment Programme approach.

Sustainable development

AS Economics, Chapter 15 discussed economic growth in the context of developed countries. It was pointed out that economic growth may have important effects on the environment, and that care needs to be taken to ensure that, in pursuing growth, countries bear in mind the importance of future generations as well as the needs of the present.

These issues are equally important for LDCs. Deforestation has been a problem for many LDCs with areas of rainforest. In some cases logging for timber has destroyed much valuable land; in other cases land has been cleared for unsuitable agricultural use. This sort of activity creates relatively little present value, and leaves a poorer environment for future generations.

Another aspect of environmental degradation concerns *biodiversity*. This refers to the way in which misuse of the environment is contributing to the loss of plant species – not to mention those of birds, insects and mammals – which are becoming extinct as their natural habitat is destroyed. In some cases the loss is of species that have not even been discovered yet. Given the natural healing properties of many plants, this could mean the destruction of plants that could provide significant new drugs for use in medicine. But how can something be valued when its very existence is as yet unknown?

Environmental degradation can have a negative impact on biodiversity.

One way of viewing the environment is as a factor of production that needs to be used effectively, just like any other factor of production. In other words, each country has a stock of *environmental* capital that needs to be utilised in the best possible way.

However, if the environmental capital is to be used appropriately, it must be given an appropriate value. This can be problematic; if property rights are not firmly established – as they are not in many LDCs – it is difficult to enforce legislation to protect the environment. Furthermore, if the environment (as a factor of production) is underpriced, then 'too much' of it will be used by firms.

There are externality effects at work here too, in the sense that the loss of biodiversity is a global loss, and not just something affecting the local economy. In some cases there have been international externality effects of a more direct kind, such as when forest fires in Indonesia caused the airport in Singapore to close down because of the resulting smoke haze.

China has been one of the fastest growing economies in the world since 1978, as can be seen in Figure 10.10. To have averaged almost 8% growth per annum over such a long period is extraordinary. In 2004 the *Asian Development Bank* reported that China's GDP had grown by 9.1% in 2003, and it predicted that in 2004 the country's growth would account for 15% of the expected expansion in the *world* economy. Exports from the rest of the world to China grew by 34.6% in 2003.

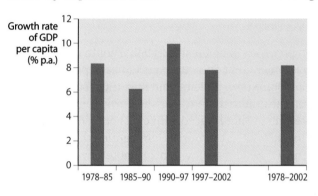

Figure 10.10 *China's economic growth, 1978–2002*

Source: H. Ungang, H. Linlin and C. Zhixiao, 'China's economic growth and poverty reduction, 1978–2002', at **www.imf.org**

In August 2004 *The Economist* reported that 16 of the world's most polluted cities are now located in China, and that around half of China's population (i.e. some 600 million people) have water supplies that are contaminated by animal and human waste. River systems are heavily polluted, and air pollution is becoming a serious issue, partly as a result of the country's heavy reliance on coal-fired electricity generation. Shanghai's environmental protection bureau estimated that 70% of the 1 million cars in Shanghai do not reach even the oldest European emission standard.

This illustrates the trade-off between rapid economic growth and protection of the environment. The other factor in the equation is the desire to alleviate poverty. The World Bank estimated that in 1999, 224 million people in China were living in poverty – defined as people living on less than $1 per day. The need to bring so many people out of extreme poverty lends urgency to the drive for economic growth. However, this needs to be balanced against the need to ensure **sustainable development**. In other words, economic growth must be achieved in such a way that it does not destroy the environment for future generations.

There are many aspects to this issue, of which protecting the environment is just one. Sustainable development also entails taking account of the depletion rates of non-renewable resources, and ensuring that renewable resources *are* renewed in the process of economic growth.

 Key term

sustainable development: 'development which meets the needs of the present without compromising the ability of future generations to meet their own needs' (Brundtland Commission, 1987)

So, although economic growth is important to a society, the drive for growth must be tempered by an awareness of the possible trade-offs with other important objectives.

The government and economic growth

There may be limits to which a government can influence the growth process. Infrastructure can be put in place, and markets encouraged to operate, but nevertheless, there may be limits to what can be done, especially as, with low levels of incomes in the LDC and inefficient tax collection, the government itself may have inadequate resources at its disposal.

Many LDCs have encountered problems of political instability, not to mention civil or international conflict. A government that does not expect to be in power for very long has little incentive to adopt long-term policies, and may thus focus on short-run fixes that it hopes will keep the public content — or short-run policies that will line their own pockets. A government that is faced with civil conflict, or war with a neighbouring state, will be forced to divert resources into fighting the war, rather than stimulating development. Political stability can promote development by encouraging leaders to take a long-term view. This was the case for Singapore, where Lee Kuan Yu, who was Prime Minister from 1957 until 1991, guided the economy through a period of rapid growth and development. However, political stability by itself does not guarantee success — as demonstrated by the case of Zimbabwe, where Robert Mugabe has enjoyed a long period of rule, but has demolished rather than built up the economy.

In the case of the tiger economies the government did have a strong influence — although less so in the case of Hong Kong. In Singapore the government kept tight reins on the macroeconomy, encouraged savings, nurtured the education system, guided the development of key strategic sectors in the economy and provided good infrastructure for trade and industry, as well as maintaining an open economy. In South Korea the government subsidised the development of large conglomerate firms that provided the foundations for economic growth.

Summary

> In pursuing economic growth, governments must remain aware of the potential costs of such growth.

> These may be seen especially in terms of possible damage to the environment.

> In this connection, deforestation and the loss of biodiversity are critical areas of concern.

> There are many international externality effects at work in the process of economic growth in LDCs.

> The recent rapid economic growth achieved in the Chinese economy has highlighted some of the environmental costs associated with growth.

> Given low per capita incomes and limited resources, LDC governments may not be able to influence growth very readily.

Exercise 10.1

Which of the following can be seen as impediments to growth?

a a lack of savings resulting from low per capita incomes

b underdeveloped financial markets

c lack of confidence in financial assets and institutions

d low real interest rates

e shortage of entrepreneurs

f inadequate infrastructure

g low levels of human capital

h foreign exchange shortage

i limited government resources

j weak governance and civil conflict

Which of these factors are likely to be present in less-developed countries?

Contrasting patterns of development

The East Asian experience

The rapid growth achieved by the East Asian **tiger economies**, as they came to be known, was undoubtedly impressive, and held out hope that other less-developed countries could begin to close the gap in living standards. Indeed, the term 'East Asian miracle' was coined to describe how quickly these **newly industrialised economies** had been able to develop. At the heart of the success were four countries: Hong Kong, Singapore, South Korea and Taiwan; others, such as Malaysia and Thailand, were not far behind.

How was their success achieved?

None of these countries enjoy a rich supply of natural resources. Indeed, Hong Kong and Singapore are small city-states whose only natural resources are their excellent harbours and good positions — but with small populations.

Key *terms*

tiger economies: a group of newly industrialised economies in the East Asian region, including Hong Kong, Singapore, South Korea and Taiwan

newly industrialised economies: economies that experienced rapid economic growth from the 1960s to the present

The tigers soon realised that to develop manufacturing industry it would be crucial to tap into economies of scale. This meant producing on a scale that would far outstrip the size of their domestic markets — which meant that they would have to rely on international trade.

By being very open to international trade and focusing on export markets, the tigers were able to sell to a larger market, and thereby improve their efficiency

through economies of scale. This enabled them to enjoy a period of **export-led growth**. In other words, the tiger economies expanded by selling their exports to the rest of the world, and building a reputation for high-quality merchandise. This was helped by their judicious choice of markets on which to focus: they chose to move into areas of economic activity that were being vacated by the more-developed nations, which were moving up to new sorts of product.

Key term

export-led growth: situation in which economic growth is achieved through the exploitation of economies of scale made possible by focusing on exports, and so reaching a wider market than would be available within the domestic economy

The export-led growth hypothesis explains part of the success of the tiger economies, but there were other contributing factors. The tiger economies nurtured their human capital and attracted foreign investment. Their governments intervened to influence the direction of the economies but also encouraged markets to operate effectively, fostering macroeconomic and political stability and developing good infrastructure. Moreover, these countries embarked on their growth period at a time when world trade overall was buoyant.

Sub-Saharan Africa

The experience of countries in sub-Saharan Africa is in total contrast to the success story of the tiger economies. Even accepting the limitations of the GDP per capita measure, the fact that GDP per capita was lower in the region as a whole in 2000 than it had been in 1975 (or even earlier) paints a depressing picture. Can sub-Saharan Africa learn from the experience of the tiger economies?

Part of the explanation for the failure of growth in this region lies in the fact that sub-Saharan Africa lacks many of the positive features that enabled the tiger economies to grow. Export-led growth is less easy for countries that have specialised in the production of goods for which demand is not buoyant. Furthermore, it is not straightforward to develop new specialisations if human and physical capital levels are low, the skills for new activities are lacking and poverty is rife. Encouraging development when there is political instability, and when markets do not operate effectively, is a major challenge. This chapter considers some of the obstacles to development that are faced by LDCs.

Latin America

Countries in Latin America followed yet another path. There was a period in which the economies of Argentina, Brazil and Mexico, among others, were able to grow rapidly, enabling them to qualify as 'newly industrialised economies'. However, such growth could not be sustained in the face of the high rates of inflation that afflicted many of the countries in this region, especially during the 1980s. Indeed, many of them experienced bouts of hyperinflation, inhibiting economic growth.

In part this reflected fiscal indiscipline, with governments undertaking high levels of expenditure which they financed by printing money. In many cases, countries in this region have tended to be relatively closed to international trade. International debt reached unsustainable levels, and continues to haunt countries such as Argentina which, in 2005, wrote off its debt by offering its creditors about 33% of the value of its outstanding debt. Around three-quarters of the creditors accepted the deal, knowing that otherwise they would probably get nothing at all. However, whether anyone will be prepared to lend to Argentina in the future remains to be seen. Latin American economies also tend to be characterised by high levels of income inequality, and poverty remains a major problem.

The Latin American economies grew strongly in the 1970s, but were hit by high inflation in the 1980s.

Summary

> A small group of countries in South East Asia, known as the East Asian tiger economies, underwent a period of rapid economic growth, closing the gap on the more-developed countries.

> This success arose from a combination of circumstances, including a high degree of openness to international trade, which was seen as crucial if economies of scale are to be reaped.

> However, the tigers are also characterised by high levels of human capital and political and macroeconomic stability.

> In contrast, countries in sub-Saharan Africa have stagnated; in some cases real per capita incomes were lower in 2000 than they had been in 1975.

> Countries in Latin America began well, experiencing growth for a period, but then ran into economic difficulties.

Population growth

Early writers on development were pessimists. For example, Thomas Malthus argued that real wages would never rise above a bare subsistence level. This was based on his ideas about the relationship between population growth and real incomes.

Malthus, having come under the influence of David Ricardo, believed that there would always be *diminishing returns to labour.* This led him to believe that as the population of a country increased the average wage would fall, since a larger labour force would be inherently less productive. Furthermore, Malthus argued that the birth rate would rise with the real wage, because if families had more resources they would have more children; at the same time, the death rate would fall with an increase in the real wage, as people would be better fed and therefore healthier.

Extension material

Figure 10.11 shows one way of looking at the relationship between population growth and real wages. The left-hand panel illustrates the relationship between population size and the real wage rate, reflecting diminishing returns to labour in agriculture. The right-hand panel shows the birth rate (B) and death rate (D) functions. When the wage is relatively high, say at W_1, the birth rate (B_1) exceeds the death rate (D_1), which in turn means that the population will grow. However, as population grows, the real wage must fall (as shown in the left-hand panel), so eventually the wage converges on W^*, which is an equilibrium situation.

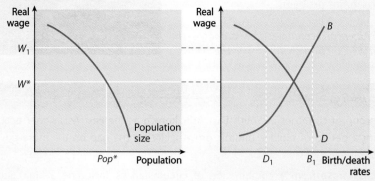

Figure 10.11 *Malthus's theory of population*

For these reasons, Malthus believed that it was not possible for a society to experience sustained increases in real wages, basically because the population was capable of exponential growth, while the food supply was capable of only arithmetic growth, because of diminishing returns.

Although he was proved wrong (he had not anticipated the improvements in agricultural productivity that were to come), the question of whether population growth constitutes an obstacle to growth and development remains. At the heart of this is the debate about whether people should be regarded as key contributors to development, in their role as a factor of production, or as a drain on resources, consuming food, shelter, education and so on. Ultimately, the answer will depend upon the quantity of resources available relative to the population size.

In global terms world population is growing at a rapid rate, by more than 80 million people per year. In November 1999 global population went through the 6 billion mark – that is about six times as many people as in 1800. But the growth is very unevenly distributed: countries like Italy, Spain, Germany and Switzerland are projected to experience declining populations in the 2000–15 period, while sub-Saharan Africa's population continues to grow by 2.4% per annum, and 'low human development' countries (by the UNDP definition) by 2.5%. A country whose population is growing at 2.5% per annum will see a doubling in just 28 years, so the growing pressure on resources to provide education and healthcare is considerable. The proportion of the population aged below 15 is very high for much of sub-Saharan Africa.

It has been observed that developed countries seem to have gone through a common pattern of population growth as their development progressed. This pattern has become known as the **demographic transition**, and is illustrated in Figure 10.12 for England and Wales between 1750 and 2000. This shows the birth rate and death rate for various years over this period. Remember that the natural rate of increase in population is given by the difference between these: the birth rate minus the death rate. (This ignores net migration.)

Notice that between 1750 and 1820 the death rate fell more steeply than the birth rate, which means that the population growth rate accelerated in this period. This was the time when Britain was embarking on the Industrial Revolution, and corresponds to the early 'take-off' period of economic growth. At this stage the birth rate remains high. However,

Key *term*

demographic transition: a process through which many countries have been observed to pass whereby improved health lowers the death rate, and the birth rate subsequently also falls, leading to a low and stable population growths

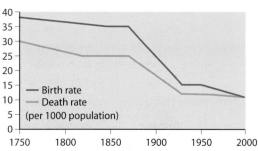

Figure 10.12 *The demographic transition in England and Wales, 1750–2000*

Source: D. Perkins et al. *The Economics of Development*, Norton/World Bank.

after 1870 there is a further fall in the death rate, accompanied by an even steeper fall in the birth rate, such that population growth slows down. You can see that by 2000 the natural population growth has shrunk to zero.

This demographic transition process has been displayed in most of the developed countries. The supporting story is that when the development process begins, death rates tend to fall as incomes begin to rise. In time families adapt to the change, and new social norms emerge in which the typical family size tends to get smaller. For example, as more women join the workforce, the opportunity cost of having children rises — by taking time out from careers to have children, their forgone earnings are now higher. This process has led to stability in population growth.

However, for countries that have undergone the demographic transition in a later period things have not been so smooth. Figure 10.13 shows the pattern of the demographic transition for Sri Lanka, which is one of the countries that have achieved some stability in the rate of population growth. Here, it is not until after about 1920 that the death rate begins to fall — and it falls more steeply than it did

in the early stages of economic growth in England and Wales. After 1950 it falls even more steeply, partly because methods of hygiene and modern medicine were able to bring the death rate down more rapidly.

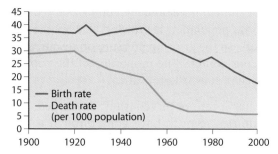

Perhaps more crucially, the birth rate in Sri Lanka has remained high for much longer — in other words, households' decisions about family size do not seem to

Figure 10.13 *The demographic transition in Sri Lanka, 1900–2000*

Source: as Figure 10.12.

have adjusted as rapidly as they did in England and Wales. This has led to a period of relatively rapid population growth.

In Figure 10.14, presenting data for a range of countries around the world, the top point of each bar represents the birth rate and the bottom point the death rate; the length of each bar thus represents the rate of natural population increase. You will see that there are three important groupings. The first is of five countries that do not yet seem to have entered the demographic transition, and for which both birth rates and death rates have remained relatively high. These are mainly low-income countries.

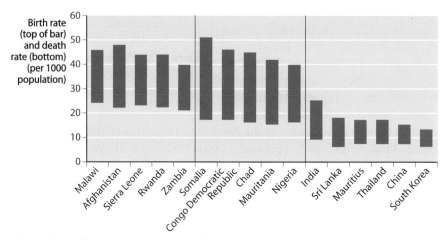

Figure 10.14 *Birth and death rates in selected countries, 1999*

Source: World Bank

The second group represents countries in which death rates have begun to fall but birth rates have remained high. As a result, these are currently going through a period of rapid population growth.

The final group represents countries that have seen falls in both birth and death rates, so that population growth has now been reduced. Notice that this includes Sri Lanka, which was discussed earlier.

Extension material: the microeconomics of fertility

To some extent, a household's choice of family size might be viewed as an *externality* issue. Figure 10.15 illustrates this. *MPB* (= *MSB*) represents the marginal benefit that the household receives from having different numbers of children (which is assumed to equal the marginal social benefit), and *MPC* represents the marginal private costs that are incurred. If education is subsidised, or if the household does not perceive the costs inflicted on society by having many children, then the marginal social cost of children (*MSC*) is higher than the marginal private cost.

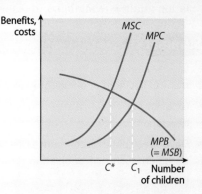

Figure 10.15 *The microeconomics of fertility*

Households will thus choose to have C_1 children, rather than the C^* that is optimal for society. In other words, a choice of large family size might be interpreted as being a market failure. Note that this discussion assumes that the household has the ability to choose its desired family size by having access to, and knowledge of, methods of contraception.

Figure 10.16 shows fertility rates for the group of countries used in the previous chapter. Remember that the countries are in rank order of GDP measured in PPP$. The fertility rate records the average number of births per woman. Thus, in Uganda the average number of births per woman is almost 7. Of course, this does not mean that the average number of *children* per family is so high, as not all the babies survive.

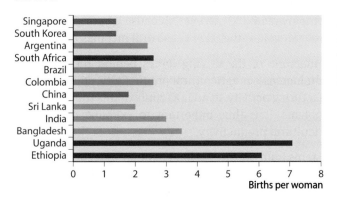

Figure 10.16 *Total fertility rates, selected countries, 2000–2005*

Source: Human Development Report 2007/08.

This pattern of high fertility has implications for the age structure of the population, leading to a high proportion of young dependants in the population. This creates a strain on an LDC's limited resources, because of the need to provide education and healthcare for so many children, and in this sense high population growth can prove an obstacle to development.

This argument might be countered by pointing out that people themselves are a resource for the country. However, it is a question of the balance between population and the availability of resources.

Summary

> Early writers such as Malthus were pessimistic about the prospects for sustained development, believing that diminishing returns to labour would constrain economic growth.

> Globally, population is growing rapidly, with most of the increase taking place in less-developed countries.

> Developed countries and some LDCs have been seen to have passed through a demographic transition, such that population growth stabilises following decreases in death and birth rates.

> However, many LDCs have not completed the transition, remaining in the rapid population growth phase.

> Coupled with the age structure of the population, rapid population growth can create difficulties for LDCs because of the pressure on resources.

Exercise 10.2

Discuss the way in which the age structure of a population may influence the rate of economic growth and development.

Dependence on primary production

Many LDCs, especially in sub-Saharan Africa, continue to rely heavily on the agricultural sector to provide employment and incomes. Because labour productivity in agriculture tends to be relatively low, this may keep rural incomes low.

It is worth remembering that one of the driving forces behind the Industrial Revolution in Britain was an increase in agricultural productivity, enabling more workers to shift into manufacturing activity. In an LDC context, this transition may run into a number of problems. It is thus important to examine if there are obstacles to increasing agricultural productivity.

In some LDCs the problem stems from the form of land tenancy agreements, which can lead to inefficiency. In other cases problems arise because of insecure property rights and the inheritance laws that pertain.

Land tenancy

One characteristic of many LDCs is that land is unequally distributed. If a landowner has more land than can be farmed as a single unit, it is likely that he will hire out parcels of land to small farmers. The way in which this is done turns out to be important for productivity and incentives.

One common form of land tenancy agreement in LDCs is that of **sharecropping**. In this system a tenant-farmer and a landlord of a piece of land have an agreement to share the resulting crop. The tenant-farmers in this case act as *agents*, farming the land on behalf of the landlord (the *principal*). The landlord would like the farmers to maximise returns from the land. However, the tenants

> **Key term**
>
> **sharecropping:** a form of land tenure system in which the landlord and tenant share the crop

will set out to balance the return received with the cost of producing the crop in terms of work effort. A *principal–agent problem* arises here, since if tenants receive only a portion of the crop, their incentive will be to supply less effort than is optimal for the landlord. There is also an asymmetric information problem, in the sense that the landlord cannot easily monitor the amount of effort being provided by a tenant. The tenants know how much of the low output results from low effort, and how much from unfavourable weather conditions — but the landlord does not. The problems that can arise from *asymmetric information* were discussed in *AS Economics, Chapter 8*.

Notice that under a sharecropping contract tenants have little incentive to invest in improving the land or the production methods, because part of the reward for innovation goes to the landlord. On the other hand, the risk of the venture is shared between the landlord and the tenant, as well as the returns.

An alternative would be for the landlord to charge the tenants a fixed rent for farming the land. This would provide better incentives for them to work hard, as they now receive all of the returns. However, it would also mean that they carry all the risk involved — if the harvest is poor, it is the tenants who will suffer, having paid a fixed rent for the land.

Yet another possibility would be for the landlord to hire tenants on a wage contract, and pay a fixed wage for their farming the land. This again would provide little incentive for the tenants to supply effort, as the wage would be paid regardless. As the landlord may not be able to monitor the supply of effort, this would create a problem. Furthermore, the landlord would now face all of the risk.

Thus, for these forms of tenancy, careful consideration needs to be given to the incentives for work effort, the incentives for innovation and investment and the sharing of risk.

Land ownership

In other circumstances inheritance laws can damage agricultural productivity, for example where land is divided between sons on the death of the household head, which means that average plot size declines in successive generations. In some societies property rights are inadequate: for example, women may not be permitted to own land, which can bring problems given that much of the agricultural labour is provided by women. Furthermore, in an attempt to make the best of adverse circumstances, over-farming and a lack of crop rotation practices can mean that soil becomes less productive over time. All of this makes it more difficult to achieve improvements in productivity in the agricultural sector.

Unsuitable land tenure, over-farming and a lack of crop rotation can all lead to low agricultural productivity.

Poverty is thus perpetuated over time; and with limited resources available for survival, farmers have no chance to adopt new or innovative farming practices. The very fact that people are struggling to make the best of the resources and arrangements available may make it difficult for them to step back and look for broader improvements that would allow the reform of economic and social institutions.

It was pointed out earlier that financial markets in many LDCs are relatively under-developed. This is especially so in the rural areas, where the lack of formal financial markets makes borrowing to invest in agricultural improvements almost impossible.

One of the problems here is that the cost of establishing rural branches of financial institutions in remote areas is high; the fixed costs of making loans for relatively small-scale projects are similarly high. This is intensified by the difficulty that banks have in obtaining information about the creditworthiness of small borrowers, who typically may have no collateral to offer.

Trade in primary goods

The difficulty of improving agricultural productivity does not make it easy for LDCs to engage in active international trade, but in practice some have little choice but to rely on primary production in their export activity, as shown in Figure 10.17. The figure shows quite a mixed pattern, reflecting the fact that some countries,

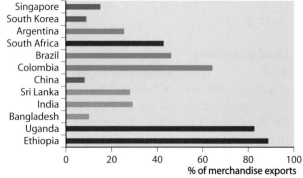

Figure 10.17 *Dependence on primary exports, selected countries*

Source: Human Development Report 2007/08.

Edexcel A2 Economics

especially in Asia, have managed to diversify away from primary production, whereas in others, e.g. Ethiopia and Uganda, the share of primary goods in exports remains extremely high.

In LDCs, even small enterprises may be involved in exporting activity. For example, many small farmers even in remote villages in Uganda grow some coffee for export. However, they rely on traders travelling around the rural areas to buy the coffee and sell it on to the exporters. This creates difficulties for the farmers, who may not be able to check up readily on the prices being charged in the cities, and who do not have the storage or market facilities to produce on a larger scale. If they do not have the communication links with which to determine what is a good price for their crop, the traders have an information advantage that may be exploited. The spread of mobile phones is helping to tackle this issue, by enabling farmers to keep in touch with market conditions, thus improving the information available to them in negotiating a fair price for their produce, and in taking decisions about what crops they should produce.

The Green Revolution

Given that agricultural productivity is much higher in developed countries than in LDCs, why is it not possible for them to learn from the experience of the more-developed countries, and bring in new technology and farming practices?

Part of the reason why this does not work is that the balance between capital and labour is very different in the two groups of countries. In the more-developed countries, productivity is high because of very intensive cultivation methods and the heavy use of capital and chemical inputs, which are neither available in, nor suitable for, LDCs. For example, given that there is already a surplus of agricultural labour in many LDCs, the introduction of labour-saving machinery would not seem to make sense — especially where running and servicing the machines would be difficult, and where field sizes tend to be too small for effective mechanisation.

In this context, the Green Revolution that began in the 1970s seemed to offer great promise. The Green Revolution was associated with the development of new, improved, *high-yielding varieties* (HYVs) of certain crops. Techniques for using these HYVs tended to be labour-intensive, and they promised greatly improved yields. They also involved food crops such as rice and wheat, which were attractive even to small-scale farmers. In addition they were fast growing, so that in some countries it was possible to increase the number of harvests per year.

These HYVs were widely adopted in Asia, and led to substantial increases in productivity, with some countries switching from being importers to exporters of the crops.

However, there was a downside. In some regions it was the richer farmers who were able to make best use of the new seeds, having had more education and thus understanding better how to grow them. Furthermore, some regions (e.g. Bali in Indonesia) already had the associated infrastructure that was required, such as irrigation systems, and this enabled their quick adoption of the new techniques.

In Africa, however, the Green Revolution had a much lower impact, partly because the main crops for which HYVs were developed (rice and wheat) were not widely grown staple crops in sub-Saharan Africa. So again, Africa seemed left behind. Only relatively recently have HYVs for crops such as maize been developed. Moreover, if the Green Revolution is to be successful in Africa, education levels need to be improved (because farmers need to be able to read and interpret instructions), and the necessary infrastructure provided. In the early part of the 21st century, the potential for improving productivity by the introduction of genetically modified crops is under debate, although this is opposed by many people.

The impact of HIV/AIDS

The HIV/AIDS epidemic has had a major impact on LDCs, especially in sub-Saharan Africa. The relative incidence of the disease across countries is illustrated in Figure 10.18. The high prevalence in sub-Saharan Africa is clearly visible. This conceals large differences between countries. There are countries in sub-Saharan Africa where the prevalence is unimaginably high; for example, in Botswana it was estimated that in 2003 some 37.3% of the population aged 15–49 were affected; and in Swaziland the prevalence rate was 38.8%.

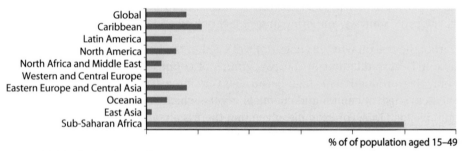

Figure 10.18 *The incidence of HIV/AIDS, selected regions*
Source: UNAIDS/WHO.

The repercussions of the disease are especially marked because of its impact on people of working age. This has affected the size of the labour force, and left many orphans with little hope of receiving an education, which in turn has implications for the productivity of future generations.

Governments have reacted to the disease in very different ways. In countries where the government has been open about the onset of the disease and has striven to promote safe sex, the chances of keeping the disease under control are much higher. For example, in 1990 the incidence of HIV/AIDS amongst adults in Thailand and South Africa was similar, at about 1%. Thailand confronted the problem through a widespread public campaign such that, by 2001, the incidence was still about 1%. South Africa did little to stop the spread of the disease, with the President choosing to downplay the problem and the Minister of Health recommending beetroot as a treatment. In 2005 the incidence of the disease was estimated to be nearly 20%. Some other governments have also kept silent, perhaps not wanting to admit that it is a problem, and here the disease has run rampant. There may also be problems in measuring the incidence of HIV/AIDS

accurately, as individuals may be hesitant to seek treatment or to report that they have the disease for fear of social stigma.

Summary

➤ Many LDCs continue to rely heavily on primary production as a source of employment, incomes and export revenues.

➤ The agricultural sector exhibits low productivity, partly arising from inefficiencies in land tenure systems and inequality in land ownership.

➤ Inadequacies in financial markets, especially in rural areas, make it difficult for farmers to obtain credit for improving productivity.

➤ The Green Revolution had a large impact on productivity in Asia, but was slow to reach sub-Saharan Africa.

➤ HIV/AIDS has been a significant obstacle to development in recent years, especially in sub-Saharan Africa, where the prevalence of the disease is higher than in other regions.

Can governments influence growth?

Faced with these and other obstacles to economic growth, how much can LDC governments do to encourage a more rapid rate of growth and development? A major factor to remember is the limitations in terms of resources. Where average incomes are low and tax collection systems are undeveloped, governments have difficulty in generating a flow of revenue domestically, which is needed in order to launch policies encouraging growth and development.

In some cases governments have tended to rely on taxes on international trade, which are relatively easy to administer, rather than on domestic direct or indirect taxes. This has not helped to stimulate international trade, of course.

Some LDC governments have responded to this problem by borrowing funds from abroad. However, in many cases such funds have not been best used. Funds have sometimes been used for prestige projects, which impress lenders (or donors) but do little to further development. Other funds have been diverted into private use by government officials, and there are well documented examples of politicians, officials and civil servants who have accumulated personal fortunes at the expense of the development of their countries. Figure 10.19 presents a Corruption Perception Index, produced regularly by the non-governmental organisation Transparency International.

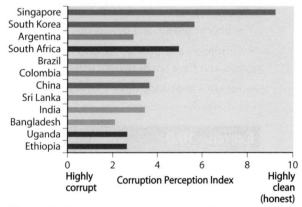

Figure 10.19 *Perceptions of corruption, selected countries, 2008*

Source: Transparency International (**www.transparency.org**)

Notice again how Singapore and South Korea, the tiger economies, score as being 'highly clean' – indeed, on this index Singapore was the fifth least corrupt nation in the world.

There is a need to be careful with such indicators, for by its nature corruption is difficult to identify and to measure. In some countries corruption may be disguised more successfully than in others. Nonetheless, the way in which firms and governments perceive the relative state of corruption in different countries may affect their decisions on where to locate foreign direct investment or provide overseas assistance.

Tendencies towards corruption are likely to be more significant in countries where there is relatively little political stability, so that the government in power knows it will not remain in power for long. Even in the absence of corruption, this discourages such governments from taking a long-term perspective.

Where borrowed funds have not been used wisely, problems inevitably follow when it is time to make repayments on outstanding debt. The debt burden that accumulated for some countries became unsustainable and will be discussed in Chapter 12. Here it suffices to say that the need to repay debt may further limit the resources available for governments to spend on development priorities such as education, healthcare or infrastructure.

Relationships with more-developed countries

In the past, the now more-developed countries have benefited from the resources of today's LDCs. For example, Britain's early success was built partly on the resources of its colonies, and on protecting its own industry at the expense of those colonies. One of the main dangers for LDCs in the twenty-first century is that the more-developed countries will continue to protect their own industries and will not allow the LDCs to develop theirs. It seems clear that sub-Saharan Africa at least will not be able to promote development without the cooperation of richer countries.

Summary

➤ Governments in LDCs have limited resources with which to encourage a more rapid rate of economic growth and development.

➤ Corruption and poor governance has meant that some of the resources that have been available have not been used wisely in some LDCs.

➤ For LDCs to develop, more cooperation is needed from the more-developed countries.

Exercise 10.3

Looking back over the nature of the economic growth process and the obstacles to growth that have been outlined, discuss the extent to which countries in sub-Saharan Africa may be able to use the pattern of development that was so successful in East Asia to promote growth.

Chapter 11

Macroeconomic policies for growth and development

Economic growth has been identified as a key objective for governments. However, there is a range of other objectives to be met, and a variety of economic policy instruments to be deployed. The targets may sometimes conflict with one another, and policy tools can have unintended consequences, so policy coordination and careful design are crucial. This chapter explores these issues and draws together analysis of the various areas of, and approaches to, economic policy.

Learning outcomes

After studying this chapter, you should:
- be familiar with the objectives of economic policy
- appreciate the role and limitations of fiscal policy in influencing the course of the economy
- understand the role and operation of monetary policy in influencing the course of the economy
- be aware of the role and significance of supply-side policies
- be familiar with the conflicts that can arise between policy objectives
- be familiar with the Phillips curve and the notion of the natural rate of unemployment
- be in a position to appraise the relative merits of alternative policy approaches
- be able to evaluate policies that can be deployed to promote growth and development

Objectives of economic policy

AS Economics, Chapter 16 identified a range of policy objectives that governments seek to pursue. Here is a brief reminder.

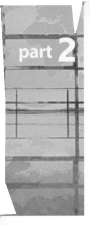

Price stability

The control of inflation has been a prime target of macroeconomic policy in the UK since the mid-1970s. Figure 11.1 shows inflation (as measured by the annual rate of change of the consumer price index in the UK since 1997). The present target for the CPI inflation rate is 2% per annum. You can see from the figure that for much of the period inflation was consistently below the target rate until mid-2005, but then rose above that target for a brief period in 2008.

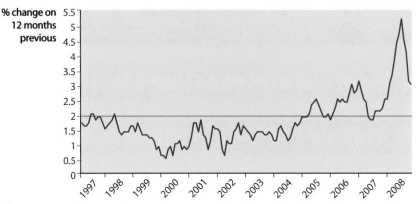

Figure 11.1 *Inflation in the UK, 1997–2008*

Source: ONS.

Prices play a key role in an economy, acting as signals that guide the allocation of resources. When prices are unstable firms may find it difficult to interpret these price signals, and this may lead to a misallocation of resources. Furthermore, instability of prices creates difficulties for firms trying to forecast future expected demand for their products, which may discourage them from undertaking investment. This in turn means that the economy's capacity to produce may expand by less than it could otherwise have done — in other words, high or unstable inflation may dampen economic growth through its effect on investment. (*AS Economics, Chapter 16* identified some other costs of inflation, and you may wish to look back to remind yourself of them. However, the effects on resource allocation and investment are widely accepted to be the most important damaging effects of inflation.)

Full employment

A second key policy objective is that of full employment. Unemployment imposes costs on society and on the individuals who are unemployed. From society's point of view, the existence of substantial unemployment represents a waste of resources and indicates that the economy is

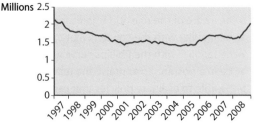

Figure 11.2 *ILO unemployment in the UK, 1997–2009*

Source: ONS.

working below full capacity. Unemployment in the UK fell steadily towards the end of the 1990s from a peak of more than 3 million in 1984. The numbers unemployed began to rise during 2008, and in December 2008 topped the 2 million mark for the first time since July 1997. This is shown in Figure 11.2.

Balance of payments

Earlier chapters have shown that under a flexible exchange rate system the overall balance of payments will always be zero, because the exchange rate adjusts to ensure that this is so. Nevertheless, the balance of payments remains an objective, not so much to ensure overall balance as to maintain a reasonable balance between the current account and the financial account. If the current account is in persistent deficit, this could cause problems in the long run, as the implication is that the country is selling off its assets in order to obtain goods for present consumption. Under a fixed exchange rate system, the need to maintain the exchange rate acts as a constraint upon economic growth, which tends to lead to an increase in imports, creating a current account deficit.

Economic growth

It is through economic growth that the productive capacity of the economy is raised, and this in turn allows the living standards of the country's citizens to be progressively improved over time. In a sense, therefore, this is the most fundamental of the policy objectives. However, attaining other policy objectives may be a pre-requisite for success with growth.

Environmental considerations

It must be recognised that it is not only resources that contribute to living standards: conserving a good environment is also important. Sustainable growth and development means growth that does not prejudice the consumption possibilities of future generations, and this consideration may act as a constraint on the rate of economic growth.

Income redistribution

The final macroeconomic policy objective considered in *AS Economics, Chapter 16* concerned attempts to influence the distribution of income within a society. This may entail transfers of income between groups – that is, from the rich to the poor – in order to protect the vulnerable. Such transfers may take place through progressive taxation (whereby those on higher incomes pay a greater proportion of their income in tax) or through a system of social security benefits such as the Jobseekers' Allowance or Income Support.

Correcting market failure

At the *microeconomic* level there are policy measures designed to deal with various forms of market failure. Competition policy is one example of this; it is designed to prevent firms from abusing monopoly power, and to improve the allocation of resources. Although such policies operate at the microeconomic level, they have consequences for macroeconomic objectives such as economic growth.

Policy instruments

The government has three main types of policy instrument with which to attempt to meet these objectives. These were introduced in *AS Economics, Chapter 17*:

1 *Fiscal policy*: the term 'fiscal policy' covers a range of policy measures that affect government expenditures and revenues through the decisions made by the government on its expenditure, taxation and borrowing. Fiscal policy is used to influence the level and structure of aggregate demand in an economy. As this chapter unfolds, you will see that the effectiveness of fiscal policy depends crucially on the whole policy environment in which it is utilised.

2 *Monetary policy*: this entails the use of monetary variables such as money supply and interest rates to influence aggregate demand. Remember that under a fixed exchange rate system monetary policy becomes wholly impotent, as it has to be devoted to maintaining the exchange rate. So here again, the effectiveness of monetary policy will depend upon the policy environment in which it is used.

3 *Supply-side policies*: such policies comprise a range of measures intended to have a direct impact on aggregate supply — specifically, on the potential capacity output of the economy. These measures are often microeconomic in character and are designed to increase output and hence economic growth.

Aggregate supply revisited

To analyse policy options, return to the model of aggregate supply and aggregate demand (*AS/AD*), first introduced in *AS Economics, Chapters 13 and 14*. Figure 11.3 shows how a shift in aggregate demand from AD_0 to AD_1 results in an increase in real output and the price level as the economy moves to a new equilibrium — a movement along the short-run aggregate supply curve (*SAS*). However, the *SAS* is called a *short-run* aggregate supply curve for a reason, and there is no guarantee that the equilibrium shown in Figure 11.3 can be sustained. For example, notice that the new equilibrium entails a higher overall

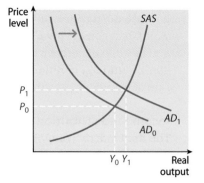

Figure 11.3 *A shift in aggregate demand*

price level. In time this will feed back into the costs faced by firms, causing the *SAS* to shift back to the left. Of more importance is thus the long-run aggregate supply curve.

In this connection, it is important to be aware of a debate that developed over the shape of the long-run aggregate supply curve: this is important because it has implications for the conduct and effectiveness of policy options.

During the 1970s, an influential school of macro-economists, which became known as the **Monetarist School**, argued that the economy would always converge on an equilibrium level of

Key term

Monetarist School: a group of economists who believed that the macroeconomy always adjusts rapidly to the full-employment level of output, and that monetary policy should be the prime instrument for stabilising the economy

output that they referred to as the **natural rate of output**. Associated with this long-run equilibrium was a **natural rate of unemployment**. If this were the case, then the long-run relationship between aggregate supply and the price level would be vertical, as shown in Figure 11.4. Here Y^* is the natural rate of output, i.e. the full-employment level of aggregate output. In other words, a change in the overall price level does not affect aggregate output, because the economy always readjusts rapidly back to full employment.

An opposing school of thought (often known as the **Keynesian School**) held that the macroeconomy was not sufficiently flexible to enable continuous full employment. They argued that the economy could settle at an equilibrium position below full employment, at least in the medium term. In particular, inflexibilities in labour markets would prevent adjustment. For example, if firms had pessimistic expectations about aggregate demand, and thus reduced their supply of output, this would lead to lower incomes because of the workers being laid off. This would then mean that aggregate demand was indeed deficient, so firms' pessimism was self-fulfilling.

These sorts of argument led to a belief that there would be a range of output over which aggregate supply would be upward sloping. Figure 11.5 illustrates such an aggregate supply curve, and will be familiar from *AS Economics, Chapter 14* (see Figure 14.6). In this diagram Y^* still represents full employment; however, when the economy is

Key terms

natural rate of output: the long-run equilibrium level of output to which Monetarists believe the macroeconomy will always tend

natural rate of unemployment: the unemployment rate that would exist when the economy is in long-run equilibrium

Keynesian School: a group of economists who believed that the macroeconomy could settle in an equilibrium that was below full employment

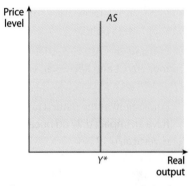

Figure 11.4 *Aggregate supply in the long run (the 'monetarist' view)*

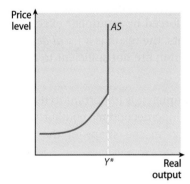

Figure 11.5 *Aggregate supply in the long run (the 'Keynesian' view)*

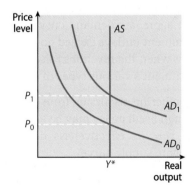

Figure 11.6 *Demand-side policy with a vertical AS curve*

operating below this level of output, aggregate supply is somewhat sensitive to the price level, becoming steeper as full employment is approached.

The policy implications of the monetarist *AS* curve are strong. If the economy always converges rapidly on the full-employment level of output, no manipulation of aggregate demand can have any effect except on the price level. This is readily seen in Figure 11.6, where, regardless of the position of the aggregate demand curve, the level of real output remains at Y^*. If aggregate demand is low at AD_0, then the price level is also relatively low, at P_0. An increase in aggregate demand to AD_1 raises the price level to P_1 but leaves real output at Y^*. In such a world, only supply-side policy (which affects the position of the aggregate supply curve) has any effect on real output.

Summary

➤ Governments pursue a range of policy objectives, including low inflation and low unemployment, a favourable balance of payments position, economic growth, maintenance of a good environment, income redistribution and the correction of market failure.

➤ In order to pursue these objectives, governments have recourse to fiscal, monetary and supply-side policies.

➤ In using the *AD/AS* model to analyse policy options, it is useful to distinguish between monetarist and Keynesian views about the shape of aggregate supply.

➤ Monetarist economists have argued that the economy always converges rapidly on equilibrium at the natural rate of output, implying that policies affecting aggregate demand have an impact only on prices, leaving real output unaffected. Aggregate supply in this world is vertical.

➤ The Keynesian view is that the economy may settle in an equilibrium that is below full employment, and that there is a range over which aggregate supply slopes upwards.

Fiscal policy

What is the role of fiscal policy in a modern economy? The traditional aim of fiscal policy was to affect the level of aggregate demand in the economy. In other words, the overall balance between government receipts and outlays affects the position of the aggregate demand curve, which is reinforced by multiplier effects. When government outlays exceed government receipts, the result is a *fiscal deficit*. This occurs when the revenues raised through taxation are not sufficient to cover the government's various types of expenditure.

Remembering discussion from earlier in the chapter, it is important to realise that although fiscal policy may be able to affect the macroeconomic equilibrium in the short run, its effectiveness depends critically on the shape of the long-run aggregate supply curve.

Figure 11.6 shows that shifting the aggregate demand curve affects only the overall price level in the economy when the aggregate supply curve is vertical — and the Monetarist School of thought argued that it would always be vertical. Hence a key issue for a government considering the use of fiscal policy is knowing whether there is spare capacity in the economy, because otherwise an expansion in aggregate demand from increased government spending will push up prices but leave real output unchanged.

Looking more closely at what is happening, you can see that there are some forces at work that are acting to weaken the multiplier effect of an increase in government expenditure. One way in which this happens is through interest rates. If the government finances its deficit through borrowing, a side-effect is to put upward pressure on interest rates, which then may cause private-sector spending — by households on consumption and by firms on investment — to

crowding out: a process by which an increase in government expenditure crowds out private-sector activity by raising the cost of borrowing

decline, as the cost of borrowing has been increased. This process is known as the **crowding out** of private-sector activity by the public sector. It limits the extent to which a government budget deficit can shift the aggregate demand curve, especially if the public-sector activity is less productive than the private-sector activity that it replaces.

Automatic and discretionary fiscal policies

It is important to distinguish between automatic and discretionary changes in government expenditure. Some items of government expenditure and receipts vary automatically with the business cycle. They are known as **automatic stabilisers**. For example, if the economy enters a period of recession, government expenditure will rise because of the increased payments of unemployment and other social security benefits, and revenues will fall because fewer people are paying income tax, and because receipts from VAT are falling. This helps to offset the recession without any active intervention from the government.

automatic stabilisers: a process by which government expenditure and revenue varies with the business cycle, thereby helping to stabilise the economy without any conscious intervention from government

More important, however, is the question of whether the government can or should make use of discretionary fiscal policy in a deliberate attempt to influence the course of the economy. As already mentioned, the key issue is whether or not the economy has spare capacity, because attempts to stimulate an economy that is already at full employment will merely push up the price level.

Balance between the public and private sectors

Even if the overall size of the budget deficit limits the government's actions in terms of fiscal policy, there are still decisions to be made about the overall balance of activity in the economy. A neutral government budget can be attained either with high expenditure and high revenues, or with relatively small expenditure and revenues. Such decisions affect the overall size of the public sector relative to the private sector. Over the years, different governments in the UK have taken different

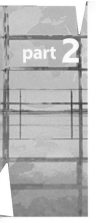

decisions on this issue – and different countries throughout the world have certainly adopted different approaches.

In part, such issues are determined through the ballot box. In the run-up to an election, each political party presents its overall plans for taxation and spending, and typically they adopt different positions as to the overall balance. It is then up to those voting to give a mandate to whichever party offers a package that most closely resembles their preferences.

Figure 11.7 shows the time path of government consumption as a share of GDP from 1949 to 2007; it shows fluctuations around a downward trend, suggesting that the public sector has been gradually reducing its share of the economy. Notice that this does not give the full picture, as public-sector investment is not taken into account in these data. There are one or two periods in the figure where the decline seems to have been especially rapid. In the early 1950s this partly reflects the

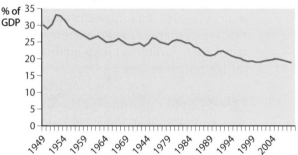

Figure 11.7 Government final consumption, 1949–2007
Source: ONS.

wind-down of government activity in the aftermath of rebuilding following the Second World War. The steep section in the 1980s reflects the privatisation drive of that period, when the government was withdrawing from some parts of the economy.

Figure 11.8 provides an international perspective, showing the share of current and capital expenditure by governments in a range of countries. This reveals something of a contrast between on the one hand North America, Australia and Japan, and on the other many European countries, where government has been more active in the economy. In part this reflects the greater role that government plays in some

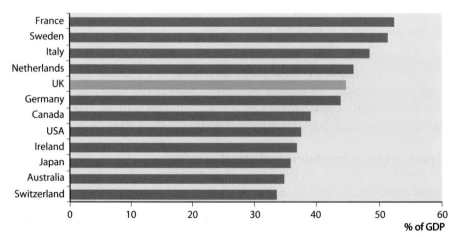

Figure 11.8 Total government expenditure as a percentage of GDP, selected countries, 2007
Source: OECD.

countries in providing services such as education and healthcare, whereas in other countries the private sector takes a greater role, often through the insurance market.

The picture in developing countries may be different again. For many LDCs, tax collection is a challenge, with no effective administrative system in place. The situation is compounded when many people in the country are living on low incomes or in absolute poverty. Furthermore, where subsistence activity is significant, taxation cannot be effectively implemented. As a consequence, governments may have to play a relatively limited role in the economy, or try to raise finance for government expenditure by other means, perhaps by levying taxes on international trade. Another possibility is to fund expenditure by printing money, but this has been seen to have disastrous consequences for inflation, and was certainly a major factor in one of the most extreme episodes of hyperinflation, which took place in Zimbabwe in the late 2000s.

Figure 11.9 shows tax revenue as a percentage of GDP for selected countries around the world — notice that these are ranked in descending order of GDP per capita. In interpreting these data, it is important to remember that tax revenue in a particular country may be low because the country does not have an effective tax collection system, or it may be that the government in power does not wish to take an active role in the economy — at least in the form of high taxes in order to finance high expenditure. This is well illustrated by the difference between the UK and the USA. Nonetheless, there is a tendency for the lower-income countries to display relatively low tax revenue relative to GDP. This is important, because if the government has a limited capacity to raise tax revenue, this may limit the extent to which it is able to introduce policies to combat poverty, or to provide social infrastructure needed in order to encourage economic growth.

Governments have also been aware that foreign firms may take account of relative tax rates in different countries when deciding where to locate their investment. Countries that are keen to attract foreign direct investment may thus feel pressured

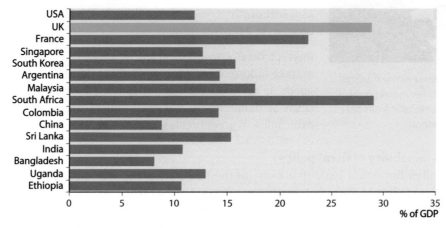

Figure 11.9 *Tax revenue as a percentage pf GDP, selected countries, 2007*
Source: World Bank.

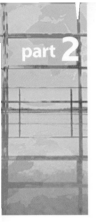

to keep corporate tax rates relatively low in the hope of attracting inflows of investment. Indeed, many multinational corporations have been able to negotiate tax holidays, leaving them free of taxation for a period after they bring their investment.

Direct and indirect taxes

Fiscal policy, and taxation in particular, has not only been used to establish a balance between the public and private sectors of an economy. In addition, taxation remains an important weapon against some forms of market failure, and it also influences the distribution of income. In this context, the choice between using direct and indirect taxes is important.

Remember that direct taxes are taxes levied on income of various kinds, such as personal income tax. Such taxes are designed to be progressive and so can be effective in redistributing income; for example, a higher income tax rate can be charged to those earning high incomes. In contrast, indirect taxes — taxes on expenditure, such as VAT and excise duties — tend to be regressive. As poorer households tend to spend a higher proportion of their income on items that are subject to excise duties, a greater share of their income is taken up by indirect taxes. Even VAT can be regressive if higher-income households save a greater proportion of their incomes.

When Margaret Thatcher came to power in 1979, one of her first actions was to introduce a switch away from direct taxation towards indirect taxes. VAT was increased, and the rate of personal income tax was reduced. In support of this move, it was pointed out that if an income tax scheme becomes too progressive it can provide a disincentive towards effort. If people feel that a high proportion of their income is being taken in tax, their incentives to provide work effort are weak. Indeed, a switch from direct to indirect taxation might be regarded as a sort of supply-side policy intended to influence the position of aggregate supply.

When she became prime minister, Margaret Thatcher moved quickly to switch the emphasis from direct to indirect taxation.

Indirect taxes can be targeted at specific instances of market failure; hence the high excise duties on such goods as tobacco (seen as a demerit good), and petrol (seen as damaging to the environment because of the externality of greenhouse gas emissions).

Sustainability of fiscal policy

Another important issue that came to the fore during the 1990s concerned the sustainability of fiscal policy. This is wrapped up with the notion that current taxpayers should have to fund only expenditure that benefits their own generation, and that the taxpayers of the future should make their own decisions, and not have to pay for past government expenditure that has been incurred for the benefit of earlier generations.

In this context, what is significant is the overall balance between receipts and outlays through time. If outlays were always larger than receipts, the spending programme could be sustained only through government borrowing, thereby shifting the burden of funding the deficit to future generations. This could also be a problem if it made it more difficult for the private sector to obtain funds for investment, or if it added to the national debt. The chancellor of the exchequer is committed to following a **Golden Rule of fiscal policy**, which states that, on average over the economic cycle, the government should borrow only to invest and not to fund current expenditure. This is intended to help achieve equity between present and future generations.

 Key term

Golden Rule of fiscal policy: rule stating that over the economic cycle net government borrowing will be for investment only, and not for current spending

Figure 11.10 shows total public-sector receipts and outlays since 1986. Outlays here include investment, but you can see how the two series tend to move in opposite directions over the cycle. To some extent this is to be expected, because of the operation of the automatic stabilisers.

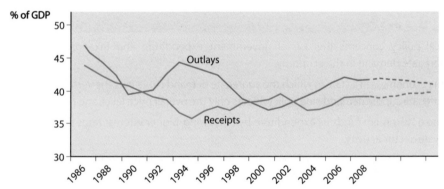

Figure 11.10 *UK public-sector receipts and outlays*

Source: HM Treasury.

Note: 2008 onwards are projected data.

If receipts and outlays more or less balance over the economic cycle, the economy is not in a position whereby the current generation is forcing future generations to pay for its consumption. However, as the economy does go through a business cycle, it is not practical to impose this rule at every part of the cycle, so the so-called Golden Rule is to apply over the economic cycle as a whole.

There is also a commitment to keep public-sector net debt below 40% of GDP – again, on average over the economic cycle. Figure 11.11 shows data for this on a quarterly basis since 1993. The financial support offered to Northern Rock and other banks in the bailout of 2008 has a noticeable effect on public sector net debt,

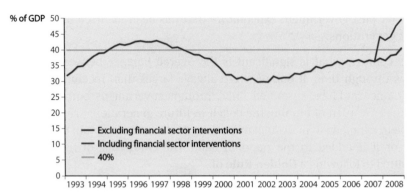

Figure 11.11 *Public sector net debt as a percentage of GDP, 1993–2008*

Source: ONS.

as is clear in the figure. Even without the financial sector interventions, net debt rose over the 40% mark in the last quarter of 2008. This reflected other measures taken by the government to try to mitigate the effects of the recession. One example was the reduction in the rate of VAT from 17.5% to 15%. This is tantamount to a fiscal expansion, but when it was introduced, it was made clear that it was intended as a temporary boost for a specified period. This statement enabled the government to maintain that it was not breaching its long-term fiscal commitment.

Summary

> Fiscal policy concerns the use of government expenditure and taxation to influence aggregate demand in the economy.

> If the economy is in a state in which the aggregate demand curve cuts the vertical segment of aggregate supply, demand-side policy affects only the overall price level, and not real output.

> If the government funds its expenditure by borrowing, higher interest rates may crowd out private-sector activity.

> The stance of the government budget varies with the business cycle, as a result of the operation of automatic stabilisers.

> The overall balance between private and public sectors varies through time and across countries.

> Direct taxes help to redistribute income between groups in society, but if too progressive they may dampen incentives to provide effort.

> The Golden Rule for fiscal policy is that the government should aim to borrow only for investment, and not for current expenditure (averaged over the economic cycle).

> There is also a commitment to keep public sector net debt below 40% of GDP.

Exercise 11.1

Discuss the extent to which the major British political parties adopt differing stances towards establishing a balance between the private and public sectors, i.e. the extent to which each is 'high tax/high public spending' or 'low tax/low public spending'. Analyse the economic arguments favouring each of the approaches.

Monetary policy

Monetary policy has become the prime instrument of government macroeconomic policy, with the interest rate acting as the key control variable. In principle, monetary policy involves the manipulation of monetary variables in order to influence aggregate demand in the economy.

It is important at the outset to realise that it is not possible to control money supply and interest rates simultaneously and independently. Firms and households choose to hold some money. They may do this in order to undertake transactions, or as a precaution against the possible need to undertake transactions at short notice. In other words there is a *demand for money*. However, in choosing to hold money they incur an opportunity cost, in the sense that they forego the possibility of earning interest by purchasing some form of financial asset.

This means that the interest rate can be regarded as the opportunity cost of holding money; put another way, it is the price of holding money. At high rates of interest, people can be expected to choose to hold less money, as the opportunity cost of holding money is high. *MD* in Figure 11.12 represents such a money demand curve. It is downward sloping.

Suppose the government wants to set the money supply (*MS*) at M^* in Figure 11.12. This can be achieved in two ways. If the government controls the supply of money at M^*, then equilibrium will be achieved only if the interest rate is allowed to adjust to r^*. An alternative way of reaching the same point is to set the interest rate at r^* and then allow the money supply to adjust to M^*. The government can do one or the other – but it cannot set money supply at M^* and hold the interest rate at any value *other than* r^* without causing disequilibrium.

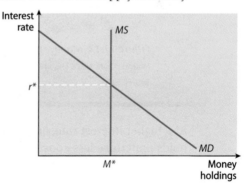

Figure 11.12 *The demand for money*

A problem with attempting to control the money supply directly is that the complexity of the modern financial system makes it quite difficult to pin down a precise definition or measurement of money. For this and other reasons, the chosen instrument of monetary policy is the interest rate. By setting the interest rate, monetary policy affects aggregate demand through the so-called **monetary transmission mechanism**.

 Key *term*

monetary transmission mechanism: channel through which changes in the interest rate feed through into the real economy

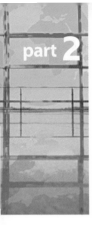
Extension material: money supply and inflation

One way of measuring the money stock is from the *monetary base*, which comprises all notes and coins in circulation and the commercial banks' deposits at the Bank of England, and is known as M0. This narrow measure has become less meaningful in recent years, and the Bank of England no longer publishes data for it.

However, there are many assets that are 'near-money', such as interest-bearing current account deposits at banks. These are highly liquid, and can readily be converted into cash for transactions. M4 is a wide measure of the money stock, and includes M0 together with sterling wholesale and retail deposits with monetary financial institutions such as banks. In other words, it includes all bank deposits that can be used for transactions, even though some of these deposits may require a period of notice for withdrawal.

Figure 11.13 presents the annual percentage rate of change of M0 and M4 since 1990, together with the annual inflation rate (measured by RPI). This shows the extent to which it is possible for M0 and M4 to follow different paths through time — in 1999, for instance, M4 accelerated while M0 decelerated (and inflation fell). Over the years, the Bank of England has introduced various changes in the way the money definitions are measured, and there been changes in the categories of institutions that are recognised for purposes of calculating M4.

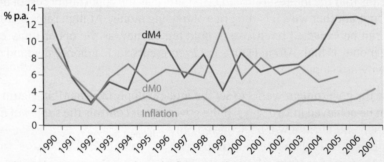

Figure 11.13 *Money supply and inflation in the UK, 1990–2007*

Note: d = annualised change in (M0 or M4).

Source: ETAS

At a higher interest rate, firms undertake less investment expenditure and house-holds undertake less consumption expenditure. Furthermore, if UK interest rates are high relative to elsewhere in the world, they will attract overseas investors, increasing the demand for pounds. This will tend to lead to an appreciation in the exchange rate — which in turn will reduce the competitiveness of British goods and services, reducing the foreign demand for UK exports and encouraging UK residents to reduce their demand for domestic goods and buy imports instead. All these factors lower the level of aggregate demand, shifting the *AD* curve to the left. Such a policy stance may be needed in order to maintain control of inflation. A reduction in interest rates would of course have the reverse effect. However, notice that the interaction of the money supply, interest rates and the exchange rate makes policy design a complicated business.

Indeed, as has been explained, under a fixed exchange rate regime monetary policy is powerless to influence the real economy, as it must be devoted to maintaining the exchange rate. Under a floating exchange rate system monetary policy is freed from this role, but even so it must be used in such a way that the current account deficit of the balance of payments does not become unsustainable in the long run. In other words, the use of interest rates to target inflation has implications for the magnitude of the current and financial accounts of the balance of payments.

As was pointed out in *AS Economics, Chapter 17*, an important aspect of monetary policy since 1997 has been the delegation of responsibility for it to the Bank of England's Monetary Policy Committee (MPC). The rationale for this is based on the observation that the effectiveness of monetary policy depends quite heavily on people's expectations. It operates much more effectively if people believe it is going to work, because then they will amend their behaviour more quickly, speeding up the process of adjustment to equilibrium. By delegating responsibility for monetary policy to the Bank of England, the credibility of policy is enhanced and it thereby becomes more effective, and the government cannot be tempted to buy election success by increasing spending financed through inflationary printing of money.

In creating a stable macroeconomic environment, the ultimate aim of monetary policy is not simply to keep inflation low, but to improve the confidence of decision-makers, and thereby encourage firms to invest in order to generate an increase in production capacity — which will stimulate economic growth and create an opportunity to improve living standards.

Monetary policy in practice

The monetary transmission mechanism explains the way in which a change in the interest rate affects aggregate demand in the economy. In summary, suppose there is a reduction in the interest rate. From firms' point of view, this lowers the cost of borrowing, and would be expected to encourage higher investment spending. Furthermore, consumers may also respond to a fall in the interest rate by increasing their expenditure, both because this lowers the cost of borrowing — so there may be an increase in the demand for consumer durable goods — and because households may perceive that saving now pays a lower return, so may decide to spend more. Thus a fall in the interest rate is expected to have an expansionary effect on aggregate demand. In terms of the *AD/AS* model, this has the effect of shifting the aggregate demand curve to the right. The effectiveness of this will depend upon the shape of the aggregate supply curve and the starting position of the aggregate demand curve.

An expansionary monetary policy intended to stimulate aggregate demand would be damaging if the economy were close to (or at) full employment, as the

main impact would be on the overall price level rather than real output. This suggests that monetary policy should also not be used to stimulate aggregate demand. However, monetary policy can still play an important role in managing the economy. This arises through its influence on the price level and hence the rate of change of prices — that is, inflation.

As has been explained, monetary policy in the UK is the responsibility of the Bank of England. The Bank's Monetary Policy Committee (MPC) meets each month to decide whether or not the interest rate needs to be altered. The objective of this exercise is to ensure that the government's inflation target is met. If the rate of inflation threatens to accelerate beyond the target rate, the Bank of England can intervene by raising interest rates, thereby having a dampening effect on aggregate demand and reducing the inflationary pressure. In reaching its decisions, the MPC takes a long-term view, projecting inflation ahead over the next 2 years.

However, decisions to change the rate of interest are not taken solely in the light of expected inflation. In its deliberations about the interest rate, the MPC takes a wide variety of factors into account, including developments in:

➤ financial markets
➤ the international economy
➤ money and credit
➤ demand and output
➤ the labour market
➤ costs and prices (e.g. changes in oil prices)

A good example was in 2008, when the UK and other countries were struggling to cope with the so-called 'credit crunch'. At this time, inflation was accelerating, and had reached a rate that was more than 1 percentage point above the target. This being so, it might have been expected that the Bank of England would raise interest rates in order to stem aggregate demand and bring inflation back into line with the target. However, this would have been damaging in other ways, pushing the economy further into recession. With house prices falling, an increase in interest rates could have damaged this sector also. It was also thought that there were other pressures affecting the world economy that would in any case mean that the rate of inflation was likely to slow down of its own accord. This was a good example of how different policy targets may come into conflict, and of how it may be prudent not to stick to a rule just for its own sake.

It is also important to remember that the transmission mechanism has a third channel in addition to the effects of the change in interest rate on consumption and investment. This third channel arises through the exchange rate, so that monetary policy cannot be considered in isolation from exchange rate policy. The channels of the transmission mechanism are summarised in Figure 11.14.

chapter *11*

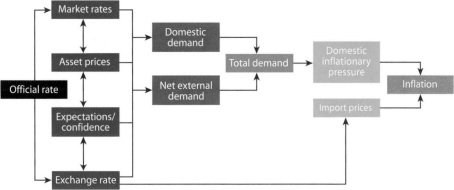

Figure 11.14 *The transmission of monetary policy*

Note: for simplicity, this figure does not show all interactions between variables, but these can be important.

Evaluation of monetary policy

For a decade after the responsibility for monetary policy was delegated to the Bank of England, monetary policy was seen to be highly effective in enabling the achievement of the inflation target. You can see this from Figure 11.15. Inflation stayed within the required one percentage point of its target, moving outside that range in only one month between May 1997 and April 2008. However, matters then took a turn for the worse, and inflation accelerated beyond its limit.

It is important to be aware that the UK was certainly not alone in facing this combination of circumstances. A number of countries had also enjoyed relative stability for several years, followed by a more turbulent period. This in itself suggests that the conduct of monetary policy cannot claim full responsibility for the period of calm, nor perhaps be entirely blamed for the subsequent problems. The process of globalisation that has been taking place means that the UK economy cannot be viewed in total isolation from events occurring elsewhere in the world, and macroeconomic policy is interconnected – through movements in the exchange rate and

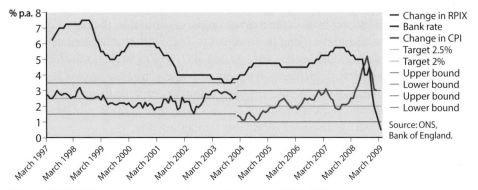

Figure 11.15 *UK interest rates and the inflation target, 1997–2009*

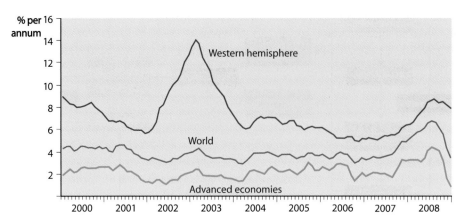

Figure 11.16 *World inflation, 2000–2008*

Source: IMF.

through trading links. This is illustrated by Figure 11.16, which shows monthly inflation (in % p.a.) from the beginning of 2000 for the world as a whole and for two country groupings. You can see how inflation in the world as a whole began to accelerate from mid-2007 onwards after a period of relative stability. Latin America displays higher inflation — and more instability than the world as a whole, whereas the advanced economies experienced inflation rates below the world average throughout the period, but also began to see inflation rates creeping up towards the end of the period before decelerating again towards the end of 2008.

In an interrelated global economy, conditions in one part of the world can rapidly have effects elsewhere. An example of this was apparent in 2007/08, when food prices began to escalate. It is difficult to identify exactly where this began, but between October 2007 and the following spring there were riots protesting at rising food prices in West Bengal, Indonesia, Mozambique, Burkina Faso, Cameroon, Côte d'Ivoire, Senegal, Yemen, Egypt, Bangladesh and Haiti. Eventually, even shoppers in supermarkets in the UK and the USA began to notice that some basic foodstuffs were increasing in price. A number of factors were identified as contributing to the situation, affecting both demand and supply sides of the market. On the demand side, the rapid economic growth in China and India — and improvements in growth in other less-developed countries as well — was fuelling the demand for food. The supply shifts may have been especially important, with increases in the price of oil affecting the price of fertilisers, and with the subsidisation of biofuels in some countries resulting in land being taken out of food production in order to provide biofuels. (For more discussion of this, see the article by Peter Smith in *Economic Review* September 2008.)

As the global recession set in, inflationary pressures eased, and you can see that inflation decelerated towards the end of 2008.

A striking feature of Figure 11.15 is the period towards the end of 2008, which corresponds to the so-called 'credit crunch' and the onset of global recession. At first glance, it would seem that the Bank of England had abandoned all its rules by cutting the bank rate at a time when inflation was way above its target. However, the MPC takes account of a range of factors other than inflation in setting the bank rate. Taking into account the growing threat of recession, the MPC expected inflation to fall drastically, and even turn negative – which would be a state of *deflation.* Hence the decision to reduce the bank rate to an unprecedented low level, reaching 0.5% in March 2009.

Having fallen to this level, further reductions become ineffective, so in March 2009, the Bank announced that it would start to inject money directly into the economy, effectively switching the instrument of monetary policy away from the interest rate and towards the quantity of money. This would be achieved by a process known as *quantitative easing*, by which the Bank purchases assets such as government and corporate bonds, thus releasing additional money into the system through the banks and other financial institutions from which they buy the assets. The hope was that this would allow banks to increase their lending, and thus combat the threat of deflation – and perhaps help to speed recovery.

It is also important to realise that for monetary policy to be and remain effective, it must be viewed in combination with other policies being implemented at the same time. In other words, monetary policy needs to be supported and augmented by other policy measures — in particular, fiscal policy and supply-side policies.

Summary

➤ Monetary policy entails the manipulation of monetary variables in order to influence aggregate demand in the economy.

➤ The prime instrument of monetary policy is the interest rate.

➤ People hold money in order to undertake transactions (among other reasons), and the interest rate can be regarded as the opportunity cost of holding money.

➤ The monetary authorities can control either the money supply or interest rates, but not both independently.

➤ In the UK, monetary policy is conducted by the Bank of England, which has had independent responsibility for meeting the inflation target since 1997.

➤ It is hoped that, by keeping inflation low, firms will be confident about the future, will invest more, and thereby increase the productive capacity of the economy.

➤ Monetary policy cannot focus solely on meeting the inflation target, but must also operate with an awareness of other developments in the macroeconomy.

➤ It is also important that monetary policy is coordinated with other policy measures being implemented that affect the macroeconomy.

Exercise 11.2

Use *AS/AD* to analyse the effect of an expansionary monetary policy on the equilibrium level of real output and the overall price level. Undertake this exercise with a monetarist vertical aggregate supply curve and with a Keynesian aggregate supply curve in which

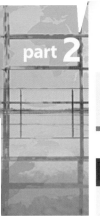

aggregate demand creates an equilibrium that is below full employment. Discuss the differences in your results.

Exercise 11.3

Discuss the evolution of the recession from 2008 onwards, and the extent to which you think that the Bank of England's policy has been successful.

Supply-side policies

Supply-side policies are directed at influencing the position of the aggregate supply curve. In Figure 11.17, Y^* represents full-employment output before the policy, with the equilibrium overall price level at P_0. Supply-side policies that lead to an increase in the economy's productive capacity shift equilibrium output to Y^{**} and the overall price level to P_1.

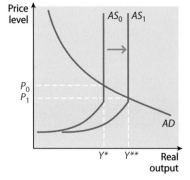

Figure 11.17 A shift in aggregate supply (with a monetarist effect)

Notice that the effect on real output is achieved from supply-side policies whether the equilibrium is in the vertical segment of the AS curve (or with a monetarist AS curve) or in the upward-sloping segment of a Keynesian AS curve, as you can see in Figure 11.18, where the shift in aggregate supply raises equilibrium real output from Y_0 to Y_1.

Such policies include measures like encouraging education and training, improving the flexibility with which markets operate and promoting competition. These policies were discussed in AS Economics, Chapter 17, so you might want to remind yourself of how they operate.

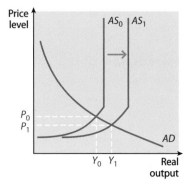

Figure 11.18 A shift in aggregate supply (with a Keynesian effect)

Notice that it is quite difficult to quantify the effects of these supply-side policies. In the case of education and training, some of the effects of increased spending become evident only after very long time lags. In the case of competition policy, again, it is not easy to identify the effects on productive capacity. It is particularly difficult to isolate the impact of these policies when so much else in the economy is changing through time. Nonetheless, these policies do have the effect of stimulating economic growth without inflationary pressure.

Conflicts between policy objectives

Having reviewed the main macroeconomic policy objectives, it should be clear that the designing of economic policy is likely to be something of a juggling act. This is especially so because there may be conflict between some of the targets of policy.

For example, there may be a conflict between economic growth and the environment, so that the pursuit of economic growth may need to be tempered by concern for the environment. Policy must therefore be designed bearing in mind that there may be a trade-off between these two objectives – at some point, it could be that more economic growth is possible only by sacrificing environmental objectives.

Unemployment and inflation

This notion of trade-off between conflicting objectives applies in other areas too. One important trade-off was discovered by the Australian economist Bill Phillips. In 1958 Phillips claimed that he had found an 'empirical regularity' that had existed for almost a century and that traced out a relationship between the rate of unemployment, and the rate of change of money wages. This was rapidly generalised into a relationship between unemployment and inflation (by arguing that firms pass on increased wages in the form of higher prices).

Figure 11.19 shows what became known as the **Phillips curve**. Although Phillips began with data, he also came up with an explanation of why such a relationship should exist. At the heart of his argument was the idea that when the demand for labour is high firms will be prepared to bid up wages in order to attract labour. To the extent that higher wages are then passed on in the form of higher prices, this would imply a relationship between unemployment and inflation: when unemployment is low inflation will tend to be higher, and vice versa.

From a policy perspective – at least within the Keynesian tradition – this suggests a trade-off between unemployment and inflation objectives. If the Phillips curve relationship holds, attempts to reduce the rate of unemployment are likely to raise inflation. On the other hand, a reduction in inflation is likely to result in higher unemployment. This suggests that it might be difficult to maintain full employment and low inflation at the same time. For example, Figure 11.20 shows

Key term

Phillips curve: a curve illustrating the trade-off relationship between unemployment and inflation

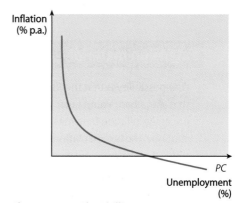

Figure 11.19 The Phillips curve

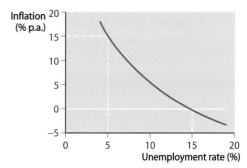

Figure 11.20 The Phillips curve inflation–unemployment trade-off

a Phillips curve that is drawn such that to achieve an unemployment rate of 5%, inflation would need to rise to 15% per annum; this would not be acceptable these days, when people have become accustomed to much lower inflation rates. Furthermore, to bring inflation down to zero would require an unemployment rate of 15%. Having said that, as recently as 1990 the UK economy was experiencing inflation of nearly 10% and unemployment of 7%, which is not far from this example.

Nonetheless, the Phillips curve trade-off offers a tempting prospect to policy-makers. For example, if an election is imminent it should be possible to reduce unemployment by allowing a bit more inflation, thereby creating a feel-good factor. After the election the process can be reversed. This suggests that there could be a political business cycle induced by governments seeking re-election. In other words, the conflict between policy objectives could be exploited by politicians who see that in the short run an electorate is concerned more about unemployment than inflation.

The 1970s provided something of a setback to this theory, when suddenly the UK economy started to experience both high unemployment and high inflation simultaneously, suggesting that the Phillips curve had disappeared. This combination of stagnation and inflation became known as **stagflation**.

> **Key** *term*
>
> **stagflation:** situation in which an economy simultaneously experiences stagnation (high unemployment) and high inflation

Extension material

One possibility is that the Phillips curve had not in fact disappeared, but had moved. Suppose that wage bargaining takes place on the basis of *expectations* about future rises in retail prices. As inflation becomes embedded in an economy, and people come to expect it to continue, those expectations will be built into wage negotiations. Another way of viewing this is that expectations about price inflation will influence the *position* of the Phillips curve.

Figure 11.21 shows how this might work. PC_0 represents the initial Phillips curve. Suppose we start with the economy at the *natural rate of unemployment* U_{nat}. (Remember this was defined earlier in the chapter.) If the economy is at point A, with inflation at π_0 and unemployment at U_{nat}, the economy is in equilibrium. If the government then tries to exploit the Phillips curve by allowing inflation to rise to π_1, the economy moves in the short run to point B. However, as people realise that inflation is now higher, they adjust their expectations. This eventually begins to affect wage negotiations; the Phillips curve then

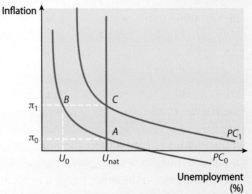

Figure 11.21 The expectations-augmented Phillips curve

moves to PC_1, and unemployment returns to the natural rate. The economy settles at C and is again in equilibrium, but now with higher inflation than before — and the same initial rate of unemployment. For this reason, the natural rate of unemployment is sometimes known as the **non-accelerating inflation rate of unemployment (NAIRU)**.

The problem that arises with this is of how to get back to the original position with a lower inflation rate. This can happen only if people's expectations adjust so that lower inflation is expected. This means that the economy has to move down along PC_1, pushing up unemployment in order to reduce inflation. Then, once expectations adjust, the Phillips curve will move back again until the natural rate of unemployment is restored. If this takes a long time, then the cost in terms of unemployment will be high.

Key *term*

non-accelerating inflation rate of unemployment (NAIRU): the rate of unemployment in an economy that is consistent with a constant rate of inflation; equivalent to the natural rate of unemployment

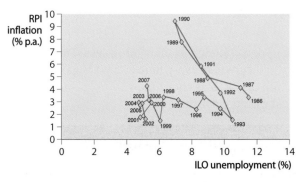

Figure 11.22 Unemployment and inflation in the UK, 1986–2007

Source: ONS.

Figure 11.22 shows some empirical data for the UK since 1986. From 1986 until 1993 (or even until 1995), the pattern seems consistent with a Phillips curve relationship. However, after that time inflation seems to have stabilised, and unemployment is gradually falling — as if, with stable inflation, people's expectations have kept adjusting and allowed unemployment to fall.

Figures 11.23 and 11.24 show the pattern of the relationship between unemployment and inflation for two other countries, Sweden and France. Sweden shows a classic Phillips curve pattern; France has experienced less variation in the unemployment rate.

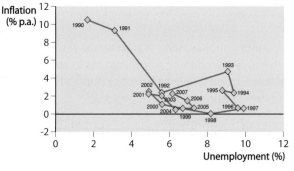

Figure 11.23 Unemployment and inflation in Sweden, 1990–2007

Source: OECD.

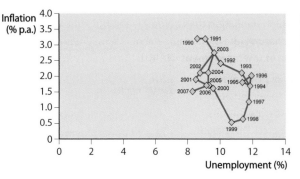

Figure 11.24 *Unemployment and inflation in France, 1990–2007*

Economic growth and the current account

In some circumstances, conflict can also arise between achieving economic growth and attaining equilibrium on the current account of the balance of payments. An increase in economic growth resulting in higher real incomes could lead to an increase in imports of goods and services, if UK residents spent a high proportion of their additional income abroad. This was seen as a major problem during the fixed exchange rate era of the 1950s and 1960s, when any deficit on the current account had to be met by running down foreign exchange reserves. This led to a 'stop–go' cycle of macroeconomic policy, where every time growth began to accelerate the current account went into deficit, and policy then had to be adjusted to slow down the growth rate to deal with the deficit.

Exercise 11.4

Given the following list of policy objectives, discuss the possible conflicts that may arise between them, and discuss how these might be resolved:

➤ low inflation

➤ low unemployment

➤ high economic growth

➤ a low deficit on the current account of the balance of payments

➤ maintenance of a high environmental quality

➤ equity in the distribution of income

Designing the policy mix

The design and conduct of economic policy may be seen as an elaborate balancing act. Differing policy objectives need to be prioritised, as in many cases there may be conflict between them. Choices have to be made about the balance to be achieved between fiscal, monetary and supply-side policies.

The consensus view in the early part of the twenty-first century is that fiscal policy should be used to achieve the desired balance between the public and private sectors. Monetary policy should be devoted to meeting the inflation target in order to create a stable macroeconomic environment; this will then encourage growth and enable improvements in the standard of living. Supply-side policies are perhaps the most important, as these contribute to a raising of efficiency and an increase in the productive capacity of the economy.

The keynote in policy design lies in enabling markets to operate as effectively as possible.

If the UK were to join the single currency area, this would create a new policy environment, in which responsibility for monetary policy would be delegated to the European Central Bank. This would leave fiscal policy and supply-side policies as the sole instruments available to a UK government.

Summary

➤ Supply-side policies aim to influence the position of the aggregate supply curve and to raise the productive capacity of the economy, primarily by helping markets to work more effectively.

➤ The achievement of the various policy objectives is complicated by the fact that some are in conflict with one another, so that the achievement of one target may endanger another.

➤ The Phillips curve claims a trade-off relationship between unemployment and inflation, although the appearance of stagflation in the 1970s cast doubt on the hypothesis.

➤ The position of the Phillips curve may be seen to depend on people's expectations about future inflation, so that in the long run the Phillips curve may be vertical at the natural rate of unemployment (or the non-accelerating inflation rate of unemployment — the NAIRU).

➤ Fiscal policy in a modern economy tends to be confined to determining the balance between the public and private sectors.

➤ Monetary policy tends to be devoted to meeting the inflation target in order to encourage economic growth.

➤ Supply-side policies are of greatest importance, influencing the efficiency with which markets work, and thus affecting the long-run capacity of the economy to produce.

Promoting growth and development

The previous chapters dealing with economic development have frequently referred to the limited resources that are available within less-developed countries (LDCs), which has constrained attempts to stimulate economic growth and development. If domestic resources are lacking, it is important to consider the possibility of mobilising resources from outside the country. This can be done by attracting foreign direct investment, accepting overseas assistance or borrowing on international capital markets. This chapter reviews these possibilities, and other ways of promoting growth and development.

Learning outcomes

After studying this chapter, you should:
➤ be aware of the need for less-developed countries to mobilise external resources for development
➤ understand the benefits and costs associated with foreign direct investment
➤ be familiar with the potential use of overseas assistance for promoting development, and the effectiveness of such flows of funds in the past
➤ be aware of the possible use of borrowing to obtain funds for development and its dangers
➤ understand the role of the Bretton Woods institutions in international development
➤ be familiar with Structural Adjustment Programmes and the HIPC initiative
➤ understand the importance of human capital in the development process
➤ be familiar with ways in which market failure may justify intervention in the economy to promote growth and development, and various ways in which this may be attempted

Market-friendly growth revisited

Chapter 10 introduced the notion of a market-friendly growth strategy. The core idea of this is that markets should be allowed to work without government intervention wherever this is possible, but that governments should intervene when there is a need to correct market failure. The persistent gap in living standards between the less-developed and the developed countries suggests that it is important to identify areas in which growth and development could be encouraged by appropriate policies. The World Bank identified four key areas that should receive a high priority in countries seeking to encourage development — namely, people, microeconomic markets, macroeconomic stability and global linkages. This chapter will examine and evaluate a range of policies that have been suggested as ways of stimulating growth and development. Many of them fit into one or other of the World Bank's key factors.

A starting point is to consider global linkages. It is clear that many LDCs have found it very difficult to mobilise resources from domestic sources. Capital tends to be scarce; labour resources are underdeveloped and underutilised; low incomes can mean low savings, and thus limited funds for investment. A natural question is whether an LDC can mobilise external resources in order to trigger the development process.

In all of this discussion, it is important to remember that LDCs have diverse characteristics, so that a one-size-fits-all approach is not likely to be successful. Different countries face different configurations of obstacles and opportunities, so need different policies and strategies. Indeed, some of the models discussed in earlier chapters may be more applicable to some countries than to others.

The role of external resources in development

The shortage of resources in many LDCs has been a severe obstacle to their economic growth and development. This was emphasised by the Harrod–Domar model of economic growth which was introduced in Chapter 10. Figure 12.1 offers a reminder.

The underlying process by which growth can take place requires the generation of a flow of savings that can be transformed into investment in order to generate an increase in capital, which in turn enlarges the productive capacity of the economy. This then enables output and incomes to grow, which in turn feeds back into savings and allows the process to become self-sustaining.

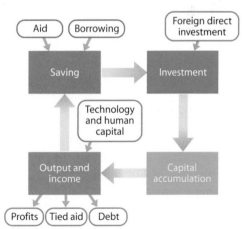

However, the process will break down if savings are inadequate, or if markets do not operate sufficiently well to maintain the chain. This chapter begins by considering the possibility that the process

Figure 12.1 *The Harrod–Domar process of economic development*

could be initiated by an inflow of resources from outside the economy. There are three possible routes to be examined: foreign direct investment, overseas aid and international borrowing. As Figure 12.1 indicates, associated with each of these inflows there are likely to be some costs, and potential leakages from the system.

Foreign direct investment

One possible source of external funding that has been attractive to many LDCs is foreign direct investment (FDI). This entails encouraging foreign multinational corporations (MNCs) to set up part of their production in an LDC. These were introduced in Chapter 6 in the discussion of globalisation.

In evaluating the potential impact of MNCs operating in LDCs, it is important to consider the characteristics of such companies. Many operate on a large scale, often having an annual turnover that exceeds the less-developed country's GDP. They tend to have their origins in the developed countries, although some LDCs are now beginning to develop their own MNCs.

MNCs are in business to make profits, and it can be assumed that their motivation is to maximise global after-tax profits. While they may operate in globally oligopolistic markets, they may have monopoly power within the LDCs in which they locate. They operate in a wide variety of different product markets — some are in primary production (Geest, Del Monte, BP), some are in manufacturing (General Motors, Mitsubishi) and some are in tertiary activity (McDonald's). These characteristics are important in shaping the analysis of the likely benefits and costs of attracting FDI into an LDC.

Chapter 6 identified three basic motivations for MNCs to locate in another country: looking for markets, resources or efficiency — or some combination of the three, of course.

To set a context for the discussion, Figure 12.2 shows the relative size of net FDI inflows for the set of countries selected previously. This reveals a very uneven pattern, with India receiving only 0.8% of GDP as inflows of FDI and Singapore receiving more than 17%.

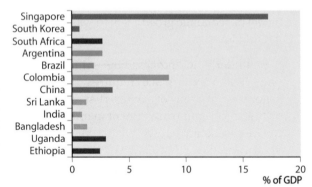

Figure 12.2 *Net foreign direct investment inflows, selected countries, 2005*

Source: Human Development Report 2007/08.

In some ways this chart is misleading, as it conceals the true size of FDI inflows into China. Remember that China's GDP is very large, so 3.5% of China's GDP represents a very substantial flow of investment. Some of this is market-seeking, as the opening up of China's market of 1.3 billion people is a major attraction. However, it may also be partly resource seeking, with MNCs wanting to take advantage of China's resource of labour.

Potential benefits

Perhaps the prime motivation for attracting FDI inflows for LDCs is the injection they provide into the Harrod–Domar chain of development. In addition to providing investment, MNCs are likely to supply capital and technology, thereby helping to remedy the LDC's limited capacity to produce capital goods. They may also assist with the development of the country's human capital, by providing training and skills development for the workers they employ, together with management expertise and entrepreneurial skills, all of which may be lacking in the LDC.

LDCs may also hope that the MNC will provide much needed modern-sector jobs by employing local workers. Given the rate of migration to the urban areas discussed in Chapter 9, such employment could be invaluable to the LDC, where employment cannot keep up with the rapid growth of the labour force.

The LDC government may also expect to be able to collect tax revenues, both directly from the MNC in the form of a tax on profits and indirectly from taxes on the workers' employment incomes. Moreover, the MNC will export its products, and thus generate a flow of foreign exchange for the LDC.

In time, there may also be spillover effects. As local workers learn new skills and gain management expertise and knowledge about technology, they may be able to benefit local firms if at some stage they leave the MNC and take up jobs with local companies — or use their new-found knowledge to start their own businesses. These externality effects can be significant in some cases.

Potential costs

In evaluating the potential benefits of FDI, however, LDCs may need to temper their enthusiasm a little, as there may be some costs associated with attracting MNCs to locate within their borders. This would certainly be the case if the anti-globalisation protesters are to be believed, as they have accused the MNCs of exploiting their strength and market power in order to damage the LDCs in various ways.

In examining such costs, it is important to be objective and to try to reach a balanced view of the matter, and to be aware that some of the accusations made by the critics of globalisation may have been overstated. On the other hand, it is also important to remember that MNCs are profit-making firms, and not humanitarian organisations seeking to promote justice and equality.

LDCs entice multinational companies to their shores, in the hope of promoting development — a hope not always fulfilled.

A first point to note is that, because most MNCs originate in more-developed countries, they tend to use technology that suits the conditions with which they are familiar. In many cases these will tend to be relatively capital-intensive, which may not be wholly appropriate for LDC factor endowments. One upshot of this is that the employment effects may not be substantial, or may be limited to relatively low-skilled jobs.

It is dangerous to generalise here. The sort of technology that MNCs tend to use may be entirely suitable for a country like Singapore, which has progressed to the stage where it needs hi-tech capital-intensive activity to match its well-trained and disciplined workforce. However, such technology would not be appropriate in much of sub-Saharan Africa. But MNCs are surely aware of such considerations when taking decisions about where to locate. A decision to set up production in China may be partly market oriented, but efficiency considerations will also affect the choice of technology.

An important consideration is whether the MNC will make use of local labour. It might hire local unskilled labour, but use expatriate skilled workers and managers. This would tend to reduce the employment and spillover effects of the MNC presence. Another possibility is that the MNC may pay wages that are higher than necessary in order to maintain a good public image, and to attract the best local workers. This is fine for the workers lucky enough to be employed at a high wage, but it can make life difficult for local firms if they cannot hold on to their best workers.

In addition, the LDC government's desire for tax revenue may not be fully met. In seeking to attract MNCs to locate within their borders, LDCs may find that they need to offer tax holidays or concessions as a 'carrot'. This will clearly limit the tax revenue benefits that the LDC will receive. It is also possible that MNCs can manipulate their balance sheets in order to minimise their tax liability. A high proportion of the transactions undertaken by an MNC are internal to the firm. Thus, it may be possible to set prices for internal transactions that ensure that profits are taken in the lowest tax locations. This process is known as *transfer pricing*. It is not strictly legal, but is difficult to monitor.

As far as the foreign exchange earnings are concerned, a key issue is whether the MNC will recycle its surplus within the LDC or repatriate its profits to its shareholders elsewhere in the world. If the latter is the case, this will limit the extent to which the LDC will benefit from the increase in exports. However, at least the MNC will be able to market its products internationally, and if the country becomes better known as a result then, again, there may be spillovers for local firms. Gaining credibility and the knowledge to sell in the global market is problematic for LDCs, and this is one area in which there may be definite benefits from the MNC presence.

The LDC should also be aware that the MNC may use its market power within the country to maximise profits. Local competitors will find it difficult to compete, and the MNC may be able to restrict output and raise price. In addition, MNCs have been accused of taking advantage of more lax environmental regulations, polluting the environment to keep their costs low. The actions of the anti-globalisation protesters in this area may have influenced MNCs to clean up their act somewhat.

Finally, MNCs tend to locate in urban areas in LDCs — unless they are purely resource-seeking, in which case they may be forced to locate near the supply of whatever natural resource they are seeking. Locating in the urban areas may increase inequality between the rural and urban areas, which has been a problem in some LDCs.

Exercise 12.1

Draw up a list of the benefits and costs of MNC involvement in an LDC, and evaluate the benefits relative to the costs. Remember that many LDCs are enthusiastic about attracting MNCs to locate in their countries. Try to identify which are the most important benefits that they are looking for.

Given the need to evaluate the benefits and costs of FDI flows, it is important that LDC governments can negotiate good deals with the MNCs. For example, countries such as Indonesia have negotiated conditions on the share of local workers that will be employed by the MNC after a period of, say, 5 years. This helps to ensure that the benefits are not entirely dissipated. Of course, it helps if the LDC has some key resource that the MNC cannot readily acquire elsewhere. There is some recent evidence that high levels of human capital help to attract FDI flows, which may help to explain why East Asia and China have been recipients of more FDI inflows than countries in sub-Saharan Africa.

Summary

➤ Multinational corporations (MNCs) are companies whose production activities are carried out in more than one country.

➤ Foreign direct investment (FDI) by MNCs is one way in which an LDC may be able to attract external resources.

➤ MNCs may be motivated by markets, resources or cost effectiveness.

➤ LDCs hope to benefit from FDI in a wide range of ways, including capital, technology, employment, human capital, tax revenues and foreign exchange. There may also be spillover effects.

➤ However, MNCs may operate in ways that do not maximise these benefits.

Overseas assistance

If LDCs could enter a phase of economic growth and rising incomes, one result would be an increase in world trade. This would benefit nations around the world, and the more-developed industrial countries would be likely to see an increase in the market for their products. This might be a reason for the governments of more-developed countries to help LDCs with the growth and development of their economies. Of course, there may also be a humanitarian motive for providing assistance, i.e. to reduce global inequality.

Indeed, there may be market failure arguments for providing aid. For example, it may be that governments have better information about the riskiness of projects in LDCs than private firms have. In relation to the provision of education and health-care, it was argued earlier that there may be externality effects involved. However, LDC governments may not have the resources needed to provide sufficient education for their citizens. Similarly, it was argued that some infrastructure may have public good characteristics that require intervention.

Official aid is known as **overseas development assistance (ODA)**, and is provided through the Development Assistance Committee of the OECD. Figure 12.3 shows the relationship between the amount of ODA received per capita and GDP per capita in 2000. It suggests that humanitarian motives are not always paramount in determining the recipients of aid. In particular, the fact that Israel receives more ODA per person than any other country, in spite of being a high-income country, suggests a political motivation. Israel actually receives more ODA as a percentage of GDP than India. Indeed, there has been much criticism of the USA over many years for the way in which aid has been used to favour countries that have been important in US foreign policy.

Key term

overseas development assistance: aid provided to LDCs by countries in the OECD

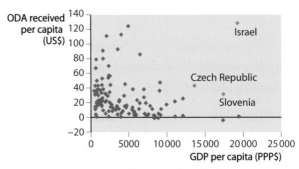

Figure 12.3 *ODA and GDP per capita, 2000*

A contentious issue is whether ODA should be channelled to those countries most in need of it, or focused on those countries best equipped to make good use of the funding. If humanitarian motives are uppermost, then you would expect there to be a strong relationship between flows of overseas assistance and average income levels. However, if other motives are important, this relationship might be less apparent.

Figure 12.4 shows the top 15 recipients of ODA as a percentage of the total aid disbursed in 2006. The fact that Iraq and Afghanistan come high up the list may reflect the importance of these countries in terms of US foreign policy in the

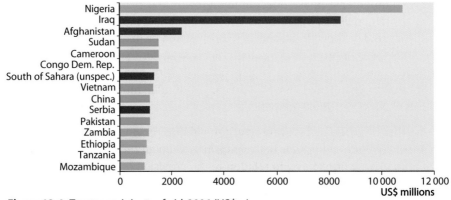

Figure 12.4 *Top ten recipients of aid, 2006 (US$m)*

Source: OECD.

aftermath of 9/11 and the Iraq war. Countries that fall in the UNDP's 'low human development' category are coloured green in this graph. You need to be careful in interpreting these data, because looking at the overall size of the flows does not take account of differing country sizes. For this reason Figure 12.5 may be more useful. This chart shows the extent to which some countries are dependent on overseas assistance by expressing receipts of ODA relative to the recipient country's gross national income. This gives a different picture, and emphasises the extent to which some LDCs rely on flows of overseas assistance.

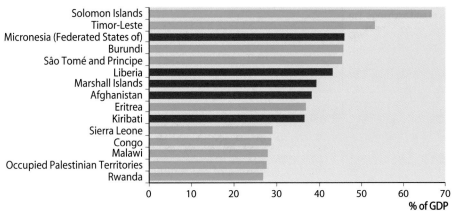

Figure 12.5 *Top ten recipients of aid, 2005 (% of GDP)*

Source: Human Development Report 2007/08.

At a meeting of the United Nations in 1974, the industrial countries agreed that they would each devote 0.7% of their GNP to ODA. This goal was reiterated at the Millennium Summit as part of the commitment to achieving the Millennium Development Goals. Progress towards this target has not been impressive. Figure 12.6 shows the performance of donor countries relative to this target, and you can see that only five countries had achieved the 0.7% UN target by 2005. The amount of ODA provided by the UK as a percentage of GNI increased after 1997, but

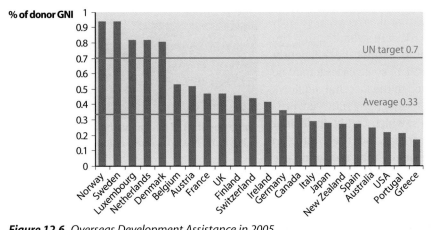

Figure 12.6 *Overseas Development Assistance in 2005*

Source: Human Development Report 2007/08.

the USA's share has fallen. However, it should be borne in mind that in terms of US$, the USA is by far the largest contributor.

An encouraging sign is that total ODA flows increased in the late 1990s and the early years of the new millennium, as can be seen in Figure 12.7. This seemed to represent an enhanced awareness of the importance of such flows for many LDCs. Indeed, at the summit meeting of G8 at Gleneagles in July 2005 the commitment to the UN target for ODA was reiterated.

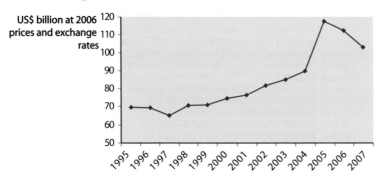

US$ billion at 2006 prices and exchange rates

Figure 12.7
Flows of ODA,
1995–2007
Source: OECD.

A World Bank study of the effectiveness of aid, published in 1997, reported that 'foreign aid to developing countries since 1970 has had no net impact on either the recipients' growth rate or the quality of their economic policies'. Some evidence was found to suggest that aid was more effective in countries where 'sound economic management' was being practised. In other words, it was argued that aid might prove effective in stimulating growth only if the country were also implementing 'good' economic policies — particularly in terms of openness to trade, low inflation and disciplined fiscal policy.

There are many possible reasons for the ineffectiveness of aid. It may simply be that providing aid to the poorest countries reduces its effectiveness, in the sense that the resources of such countries are so limited that the funding cannot be efficiently utilised. In some cases it may be related to the fact that aid flows are received by LDC governments, which can be inefficient or corrupt, so there are no guarantees that the funds are

Large amounts of foreign aid have been supplied to LDCs, but it has not always helped.

used wisely by these governments. Or it might simply be that the flows of aid have not been substantial enough to have made a difference.

There are other explanations, however. For example, some donor countries in the past have regarded aid as part of their own trade policy. By tying aid to trade deals, the net value of the aid to the recipient country is much reduced: for instance, offering aid in this way may commit the recipient country to buying goods from the donor country at inflated prices.

In other cases, aid has been tied to use in specific projects. This may help to assure the donor that the funds are being used for the purpose for which they were intended. However, it is helpful only if appropriate projects were selected in the first place. There may be a temptation for donors to select prestige projects that will be favourably regarded by others, rather than going for the LDC's top-priority development projects.

Such deals are becoming less common, as now more ODA is being channelled through multilateral organisations than bilaterally between donor and recipient directly. This may mean that aid flows will be more effective in the future. In 1994, 66.1% of total aid was untied (45.8% in the case of aid from the UK), but by 1999 this proportion had increased to 83.8% (91.8% from the UK).

An important issue for all sorts of aid is that it should be provided in a way that does not damage incentives for local producers. For example, dumping cheap grain into LDC markets on a regular basis would be likely to damage the incentives for local farmers by depressing prices.

Summary

➤ Overseas development assistance (ODA) comprises grants and concessional funding provided from the OECD countries to LDCs.

➤ The countries most in need of ODA may not be in a position to use it effectively.

➤ In some cases the direction of ODA flows is influenced by the political interests of the donor countries.

➤ The more-developed countries have pledged to devote 0.7% of their GNPs to ODA, but few have reached this target.

➤ Some evidence suggests that aid has been ineffective except in countries that have pursued 'good' economic policies.

➤ The tying of aid to trade deals or to specific projects can limit the aid's benefits to recipient LDCs.

Exercise 12.2

Examine the arguments for and against providing assistance to those countries in most need of it, as opposed to those best equipped to make good use of it.

International borrowing

The final option for LDCs is to borrow the funds needed for development. This may be on concessional terms from the World Bank or the IMF, or on a commercial basis from international financial markets.

It is important to notice that when countries borrow from the World Bank or the IMF, the loans come with strings attached. In other words, these bodies impose conditions on countries wanting to borrow, typically in relation to the sorts of economic policy that should be adopted. Such policy programmes will be considered below.

As with other forms of external finance, problems have arisen for some LDCs that have tried to borrow internationally. These problems first became apparent in the early 1980s, when Mexico announced that it could not meet its debt repayment commitments. The stock of outstanding debt has been a major issue for many LDCs, especially in sub-Saharan Africa.

Figure 12.8 presents some data about this. It can be seen that in 1990 the debt position for many of these countries was serious indeed. In the case of Uganda, in 1990 more than 80% of the value of exports of goods and services was needed just to service the outstanding debt. For a country with limited resources, this leaves little surplus to use for promoting development. The encouraging aspect of Figure 12.8 is that for most of these countries the situation was much improved in 2005 – in some cases dramatically so, as in Uganda, for example.

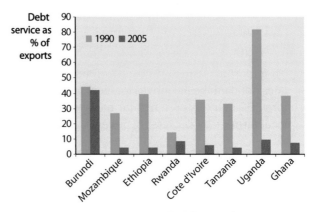

Figure 12.8 *Debt servicing in sub-Saharan Africa, 1990 and 2005*

Source: Human Development Report 2006/07.

Figure 12.9 shows the relationship between stocks of external debt and the growth of GNP per capita in the late 1990s. Nicaragua is excluded because its debt level at that time was way off the scale. The striking aspect of this

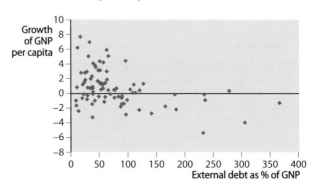

Figure 12.9 *Debt and growth*

Source: Human Development Report 1999.

figure is that the countries with the highest levels of debt experienced low or negative growth, supporting the contention that debt is a constraint on growth.

But how did this situation arise? The story begins in the mid-1970s with the first oil price crisis. In 1973–74 oil prices quadrupled. Countries that were not oil producers were suddenly faced with a deficit on the current account of the balance of payments, as the demand for oil in the short run was highly inelastic.

For LDCs, this was a major problem. They knew that if they went to the IMF for a loan they would be forced to accept onerous conditions, so they were reluctant to do this. On the other hand, the oil producers were enjoying windfall gains, and their surpluses were lodged with the banks, which were thus keen to lend. LDCs were therefore encouraged to borrow from the banks rather than the IMF, and they took out loans at variable interest rates.

The second oil price crisis came in 1979–80, when prices tripled. Many LDCs were now in deep trouble, carrying a legacy of past debts and now needing to borrow still more. Furthermore, countries like the USA and the UK were adopting macro-economic policies that were pushing interest rates to high levels, making it more difficult for LDCs to meet their existing commitments.

This resulted in the debt crisis of the 1980s, when a number of countries were threatening to default on their debts. A number of plans (including the Baker and Brady Plans) were introduced to safeguard the international financial system, but from the LDC viewpoint these entailed mainly a rescheduling of existing debt; in other words, they were given longer to pay. A consequence was that debt levels continued to grow.

The problems were made worse because in some countries the borrowed funds were not used wisely. Development through borrowing is sustainable only if the funds are used to enable exports to grow, so that the funds can be repaid. When they do not lead to increased export earnings, repayment problems will inevitably result.

Before looking at more recent events, this chapter examines the role of the so-called Bretton Woods institutions – the World Bank, the IMF and the World Trade Organisation.

Summary

➤ A third way for LDCs to obtain external funds is through borrowing.

➤ Loans provided by the World Bank and the IMF have conditions attached that are not always palatable for LDCs.

➤ Many LDCs have borrowed in the past, but have then been unable to meet the repayments.

➤ In some cases this was because the funds were not well used.

Exercise 12.3

Discuss the extent to which good government within a developing country is a necessary condition for the successful mobilisation of internal and external resources.

The Bretton Woods institutions

At the end of the Second World War in 1945, a conference was held at Bretton Woods, New Hampshire, USA, to establish a system of fixed exchange rates. This became known as the Dollar Standard, as countries agreed to fix their currencies relative to the US dollar. John Maynard Keynes was an influential delegate at the conference. In addition to establishing the exchange rate system (which operated until the early 1970s), the conference set up three key institutions with prescribed roles, in support of the international financial system.

International Monetary Fund

The **International Monetary Fund (IMF)** was set up with a specific brief to offer short-term assistance to countries experiencing balance of payments problems. Thus, if a country were running a deficit on the current account, it could borrow from the IMF in order to finance the deficit. However, the IMF would insist that, as a condition of granting the loan, the country put in place policies to deal with the deficit — typically, restrictive monetary and fiscal policies.

World Bank

The International Bank for Reconstruction and Development was the second institution established under the Bretton Woods agreement. It soon became known as the **World Bank**. The role of the World Bank is to provide longer-term funding for projects that will promote development. Much of this funding is provided at commercial interest rates, as the role of the Bank was seen to be the channelling of finance to projects that normal commercial banks would perceive as being too risky. However, some concessional lending is also made through the International Development Association (IDA), which is part of the World Bank.

Key terms

International Monetary Fund (IMF): a multilateral institution that provides short-term financing for countries experiencing balance of payments problems

World Bank: multilateral organisation that provides financing for long-term development projects

General Agreement on Tariffs and Trade (GATT): precursor of the WTO, GATT organised a series of 'Rounds' of tariff reductions

World Trade Organisation (WTO): multilateral body responsible for overseeing the conduct of international trade

World Trade Organisation

Initially, Bretton Woods set up the **General Agreement on Tariffs and Trade (GATT)**, with a brief to oversee international trade. This entailed encouraging countries to reduce tariffs, but the GATT also provided a forum for trade negotiations and for settling disputes between countries. The GATT was replaced by the **World Trade Organisation (WTO)** in 1995. Between them, these organisations have presided over a significant reduction in the barriers to trade between countries — not only tariffs, but other forms of protection too. The role of the WTO was discussed in Chapter 6.

Heavily Indebted Poor Countries (HIPC) Initiative

In the run-up to the Millennium it was clear that many countries' international debt burdens had become unsustainable. Pressure was put on the World Bank and the UN to offer debt forgiveness to LDCs to herald the Millennium.

The World Bank was reluctant to consider this route. One of the reasons for its reluctance concerns *moral hazard.* It is argued that if a country expects to be forgiven its debt it will have no incentive to behave responsibly. Furthermore, a country that has been forgiven its debt may have no incentive to be more responsible in the future — and other countries too will have less of an incentive to pay off their debts.

The response was the **HIPC Initiative**, which allows for debt forgiveness on condition that the country demonstrates a commitment to 'good' policies over a period of time. The HIPC Initiative was first launched in 1995, but the conditions were so restrictive that few countries were able to benefit. Thus, a number of pressure groups, including Jubilee 2000, lobbied the World Bank to allow the initiative to be more accessible. The original HIPC measures required countries to follow the policy package for a period of 6 years before they would qualify for any debt relief.

The policies concerned overlap with a previous package of measures, which came to be known as a **Structural Adjustment Programme (SAP)**. SAPs have been on the World Bank agenda for many years, and comprise a package of policies designed to help a country initiate a process of growth and development. Under the HIPC Initiative, a new set of measures was added to encourage countries to devote funds to poverty alleviation programmes.

Key terms

HIPC Initiative: initiative launched in 1995 to provide debt relief for heavily indebted poor countries

Structural Adjustment Programme (SAP): package of policy measures recommended by the World Bank to LDCs

The HIPC policy package incorporates four main steps:

1 successful implementation of policies to enhance economic growth (the World Bank's model of market-friendly growth was discussed in Chapter 10)

2 development of a Poverty Reduction Strategy Paper (PRSP)

3 encouragement of private enterprise

4 diversification of the export base

Uganda was the first country to qualify for debt relief under HIPC, and Figure 12.8 seems to suggest that this has had an effect, with debt service having been reduced substantially. Indeed, there is some evidence that debt levels for low-income countries are coming under control, as can be seen in Figure 12.10, showing that the ratio of total

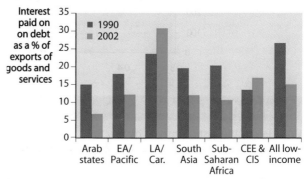

Figure 12.10 *Debt service, selected regions, 1990 and 2002*
Source: Human Development Report 2004.

debt service to exports has fallen for all low-income countries from 27% in 1990 to 15% in 2002. Indeed, for the least-developed countries the ratio is down to 7.7% in 2002, from 16.2% in 1990. However, the regional pattern shown in Figure 12.10 indicates that debt levels continue to grow in Latin America and the Caribbean and in Central and Eastern Europe and the CIS.

In July 2005 government leaders from the G8 countries met at a summit meeting in Gleneagles. At this meeting the countries present pledged to cancel the debt of the world's most indebted countries — which effectively meant those countries that had qualified under the HIPC initiative. It remains to be seen as to how this recommitment will work out in practice. Jubilee 2000 has continued to argue that HIPC remains overly restrictive, and has pointed out that there are countries that face heavy debt burdens that have been excluded from HIPC, and are therefore also excluded from the Gleneagles statement. This includes such countries as Bangladesh, Cambodia, the Philippines, Nigeria and Peru.

What is not entirely clear is the extent to which improvements in debt service levels can be attributed to the HIPC Initiative. A number of commentators have pointed out that it is not only the HIPC countries that have witnessed a reduction in debt service levels in recent years. Figure 12.11 presents some evidence on this. On the vertical axis is a debt service index for 2005 based on 1990 = 100. This is to be interpreted as saying that countries with an index below 100 have seen a reduction in debt service levels in 2005 compared with 1990. On the horizontal index are values of the Human Development Index for the same year. The HIPC countries are coloured red in the figure, and you can see that only one of these countries saw debt service rise in this period. However, the countries coloured blue on the graph are countries that were excluded from HIPC, and you can see that the majority of these countries also experienced a reduction in debt service levels in the period — especially those with relatively low human development levels. Some big increases in debt service were registered by some countries with relatively high human development.

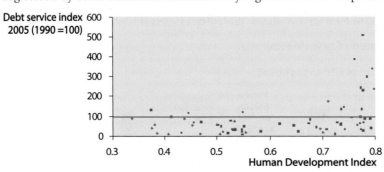

Figure 12.11
The impact of HIPC on debt service?

Case study Uganda

Uganda was the first country to qualify for debt relief under the HIPC Initiative and illustrates some of the key issues.

Uganda is a landlocked country in East Africa, bordering a range of countries and with ongoing civil conflict in the north.

The country gained independence from Britain in 1962, and was governed initially by Milton Obote. There was some political instability in this period, although GDP per capita remained fairly constant. Obote stayed in power partly by using the army to carry out a coup against his own government. Then in 1971 he was overthrown by Idi Amin, who ruled through military power. During this period the Ugandan economy essentially collapsed, as you can see in Figure 12.12, which shows the time-path of Uganda's real GDP per capita. This was partly through Amin's expulsion of all Asian Ugandans, who had run the country's limited manufacturing industry and distribution sector. He also killed an estimated 300,000 people during his regime.

Amin was illiterate, and allowed no written instructions, which impeded the bureaucracy. In 1978 he invaded Tanzania, but the Tanzanian army, with the help of exiled Ugandans, fought back and took Kampala in 1979. Elections were held in 1980, and Milton Obote came back to power, albeit under

allegations of election fixing. Obote's second period was characterised by civil war, and lasted until the next coup in 1985 (Okello). The Okello regime lasted only until 1986, when the present President Museveni took over, bringing some stability and economic recovery. Indeed, the introduction of an SAP followed soon after Museveni came to power.

In terms of the HIPC requirements, Uganda has done everything expected of it. It has established a strong record of sound macro-economic policies and structural adjustment reforms. It has produced its Poverty Reduction Strategy Paper (PRSP) and tried to implement it. The Plan included a drive for universal primary education initiated in 1997, supported by $75 million from the World Bank. Figure 12.13 shows the time-path of Uganda's external debt relative to gross national income. The dramatic fall in the last years of the figure may reflect the effect of the HIPC debt relief.

I visited Uganda in November 1997 to undertake a survey in the rural areas. Even at this early stage in the new policy, some of the effects of the HIPC Initiative were evident. In some cases children had been held back from attending school in anticipation of the new measures. In other cases, some older children had returned to school — there were several 13-year-olds in the first year of primary education, and 'children' of up to 19 years old enrolled in primary education.

However, although the debt burden has lessened, and in spite of rapid growth during

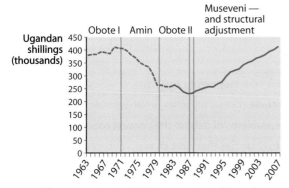

Figure 12.12 *Real GDP per capita in Uganda*

Source: data from 1982 from the World Bank; earlier data from Ugandan sources

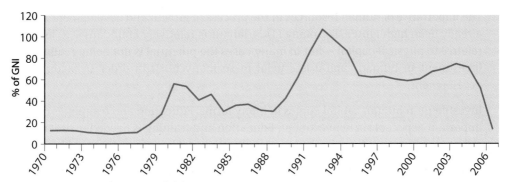

Figure 12.13 *Uganda's external debt, 1970–2006*

the 1990s (Uganda was one of the fastest-growing economies in the world in this period), the country remains poor. However, in terms of the HDI, Uganda moved out of the 'low human development' group of countries in 2003.

There seem to be a number of factors that have affected Uganda's situation. First, the international price of coffee has fallen to unanticipated low levels. With Uganda continuing to rely heavily on coffee for export earnings, this is a major setback. Efforts have been made to bring about greater diversification, and this is beginning to show results. However, the IMF also concedes that 'further cooperation of the international community is needed to help remove the barriers to trade'. There is a major issue lurking here: it is all very well persuading LDCs to stimulate and diversify their exports, but if they cannot find buyers the impact will be limited.

In addition, some countries have not conceded the debt relief that is due under the agreements, another indication that international cooperation is crucial in enabling the HIPC measures to become effective.

There is some further evidence that one of the reasons for the persistence of poverty in the rural areas, in spite of the macroeconomic success, was the lack of integration of these rural areas into national markets. In part this is a result of poor infrastructure — poor roads, lack of market facilities and poor information about national trading conditions.

THE AUTHOR

Summary

> The Bretton Woods conference in 1945 set up three major multilateral organisations: the IMF, the World Bank and the GATT (which later became the WTO).

> The IMF has the role of providing short-term finance for countries experiencing balance of payments problems.

> The World Bank provides longer-term financing for development projects.

> The WTO oversees the conduct of international trade.

> The HIPC Initiative was designed to address the problems of debt in the poorest countries.

> Under the HIPC Initiative, debt relief is provided to countries that have shown a commitment to World Bank-approved policies and have implemented a Poverty Reduction Strategy Paper (PRSP).

Human resources

The importance of human resources in the process of growth and development has already been highlighted. For many LDCs, labour is relatively abundant — at least relative to physical capital — but in many cases the potential is not being realised. Investment in human capital is crucial in so many LDCs in order to facilitate development.

Investment in human capital comes in many forms. Education and training is one important aspect of such investment. Education and training is needed in order to raise agricultural productivity, and to provide a skilled labour force that enables the growth of modern sector economic activity such as manufacturing industry — and for the increased utilisation of technology. Certainly the absence of skilled labour

Improved healthcare provision is important in raising the productivity of workers.

is a substantial obstacle to economic growth. However, human capital does not only involve education and training, important as that is. For many LDCs, improved provision of nutrition and healthcare can be equally important in raising the productivity of workers — and in contributing directly to the quality of life.

An important question in the context of the market-friendly approach to growth and development is whether markets can be relied upon to ensure the appropriate provision of education and healthcare, or whether there is some form of market failure that required government intervention.

In the case of both education and healthcare, it can be argued that there are significant externality effects. In the case of education, it has been shown that there are spillover effects, in the sense that a group of educated workers cooperating together becomes more productive because the members of the group interact with each other. This implies that the marginal social benefits of education exceed the marginal private benefits — because society gains from the way in which workers are able to work together. In terms of healthcare, consider the example of a vaccination programme against a communicable disease. An individual may perceive that the marginal benefit of having their child vaccinated is relatively low, because the probability of becoming infected may be low. However, if everyone thinks in the same way, then this increases the likelihood of there being an epidemic of the disease. Thus the social benefits that arise from a vaccination programme may exceed the private benefits — so in the absence of intervention, too few individuals will invest in vaccination.

There may also be information failures in education and healthcare. A poor rural household may not perceive the full benefits of education — especially where uneducated parents are taking decisions on behalf of their children. They may then decide to keep their children out of school, perhaps believing that the benefits to the household from child labour exceed the benefits of sending their children to school. In many LDCs, there has been a tendency to keep female children away from school, as the household may not see any benefit from female education. In healthcare, there may also be situations in which households do not understand the potential benefits from medical treatment (especially preventative treatment), or may not perceive the value of good nutrition.

Given these arguments about market failure, there may be a case for some form of intervention in order to ensure better take-up of education and healthcare. This might take the form of subsidising education, perhaps by providing free primary school education, or it might be through regulation – enforcing a minimum school-leaving age.

The question then arises of how an LDC government can raise the finances needed in order to improve education and healthcare, especially given the problems (discussed in Chapter 11) associated with tax collection systems. For many LDCs, this has proved a major stumbling block. Some progress has been made through the use of overseas assistance. For example, Uganda was able to launch a scheme to encourage primary education by making use of funds provided by the World Bank as part of the HIPC Initiative. These funds were earmarked for the purpose in the poverty reduction strategy produced by Uganda. However, it is clear from the data that much more is needed in this area.

Exercise 12.4

Using appropriate diagrams, explain how the provision of education and healthcare may be subject to externality effects. Discuss possible policies to ensure improved healthcare provision in LDCs.

Making microeconomic markets work

The discussion of education and healthcare in the previous section made reference to externality effects as one reason for market failure in those areas. However, there are many other ways in which microeconomic markets have been seen to be inefficient in LDCs. This is partly because markets have not fully developed in some LDCs, but also may reflect the way that governments in the past have tended to intervene inappropriately. For example, many LDC governments have been tempted to try to fix prices of goods, rather than allowing market forces to dictate prices. This can then have unintended effects on incentives. If a government decides to hold food prices down in the urban areas, in order to help the urban poor (or to keep their electorates happy), this then distorts the market and provides insufficient incentive for farmers.

Microfinance

A particular problem has been the provision of finance for small (but important) projects in rural areas of LDCs. Where a large portion of the population live in the rural areas, the difficulty of raising funds for investment has been an impediment to improving agricultural productivity — in spite of the significance of this sector in many LDCs. This was mentioned in Chapter 11.

Attempts have been made to remedy this situation through **microfinance** schemes. This approach was pioneered by the Grameen Bank, which was founded in Bangladesh in 1976. The bank made small-scale loans to groups of women who otherwise would have had no access to credit, and each group was made corporately responsible for paying back the loan. The scheme has claimed great success, both in terms of the constructive use of the funds in getting small-scale projects off the ground and in terms of high pay-back rates.

Key **term**

microfinance: schemes that provide finance for small-scale projects in LDCs

Case study The Grameen Bank

In 1974 a severe famine afflicted Bangladesh, and a flood of starving people converged on the capital city, Dhaka. Muhammad Yunus was an economics professor at Chittagong University. He tells how he was struck by the extreme contrast between the neat and abstract economic theories that he was teaching, and the plight and suffering of those surviving in bare poverty, and suffering and dying in the famine.

He also tells how he decided to study the problem at first hand, taking his students on field trips into villages near to the campus. On one of these visits they interviewed a woman who was struggling to make a living by making bamboo stools. For each stool that she made, she had to borrow the equivalent of 15 pence for the raw materials. Once she had paid back the loan, at interest rates of up to 10% per week, her profit margin was just 1p. The woman was never able to escape from her situation because she was trapped by the need to borrow, and the need to pay back at such punitive rates of interest. Her story was

by no means unique, and Yunus was keen to find a way of enabling women like her to have access to credit on conditions that would allow them to escape from poverty. He began experimenting by lending out some of his own money to groups in need.

Muhammad Yunus launched the Grameen Bank experiment in 1976. The idea was to provide credit for small-scale income-generating activities. Loans would be provided without the need for collateral, with borrowers being required to form themselves into groups of five with joint responsibility for the repayments. The acceptance of this joint responsibility and the lack of collateral helped to minimise the transaction costs of making and monitoring the loans.

On any criteria, the project proved an enormous success. The repayment record has been impressive, although the Grameen Bank charges interest rates close to those in the formal commercial sector — which are much lower than the informal money-lenders. After the initial launch of the Bank, lending has

The Sheffield College

Hillsborough LRC
Telephone: 0114 260 2254

been channelled primarily to women borrowers, who are seen to invest more carefully and to repay more reliably — and to be most in need. Table 12.1 offers some information about the scale and scope of the Grameen Bank by the late 1990s.

By the end of May 1998 more than $2.4 billion had been loaned by Grameen Bank, including more than 2 million loans for milch cows, nearly 100,000 for rickshaws, 57,000 for sewing machines and many more for processing, agriculture, trading, shop keeping, peddling and other activities. Grameen-type credit programmes are now operating in 59 countries in Africa, Asia, the Americas, Europe and Papua New Guinea.

As for the impact of Grameen loans in economic terms, the loans are seen to have generated new employment, to have reduced the number of days workers are inactive, and to have raised income, food consumption and living conditions of Grameen Bank members — not to mention their social impact on the lives of millions of women.

No. of villages where Grameen operates	38,551
No. of Grameen centres	65,960
No. of branches	1,112
No. of staff	12,589
No. of Grameen members	
Female	2,210,160
Male	124,620
Total	2,334,780
Cumulative no. of houses built with	
Grameen housing loans	438,764

Table 12.1 *The Grameen Bank as of 31 May 1998*

Source: *Muhammad Yunus, Banker to the Poor*, Aurum Press, London, 1998.

Other schemes have involved groups of households coming together to pool their savings in order to accumulate enough funds to launch small projects. Members of the group take it in turns to use these joint savings, paying the loan back in order for the next person to have a turn. These are known as *rotating savings and credit schemes (ROSCAS)*, and they have had some success in providing credit for small schemes. In spite of some successful enterprises, however, such schemes have been found to be less sustainable than Grameen-style arrangements, and have tended to be used to obtain consumer durable goods rather than for productive investment and innovation.

Case study Example of a ROSCA

Suppose that 12 individuals are saving for a bicycle (a key form of transport in many developing countries). A bicycle costs $130, and each individual saves $10 per month. Simple arithmetic indicates that it would take 13 months for enough funds to have accumulated for the 12 individuals to buy their bicycles. Suppose that the 12 people agree to work together. First, they explain to the bicycle dealer that there is a guaranteed order for 12 bicycles, and they negotiate a discount of $10 per bicycle. They then meet at the end of each month, and each pays $10 into the fund. At the end of the first month, there are sufficient funds for one person to buy a bicycle — usually chosen by a lottery. As a result, even the last person in turn gets the bicycle earlier because of the discount they negotiated. Of course, without the discount, one unfortunate person would have to wait the full period, but clearly this is a very efficient way of making use of small amounts of savings. With more people, or higher contributions, the funds can be used for more substantial projects. Administration costs are minimal, but the schemes do rely on trust,

such that the first person to win the lottery does not then stop making payments.

In the absence of such schemes, households may be forced to borrow from local moneylenders, often at very high rates of interest. For example, the Bank of Uganda survey mentioned earlier found that households were paying rates between 0% (when borrowing from family members) and 500%. In part this may reflect a high risk of the borrower's defaulting, but it may also reflect the ability of local money-lenders to use market power. The absence of insurance markets may also deter borrowing for productive investment, especially in rural areas.

Fair trade

Given the relatively weak position that LDCs hold when they try to compete in global markets, there has been increasing interest in the notion of **fair trade schemes**. These had small beginnings, with a number of charities campaigning for small producers in LDCs to be given a 'fair' price for their products. This has flourished and proliferated, to the extent that most supermarkets now stock items labelled as being 'fair trade' — often with a premium price, although this can be difficult to judge because of quality differences between products. If consumers in the rich countries are prepared to pay more for produce in the knowledge that a larger amount goes to the producer, then this may be a way of giving better incentives to farmers in LDCs.

However, it is important also to consider the economic arguments that underlie this sort of scheme. There are two key issues. First, are there good economic grounds for intervening through the provision of subsidies through fair trade schemes? Second, what would be the effect of those subsidies?

A Guatemalan coffee farmer — fair trade schemes may not always help small producers.

The market failure argument in this case is based on the abuse of market power, under which small producers in LDCs are unable to receive a 'fair' price for their output. This may partly reflect information failure as well, as small producers may not always be in a position to discover the going market price for the crops that they produce. The increased use of mobile phones in some countries may be helping to overcome this information failure, but there is a long way to go before it is eliminated. The problem is made worse by the time lags involved in responding to changes in market conditions. It takes 3 to 4 years for a newly planted coffee plant to produce marketable coffee, so it is impossible to respond quickly to an increase in price. Indeed, given that prices are set in world markets, and are subject to fluctuations, it is possible that a farmer may manage to increase output only to find that prices have plummeted.

If the issue is one of market power, then using the power of the consumer to affect the bargaining power of the small producer could potentially improve the distribution of the gains from production and provide improved incentives for the producer. If the issue is one of information failure, then the appropriate targeted response would be to take steps to resolve that failure by providing better information to the producers. A fair trade scheme may be able to help by providing advice and guidance to farmers. If the issue is with price fluctuations, then it is not clear how a fair trade scheme by itself can deal with the problems of gestation lags.

In the longer term, there are a number of unanswered questions to be addressed. Some critics have argued that providing subsidies to small producers can produce some anomalous and unintended defects. One danger is that farmers may be subsidised to continue production in a market in which prices may already be on a downward spiral, rather than switching to alternative commodities with better long-term prospects.

Exercise 12.5

Discuss the economic arguments for and against fair trade schemes, and come to a view about whether *you* regard them as benefiting LDC producers.

Macroeconomic stability

The macroeconomic policies needed to promote growth and development were discussed in Chapter 11. In the context of LDCs, a stable macroeconomic environment may be seen as a prerequisite for encouraging investment – in particular for attracting foreign direct investment. At times, some LDCs have struggled to achieve such stability, notably in Latin America where inflation became a major problem that interfered with the growth process. More recently, one of the symptoms of economic disaster in Zimbabwe was the hyperinflation that officially reached 231 million per cent, but was thought unofficially to be in the billions. This effectively meant that some 80% of the population were relying on subsistence and barter.

Without macroeconomic stability, the other components of a market-friendly strategy cannot operate; as microeconomic markets will fail when price signals are not clear, people will be reluctant to invest in human capital, and MNCs and governments will be reluctant to invest in the country. Indeed, when domestic markets do not operate effectively, and where financial markets do not pervade the whole economy, then traditional methods of achieving macroeconomic stability will not work.

Summary

> Investment in human capital is a critical part of the growth and development process, in terms of education, healthcare and nutrition.

> It is important to enable microeconomic markets to work wherever this is possible, as this can encourage efficiency in resource allocation.

> Intervention may be needed to deal with failure in rural credit markets; this could take the form of microfinance initiatives.

> Fair trade schemes have tried to address problems caused by market failure in aspects of international trade, but these remain somewhat contentious.

Other policies to encourage growth and development

What else can be done to encourage growth and development? If markets were working effectively, then prices would guide resource allocation, and LDCs would be in a position to engage in beneficial trade with the rest of the world. If markets do not work, then LDCs may find themselves disadvantaged in the global market, and may find that the structural transformation that is desirable for development will not take place sufficiently quickly, leaving countries over-dependent on traditional economic activities.

Trade policy

It is important for LDCs to be able to adopt an appropriate trade policy if they are to reap the potential gains from international trade. In turn, trade is important because LDCs need to be able to obtain foreign exchange with which to import the capital and technology that is needed to transform the structure of the domestic economy.

If a country is short of foreign exchange, there are two broad approaches that it can take in drawing up its trade policy to deal with the problem. One is to reduce its reliance on imports in order to economise on the need for foreign currency — in other words, to produce goods at home that it previously imported. This is known as an **import substitution** policy.

An alternative possibility is to try to earn more foreign exchange through **export promotion**.

Key *terms*

import substitution: policy entailing the encouragement of domestic production of goods previously imported in order to reduce the need for foreign exchange

export promotion: policy entailing the encouragement of domestic firms to export more goods in order to earn foreign exchange

Import substitution

The import substitution strategy has had some appeal for a number of countries. The idea is to boost domestic production of goods that were previously imported, thereby saving foreign exchange. A typical policy instrument used to achieve this is the imposition of a **tariff**. Tariffs were discussed in Chapter 6.

However, not all the effects of a tariff are favourable for the economy. Look back at Figure 6.6 to remind yourself of how a tariff operates. Consumers are certainly worse off, as they have to pay a higher price for the good. They will therefore consume less, so there will be a loss of consumer surplus. Some of what was formerly consumer surplus will now be redistributed to others in society. The government gains the tariff revenue, as mentioned. In addition, producers gain economic rent, given by the dark blue area in Figure 6.6. There is also a deadweight loss to society, such that, overall, society is worse off as a result of the tariff. Effectively, the government is subsidising inefficient local producers, and forcing domestic consumers to pay a price that is above that of the good if imported from abroad.

Some would defend this policy on the grounds that it allows the LDC to protect an infant industry. In other words, through such encouragement and protection, the new industry will eventually become sufficiently efficient to compete in world markets.

There are two key problems with this argument. First, unless the domestic market is sufficiently large for the industry to reap economies of scale, local producers will never be in a position to compete globally. Second, because of such protection domestic firms are never exposed to international competition, and so will not have an incentive to improve their efficiency. In other words, tariff protection fosters an inward-looking attitude among local producers that discourages them from trying to compete in world markets. They remain happy with the protection that provides them with economic rent.

Export promotion

Export promotion requires a more dynamic and outward-looking approach, as domestic producers need to be able to compete with producers already established in world markets. The choice of which products to promote is critical, as it is important that the LDC develops a new pattern of comparative advantage if it is to benefit from an export promotion strategy.

For primary producers, a tempting strategy is one that begins with existing products and tries to move along the production chain. For example, in 1997 (under encouragement from the World Bank) Mozambique launched a project whereby, instead of exporting raw cashew nuts, it would establish processing plants that would then allow it to export roasted cashew nuts. In the early 1970s Mozambique was the largest producer

By the late 1990s, Brazil and India had overtaken Mozambique in cashew nut production.

of cashew nuts in the world, but by the late 1990s the activity had stagnated, and the country had been overtaken by producers in Brazil and India.

This would seem to have been a good idea, because it makes use of existing products and moves the industry into higher value-added activity. However, the project ran into a series of problems. On the one hand, there were internal constraints: processing the nuts requires capital equipment and skilled labour, neither of which was in plentiful supply in Mozambique. In addition, tariff rates on processed commodities are higher than on raw materials, so the producers faced more barriers to trade. In addition, they found that they were trying to break into a market that was dominated by a few large existing producers which were reluctant to share the market. Furthermore, the technical standards required to sell processed cashew nuts were beyond the capability of the newly established local firms.

These are just some of the difficulties that face new producers from LDCs wanting to compete in world markets. Indeed, the setting of high technical specifications for imported products is one way in which countries have tried to protect their own domestic producers – it is an example of a **non-tariff barrier**.

Key *term*

non-tariff barrier: an obstacle to free trade other than a tariff, e.g. quality standards imposed on imported products

The East Asian tiger economies pursued export promotion strategies, making sure that their exchange rates supported the competitiveness of their products and that their labour was appropriately priced. However, it must be remembered that the tiger economies expanded into export-led growth at a time when world trade itself was booming, and when the developed countries were beginning to move out of labour-intensive activities, thereby creating a niche to be filled by the tigers. If many other countries had expanded their exports at the same time, it is not at all certain that they could all have been successful.

As time goes by, it becomes more difficult for other countries to follow this policy. It is particularly difficult for countries that originally chose import substitution, because the inward-looking attitudes fostered by such policies become so deeply entrenched.

It should also be remembered that there will always be dangers in trying to develop new kinds of economic activity that may entail sacrificing comparative advantage. This is not to say that LDCs should remain primary producers for ever, but it does suggest that it is important to select the new forms of activity with care in order to exploit a *potential* comparative advantage.

Exercise 12.6

Discuss the possible effects on developed countries if LDCs characterised by low wage labour become more active in world markets.

The Sheffield College

Norton LRC
Telephone: 0114 260 2334

Summary

> In designing a trade policy, an LDC may choose to go for import substitution, nurturing infant industries behind protectionist barriers in order to allow them to produce domestically goods that were formerly imported.

> However, such infant industries rarely seem to grow up, leaving the LDC with inefficient producers which are unable to compete effectively with world producers.

> Export promotion requires a more dynamic and outward-looking approach, and a careful choice of new activities.

Exercise 12.7

Discuss the relative merits of import substitution and export promotion as a trade strategy. Under what conditions might import substitution have a chance of success?

Industrialisation and structural change

So what are the prospects for a country wanting to move towards industrialisation, and to reduce its reliance on primary production? If the Lewis model were valid (see Chapter 10), then a small wage differential would be sufficient to encourage the growth of the modern sector. Unfortunately, the process did not prove to be as smooth as Lewis suggested. One reason relates to human capital levels. Agricultural workers do not have the skills or training that prepare them for employment in the industrial sector, so it is not so straightforward to transfer them from agricultural to industrial work.

Furthermore, to the extent that they were able to transfer, the expanding industry did not always reinvest the surplus in order to enable continuous expansion of the industrial sector. Foreign firms tended to repatriate the profits, and in any case tended to use modern, relatively capital-intensive technology that did not require a large pool of unskilled labour.

Perhaps more importantly, Lewis's model encouraged governments to think in terms of industry-led growth, and to neglect the rural sector. This meant that agricultural productivity often remained low, and inequality between urban and rural areas grew.

Urbanisation

A natural result of the perceived disparity in living conditions between urban and rural areas was to encourage migration from the villages to the towns, a process known as urbanisation.

Migration occurs in response to a number of factors. One is the attraction of the 'bright lights' of the cities – people in rural areas perceive urban areas as offering better access to education and healthcare facilities, and better recreational opportunities.

*A township on
the outskirts of
Cape Town —
urbanisation
results when rural
populations are
lured to cities in
search of work.*

Perhaps more important are the economic gains to be made from migrating to the cities, in terms of the wage differential between urban and rural areas.

Urban wages tend to be higher for a number of reasons. Employment in the manufacturing or service sectors typically offers higher wages, in contrast to the low productivity and wages in the agricultural sector. Furthermore, labour in the urban areas tends to be better organised, and governments have often introduced minimum wage legislation and social protection for workers in the urban areas — especially where they rely on them for electoral support.

Such wage differentials attract a flow of migrants to the cities. However, in practice there may not be sufficient jobs available, as the new and growing sectors typically do not expand sufficiently quickly to absorb all the migrating workers. The net result of this is that rural workers exchange poor living conditions in the rural areas for unemployment in the urban environment.

Furthermore, as employment in the newer sectors cannot expand at such a rate, the result is an expansion of the *informal sector*. Migrants to the city who cannot find work are forced to find other forms of employment, as most LDCs do not have well-developed social security protection. The cities of many LDCs are therefore characterised by substantial amounts of informal activity, as was explained in an earlier chapter.

Tourism

The analysis so far suggests that LDCs need to diversify away from primary production and into new activities that do not require large amounts of capital, preferably involving the production of goods or services that can earn foreign exchange and that have a high income elasticity of demand. On the face of it, tourism would seem to fit the bill.

In the first place, the income elasticity of demand for tourism is strongly positive. This means that, as real incomes rise in the more-developed countries, there will be an increase in the demand for tourism. Within the domestic economy in the LDC, the development of the tourist sector will have an impact on employment. In the early stages there will be a demand for construction workers, and later there will be jobs in hotels and in transport and other services. Tourism is also the sort of activity that is likely to have large multiplier effects on the domestic economy. The World Bank has reported that visitor expenditures outside the hotel sector can range from half to nearly double the in-hotel spending. In addition, there is likely to be scope for small labour-intensive craft-based activities to sell goods to foreigners without actually having to go into the export business – because the tourists come to the producers. Tourism may also attract foreign direct investment if international hotel chains move in to cater for the visiting tourists.

Tourism will require an improvement in the country's infrastructure. For example, it may require road improvements, and upgraded transport and communications facilities. However, such facilities not only help the tourist sector, but also generate externality effects, in the sense that local businesses (and residents) benefit from the improvements as well.

Another potentially important aspect of tourism from the government's perspective is that it may generate a flow of tax revenue. This may come partly from taxes on goods and services, but also from airport taxes and landing fees.

As usual, however, there is a potential downside as well. Tourists will also demand goods that cannot be produced locally, so there may be a need to increase imports, adding to the current account deficit on the balance of payments. This may be reinforced by the outflow of profits from the foreign direct investment. In addition, there may be negative externality effects arising from the erosion of the environment. And tourists exhibit different lifestyles, which may alter the aspirations of the local population, and encourage the consumption of inappropriate (and perhaps imported) products.

It is also important to keep opportunity costs in mind. The development of any new activity entails the sacrifice of some alternative. In deciding to develop tourism, some other option will have to be forgone. For example, resources that are used to improve the transport and communications infrastructure cannot be used to improve education or healthcare. Of course, tourism may prove to be so successful that it will generate resources that can be devoted to education or healthcare, but it is not an issue that can be ignored in the present.

Case study Tanzania

Tanzania is among the lowest-income countries in the world. It is located in sub-Saharan Africa, and relies heavily on agriculture for employment, income and export earnings. In 2001, 84% of its merchandise exports consisted of primary goods, and the terms of trade had declined to 44 based on 1980 = 100. Could Tanzania benefit from tourism?

In its favour, Tanzania has a rich wildlife and the potential to offer safari holidays, so there are resources that could attract foreign visitors. However, how widespread would the benefits from tourism be in the society?

Traditionally, the farmers that work the fields on the outskirts of Tanzania's capital city, Dar es Salaam, sold their produce in the outdoor markets in the city. This entailed an early start to the day, and a trek to the city over poor paths and roads, with the farm produce loaded on to bicycles. In 2001 the Royal Palm Hotel in Dar es Salaam was taken over by new management, which needed a regular supply of fresh vegetables and flowers to serve its guests. It was decided to obtain these by sending a truck into the villages to buy produce directly from the farmers. This meant that the hotel got its produce fresh from the fields, and that the farmers had a new and more convenient market in which to sell their produce. This is one example of how the multiplier effect can extend the benefits from tourism beyond those directly affected.

*The story about the farmers was taken from a World Bank website, **www.miga.org**.*

Summary

> Sir Arthur Lewis argued that the agricultural sectors in many LDCs are characterised by surplus labour, which could be transferred into the manufacturing and service sectors and thus generate structural change and economic growth.

> However, this process has not been as smooth as Lewis predicted, and in some cases has led to rural neglect and a bias of resources towards the urban areas.

> Migration to the cities has been a feature of many LDCs in recent years, bringing negative externality effects.

> Tourism has been recommended as a potentially profitable area for LDCs to develop, but here again there may be costs as well as benefits.

Exercise 12.8

Identify the factors that an LDC should take into account if planning to change its pattern of comparative advantage by developing new economic activities.

Prospects for the future

This analysis of the situation facing LDCs does not seem to give many grounds for optimism, especially for countries in sub-Saharan Africa, where so many countries seem to have stagnated, and where the combination of problems to be overcome seems so great. However, the early years of the 21st century do seem to have shown some promise, with some signs of economic growth. It is to be hoped that this can be maintained, so that countries around the world and their citizens can become full partners in the global economy.

Page numbers in **bold** refer to **key term definitions**.

import substitution **283**, 284
income distribution 185–86, 187, 188, 194, 198
income gap 193
income redistribution 237
income tax 199, 244
indirect taxes 199–**200**, 244
indivisibilities 12
industrialisation **209**, 286
industry long-run supply curve (LRS) **33**
inequality 185–89, 193–201
inflation 157, 176, 236, 248, 250–52, 255–58
informal economic activity 185, 197, 287
information failures 277, 281–82
interest rates 157, 158–59, 176, 247–49, 250–51
international borrowing 269–71
international competitiveness 165–68
International Monetary Fund (IMF) 119, 269, 271, **272**
international trade 106, 110–13, 147, 171, 172–73
internet 6, 64, 105
investment 163–64, 205, 210, 211–12, 261
invisible trade **130**

J
Jacobs Bakery Ltd 89
J-curve effect 137
Jubilee 2000 273, 274

K
Keynes, John Maynard 272
Keynesian School **239**, 254, 255
kinked demand curve 56–57
Krueger, Ann 104
Krugman, Paul 160
Kuznets curve 201

L
labour 7, 8, 11, 215
labour markets 174, 196–98

labour productivity 169–70
land ownership 229–30
land tenancy 228–29
Latin America 222–23
law of comparative advantage **111**, 147
law of diminishing returns **8**, 9, 13–14
less-developed countries (LDCs) 183–84
Lewis model **209**, 286
life expectancy 190
limited liability 3
limit pricing **71**–72
long run 7, **8**, 11–15
long-run equilibrium 32–33, 49
Lorenz curve **187**–88, 198
low-cost airlines 69, 70, 75–77
low-level equilibrium trap 205, 207, 210

M
Maastricht Treaty 156–58
macroeconomic policies 143–44, 148, *Chapter 11*
macroeconomic stability 216, 282–83
malaria 181
Malthus, Thomas 223–24
managers 20–22
marginal costs **9**
marginal revenue **19**
marginal tax rate **199**
market access 182
market concentration 45–46
market failure 237, 244, 278
market-friendly growth **214**–17, 260–61, 277, 282
market power 4, 5, 53, 281–82
market-seeking FDI 121
market share 4, 45–46, 61–62, 90–91
market structure **25**–28, 74–77
mark-up pricing 68
Marshall–Lerner condition 137
maternal health 181
MERCOSUR 118, 146
mergers and acquisitions 4–6, 16–17, 85, 122, 153

Stiglitz, Joseph 105
stop–go cycle of growth 136, 142, 258
Structural Adjustments Programmes
    (SAPs) **217**, 273
structure–conduct–performance
    paradigm 81, 83
sub-Saharan Africa 222, 232
subsidies 281
substitutes 48, 87
sunk costs **9**, 72, 73, 74, 83
supermarkets 89–91
supernormal profits **18**, 35
supply-side policies 175–76, 238, 254
surplus labour 209
sustainable development **106**–7,
    181–82, 218–20, 237
Sweezy, Paul 56

T
tacit collusion **62**
Tanzania 288–89
tariffs **113**–14, 147, 152, 175, 284
taxation 198–200, 244
tax revenue 243–44, 288
technology 212, 213, 216, 263–64
terms of trade **168**
terrorist attacks 64, 122, 164, 195
textile industry 115–16
Thatcher, Margaret 244
tiger economies 212, 217, 220,
    221–22, 285
tourism 287–89
trade barriers, reduction of 106
trade creation **119**, 147–48
trade disputes 120
trade diversion **119**, 148
trade groupings 118–19
trade liberalisation 113–17
trade policy 283–85

trade unions 174, 197
trading blocs 120
transaction costs 3, 152–53, 159
transfer pricing 264
transportation 6, 105–6, 146
travel agents 63–64
trickle-down effect 191
Tucker, Albert 58
two-part tariff system 96

U
Uganda 273, 274–76
UK and the euro 161–65, 259
UK economy and trade performance
    170–72
UK trade 108–9, 155, 173–74
unemployment 158, 164–65, 236,
    255–58
United Biscuits (UK) Ltd 89
urbanisation 286–87
USA 124–25, 136

V
value added tax (VAT) 200, 244
variable costs **9**, 18
vertical mergers **5**
visible trade **130**
voluntary export restraints (VERs) **114**

W
wealth 195
World Bank 119, 214, 217, 261, 269,
    272, 273
world trade 107–8
World Trade Organisation (WTO) **106**,
    115, 119–20, 125, 126, 272

X
X-inefficiency **21**, 50, 80, 97, 114, 173